SOUL MATES

Sonali Fernando is a writer and film-maker who has directed 30 films for Channel Four, the BBC and independent release. Working in documentary and drama, she has explored themes ranging from the contemporary art market to the new face of imperialism. Her credits include *Nine Days That Shook London*, *India Calling*, *Mary Seacole: The Real Angel of the Crimea*, the multi-award-winning *The Body of a Poet* and the series *Great Excavations*, which was filmed in 14 countries and shown around the world.

She has written on cultural issues for a number of publications, and studied at the University of Oxford.

D0815704

For Angela

SOUL MATES

TRUE STORIES FROM THE WORLD OF ONLINE DATING

SONALI FERNANDO

guardianbooks

Published by Guardian Books 2010

2 4 6 8 10 9 7 5 3 1

Text copyright © Sonali Fernando 2010
Stories copyright © Guardian News and Media 2010

Sonali Fernando has asserted her right under the Copyright, Designs and
Patents Act, 1988, to be identified as the author of this work

This book is sold subject to the condition that it shall not, by way of trade
or otherwise, be lent, resold, hired out, or otherwise circulated without the
publisher's prior consent in any form of binding or cover other than that
in which it is published and without a similar condition, including this
condition, being imposed on the subsequent purchaser.

All names and aliases used in this book are entirely fictitious

First published in Great Britain in 2010 by
Guardian Books
Kings Place, 90 York Way
London N1 9GU

www.guardianbooks.co.uk

A CIP catalogue record for this book
is available from the British Library

ISBN 978-0-85265-202-2

Design by Two Associates
Typeset by seagulls.net

Printed and bound in Great Britain by
CPI Bookmarque Ltd, Croydon, Surrey

Contents

Introduction

It wasn't the flip-book of gorgeous twentysomethings on the *Guardian* homepage that did it. Or the juicy brag of Britain's biggest dating website – 'match.com has got too many women!'– in a commercial sandwiched artfully between two halves of a Premier League football match on ITV. Or even the endless friends-of-friends' stories of civil partnerships and weddings and baby-making forged by the great matchmaking satellite in the sky. No. What proved to me, beyond all else, that online dating had come of age, was the unlikely tribute paid by a contestant on *The Weakest Link*, when quizzed by Anne Robinson as to how he had met his wife: 'It was all thanks to Bill Gates'. He chuckled, the other contestants erupted and Robinson punctuated the moment with a tiny chevron of the eyebrow. The taboo had finally been broken. Internet dating had leapt out of the closet and into our living rooms through one of the most popular shows on television.

Online dating has become *the* socialising phenomenon of our times. There is now a 50:50 chance that a singleton you know logs on to find love. In 2007, 7.8 million British people – half the nation's population of singles – used some form of online dating service in pursuit of romance, according to Europe-wide dating service parship.co.uk.[1] A *Which?* survey in 2009 found that one in five online daters has either met the love of their life this way or knows someone who has.[2] A fifth of all people who marry between the ages of 19 and 25 met their partner online.[3] And a thousand people join Guardian Soulmates every week. The websites are positively heaving with good-looking, educated, successful people seeking long-term relationships.

Internet dating has become a recreational pastime every bit as much as a quest to find 'the one'. The style of light, non-committal multiple dating, of free-wheeling exploration prior to commitment, fits our modern taste for 'shopping around', the relentless comparing and contrasting to find 'the best' that is the hallmark of neo-liberal society. According to parship.co.uk, 'the average single person in Britain has been on six dates in the last 12 months', which is three times as many as three years ago. Ironically, despite fears that the internet would atomise society, creating Facebook-addicted cyberhermits devoid of the power of speech, profuse online communication has translated into prolific real-world meetings. Of the 18 million first dates in Britain last year, 12 million were hatched in cyberspace. Most 'dates' will stay strictly platonic and some will lead to friendship. Online dating has become a new way for people to converse, one-to-one, with strangers.

All these figures add up to an eruption of sociability similar to the dating craze that spread through the United States in the 1920s. Like that fervour, in which, as the historian Theodore Zeldin says, the American economy benefited from a 'devotion to spending, which not long before had been very un-American',[4] British daters are funnelling an average of £120 per month into the service industries in the name of dating – even now, during a recession.[5]

It is nothing short of a revolution in Britishness. Online dating will do for social mixing what Elizabeth David's paean to garlic and good living, *A Book of Mediterranean Food*, did to improve food in postwar Britain, and what the Boeing 747's affordable flights did to increase British globetrotting. Cyberdating adds a new mobility to our relationships. By facilitating romantic – and child-bearing – unions that span cities, countries and continents, it will change the demographics of our society.

All age groups are involved in this revolution. For people in their 20s, the dating website has become a first port of call when seeking a mate, sitting comfortably next to the club, workplace or bar. It is social networking in reverse: whereas Facebook and MySpace have historically been used to develop and reinforce real-world friendships, cyberdating happens the other way round. The twentysomethings weaned on Facebook – who already shop, bank, chat, share music, show their movies and meet friends online – have graduated to online dating as effortlessly as school-leavers going up to university. **2leggedtree**, a 21-year-old female online dater who contributes to this book, says: 'Online dating feels like MySpace without the music and teen angst.'

Cyberdating has become the intuitive choice for young professionals throughout the west. In the United States, Rufus Griscom, the co-founder of nerve.com, a literary magazine with a personals section, reflected on online dating's take-up by people who were 'young, over-educated professionals' way back in 2002: 'Newly minted doctors, lawyers, journalists, and media executives are flocking to these systems.'[6] A similar pattern emerged a few years later in the UK, where, in the case of a site like Guardian Soulmates, the demographic comprises 30 per cent who work in the media or marketing, 20 per cent in education and 13 per cent in finance or law.

There is an increase among the new 'middle-youth' too. The dating juggernaut match.com, which has 15 million members across the world, claims exponential growth among the Baby Boomers – the postwar generation born between the late 1940s and the early 1960s that comprises the wealthiest population of singles in the US.[7] According to a 2008 survey, 'around 30 per cent of the nation's 80 million Baby Boomers are single, and they have money. Yahoo Personals and eHarmony.com report double-digit growth in the 50-plus market.'[8] And it doesn't end there. Alongside the influx of affluent young and middle-aged people, older people, well into their 80s, have joined the club, realising in greater numbers that the internet can catalyse more interesting encounters than those offered by the somewhat anachronistic knees-ups available in the community. For many people, the desktop number-cruncher has become the unlikeliest gateway to a romantic renaissance. For those who want it, there is now an alternative to signing off from love when a long-term relationship comes to an end.

The stigma is fading: people worry less than they once did about being spotted advertising their charms online. Guardian Soulmates even places a rotating gallery of photographs of its most popular daters on guardian.co.uk – the newspaper's online edition – selected from the 200 profiles that are most clicked on and messaged by other users of the site. It's now a matter of pride to be seen there: the computer only selects the most popular.

What a different picture it was 10 years ago. Few of the entrepreneurs scouting for business predicted that online dating would be the new frontier of the much-vaunted dotcom gold rush. In Britain, at the turn of the millennium, the words *social* and *networking* had not been hitched: online networks were more exclusive and counter-cultural than that. There was a thriving underground scene where netheads communed online in sci-fi roleplay games, activists built virtual communities on political bulletin-boards, and swingers arranged 'scenes' via instant messaging. The pioneers in the take-up of online personals in the late 1990s were lesbians and gay men, who spotted an opportunity to widen their social and romantic networks. Industry chiefs took note: as David Eisner, America Online's vice president of public relations, remarked, 'The gay and lesbian community was one of the first to take advantage of the anonymity online. From the beginning up until now, the community has been an early adopter of all the functionality available,' progressing from bulletin boards to chat, partner-searching and instant messaging.[9] Tom Rielly, the founder of US website planetout.com, described an earlier prototype as his vision of 'a national electronic town square that people can access from the privacy of their closet – from any small town, any suburb, any reservation in America. It's like bringing Christopher Street or the Castro to them.' It was a small leap for internet entrepreneurs to see that online dating's capacity for anonymous advertising and interaction could benefit millions of other people who were hitherto isolated from their kindred spirits.

One of the people to make the connection was a young businessman named Anupam Mittal, who returned to India in 1996 after a stint in the United States. He describes his eureka moment:

> One day I met a traditional matchmaker. In India, as you know, you don't marry one person, you marry a family. So

these matchmakers go from home to home, build relationships with families and try to make a match within their network. They carry an attaché case full of the CVs and references of the potential spouses. I asked him: 'How many people can you carry in your attaché case?' He said: 'About 50 or 60.'[10]

Mittal realised that the range of possible spouses open to a young man or woman who was planning to marry in this way was entirely limited by the size and weight of the matchmaker's attaché case. He soon developed a website that could combine the minute distinctions of caste, class, community, religion and language that are central to traditional Indian matchmaking with the processing power of the internet, and created shaadi.com, which is now the most visited matrimonial site in the world.

Whether facilitating marriages, love affairs or one-night-stands, online matchmaking is jaw-droppingly brilliant from a business point-of-view: it has targeted something that people do anyway, and will always do – meet other people speculatively with a view to romance – and standardised certain aspects of it (such as one's tastes and preferences), added value (the search tools, the match functions, the chat features), and slapped a price tag on it. It has effectively stepped into the cross-currents of sexual electricity that flow between people, and monetised them.

To reach critical mass, the dating moguls had to overcome our fears. A wariness of fraudsters, spammers and the unknown had deterred us from online dating, just as it had warded us off internet shopping. It was with trepidation that most of us first tapped our credit card details into an online checkout. But in a few short years, an internet company with no high street presence – Amazon – has become the second most popular retailer in Britain.[11] Online dating has followed this trend: just as we now trust a company with no physical shop, we now arrange dates with people we haven't met. Improvements in security, vetting and site moderation have made us trust the web – to such an extent that many people, especially women, tend to consider online introductions *safer*, more pleasurable and less random than meeting someone in a pub.

On their voyage to the mainstream, the websites have tried hard to be loved. They shower us with robot-love: send us matey emails about our 'fans' and ego-stroking birthday greetings. Th ey offer increasingly swanky online shop windows, with bigger spaces for self-description in which wordsmiths can flaunt their skills. Th ey provide all the instruments of modern courtship, from instant messaging to in-house email, video to mobile links. And some have chatrooms or chat features, which crackle with the sexy charge of quickfire messaging or newsgroup banter. The ubiquity of broadband and text bundles has played a part, creating a textual 'connected' life where there's a constant checking-in, an always-on self-awareness in which it is normal to account for even our most banal actions on a moment-by-moment basis: in this culture, a fresh style of written courtship – exciting, rapid and intimate – has been able to flourish.

There has also been a paradigm shift in the depiction of people who advertise for love. For much of its three-hundred-year existence, the personal column has been regarded with a mixture of pity and scorn by genteel society, even though many of the members of that society advertised there, as HG Cocks shows in *Classified: The Secret History of the Personal Column*.[12] The *Guardian* itself conformed to this trend: in 1964, exactly 40 years before it launched the Soulmates website, it ran an article under the headline 'The Marriage Market', conveying disdain for the infra dig matchmaking industry and mocking pity for its participants:

> Throughout all crises, alarms, and slumps certain commodities continue to be in steady demand. And among the enviable purveyors of such universal wants are the undertakers and the dealers in matrimony … every day hundreds of men and women feel impelled to spend good money seeking matrimony through the efforts of a professional undertaker in that line. There are in England to-day in flourishing existence several monthly newspapers which are entirely devoted to matrimonial advertisements (one of these claims an existence of well over 70 years), and a brief study of their columns and scale of prices for insertions is enough to convince anybody that here is the safest form of journalistic venture of our times

... And what sort of Ladies and Gentlemen are those that are so circumstanced that they cannot or dare not set about finding mates for themselves? ... Their literary style is alike in all cases and they draw touching pictures of their plight and their lovable qualities. Most of the men are 'home-loving' and 'fond of music'. The women are 'considered nice-looking' and are good-natured. What they most wish to find in a mate is a slim figure, refinement, quiet tastes, cheerfulness, and – above all – 'a keen sense of humour'... Inevitably one asks oneself what is wrong here that [a] man cannot seek and find such a wife as he wants without setting about it this way. The most reasonable reply is that far more people than we imagine are either too busy earning their keep or too completely cut off from social life to have the chances of useful propinquity.[13]

For all the delicious augurs of dating in our times (KSOH for 'keen sense of humour'?), the attitude to personal advertisers now could not be more different. Unlike the people who bought space in the personal columns in the past, today's love-seekers are not viewed as advertisers at all. They would baulk at this condescension. Online daters are not 'placing classified ads' but 'uploading profiles'. They are not 'lonely hearts', solitary souls on the outside looking in, but well-adjusted 'members' of a dating 'community': people who have joined, who belong. Not desperadoes hungry for love, but 'daters' up for non-committal fun.

This sea-change in our culture could not have happened without the new British vogue for self-disclosure. Like its younger sister, social networking, cyberdating sits comfortably in the confessional culture that has dominated our mass media for over a decade. In the 10 years that have given us *Oprah*, *Jerry Springer*, *Big Brother* and *I'm a Celebrity* ... , our media has been dominated by the dissection of our lives, screening real-time operations, childbirth, autopsies and counselling. Self-disclosure is the unlikely child of feminist politics – which sought to draw open society's hypocritical net-curtains and bring secrets such as domestic violence and abuse into the light of day – and pop psychology, which says, 'This is how I am. Accept me'. One of its effects has been to challenge people to redraw the boundaries between public and private and overcome their fear of being exposed – with all the vulnerability that entails in a society whose members have traditionally guarded their privacy like hawks. That redrawing of the boundaries is an essential prerequisite of 'putting yourself forward' to strangers, and of dating online.

There are around 820 dating sites in the UK, according to research firm hitwise.com/uk. Th ey persuade British people to part with £76m of their hard-earned cash, and, unlike the US industry, which is thought to have reached saturation-point, the British market is predicted to grow over the next two years to a point where it will attract 6 million paying members and annual revenues of more than £350m.[14]

But what lies beyond the hype? Is it now just too easy to be wowed into a crazy mental promiscuity by the conveyor belts of people whizzing before your eyes? To be spellbound by the consumerist illusion that more choice equals more happiness? To become a greedy gannet at the people buffet? Does it make us, paradoxically, lose interest in other people even as we pursue them?

From the first online dating stories I heard from a friend five years ago to the many others I've heard since, I have been intrigued by their resemblance to quests: rollicking, 21st-century adventure stories, in which people launch themselves into the unknown on a search for love like modern-day Jasons tracking down their Golden Fleeces or Psyches searching for their Cupids. It is these tales, both fascinating and frustrating, overpowering and underwhelming, that prompted the idea for this book. My first interviews were with friends, which soon rippled out to friends of friends, and then associates of our small team at Guardian Books. I contacted a number of the people who had posted their heartfelt success stories on the Guardian Soulmates website. And lastly, as the whole *Guardian* edifice got the dating bug, we ran a major competition in the print and web versions of the paper, asking people to submit their online dating stories to us.

We received over 200 entries of an extraordinarily high standard which, with difficulty, we whittled down to the selection in the book. By turns revelatory and life-enhancing, hilarious and edifying, touching and toe-curlingly embarrassing, the stories created a fascinating mosaic of modern romance. Beautifully observed, touching and witty, some of them moved us to tears, while others had us howling with laughter. There were tales of simple beauty – of love found and confidence restored – and scathing accounts of rudeness, stoically endured. Resilient to a fault, our contributors have dusted themselves off after dates where they've been stood up, snubbed or lied to, potting their pique in hilarious tracts on the hazards of the game. But they have also taken pure delight in the love, friendship and passion they have found.

The pattern of submissions was fascinating. We were inundated in the first fortnight of the month-long entry period with tales of terrible dates, as a cohort of women in their 30s, 40s and 50s grabbed the chance to vent their dismay at the men (and occasionally women) they had met, their sulphuric stories small acts of redress that fizzed with humour and indignation. The men soon returned the favour, giving as good as they got. Next, there were the haunting stories: of people becoming intoxicated by the drug of online courtship, by an exquisite, hallucinogenic reality that was so rarely matched in the flesh; or of meetings that were *nearly* wonderful, where love went whistling past, fleeting and uncatchable. In the remaining two weeks, we had a deluge of joyous and uplifting tales of love found as if by magic, from people aged between 24 and 83. Even self-confessed former cynics were shouting their non-ironic delight from the rooftops, rejoicing in relationships that could have originated in no other way than online, sometimes between people who had, *Sliding Doors*-style, passed each other for years without meeting.

It would have been futile to try and represent all the websites used by the 7.8 million unique online daters that frequent the web. But, fortuitously, stories flowed in from people who had used a wide spectrum of sites – from match.com to gaydargirls.co.uk – as well as the majority we expected from Guardian Soulmates.

The winning stories and runners-up are listed on page 245. It has been crucial to guarantee people's anonymity, and we have, in all cases, changed aliases and the names of people described. The team that runs Guardian Soulmates has been absolutely hands-off editorially – remarkable perhaps, given that the book bears the same name. It is to their credit that they have been confident enough in the high approval ratings of the service they provide not to flinch at those stories of hilariously dreadful dates that were brokered by the site.

It has been a privilege, in working on this book, to talk to, and read the words of, some of online dating's pioneers: people with humanity, grace, style and wit, who have embraced the possibilities offered by technology to set their lives on a new path.

There are many doubters and dissenters, of course; many people who remain unconvinced that online introductions are effective or even desirable. Cyberdating is, after all, a strange inversion of the usual course of human attraction. It can readily be satirised as partner-shopping; it sometimes seems to have all the elegance of an online supermarket and to suggest you can find your soulmate as simply as your semi-skimmed milk. But are people really that naïve? The answer, overwhelmingly, is no.

As **sugar_hiccup**, a 41-year-old woman who contributes to the book says, 'It's easy to conflate the cyberworld with a loss of humanity. My thing is that a dating website's only a tool. I instinctively think we need to use these tools *as tools*, and keep coming back to our humanity'.

Humanity is what the people who share their stories here have in abundance. Their experiences demonstrate, in hundreds of ways, both a romantic belief in the value of love, and a refreshing realism about the cleverest means yet invented of getting people to meet.

Sonali Fernando, 2010

Chapter 1:
Who said saddo?

Why 8 million Brits are now dating online

For self-styled bohemian goddess **LadyAms**, 24, there was only one place to go when she broke up with yet another short-term boyfriend: far away. 'I planned to do what I always did – pack a bag and go travelling.' **LadyAms** was going to lock up her fancy dress shop in a small Essex village and head for San Francisco. For now, that meant alone. 'I wasn't shy, lonely or at the end of my tether, although "finding Mr Right" *was* on my To Do list.' Unbeknown to **LadyAms**, her mother was hatching a plan.

> Would you believe it, she was scouring the internet for a travel buddy for me as she was fed up with me doing everything by myself! And while she was cruising the net, being this comedy version of an interfering mother, a pop up 'popped up' on her screen. She rang me and told me to come home that instant because she'd found my Mr Right. I assumed that he hadn't just popped round and asked to borrow a cup of sugar, so I asked her where she'd 'found him'.
>
> 'Err, well, that's not important – just come home.'
>
> 'Mum ... have you just found me a mail-order husband?'

Why do people date online? Because they already do everything else online. Because they're looking for fun. Because they want to be loved-up and sexy with someone. Because they've just moved home. Because they're grieving, divorced or lonely. And of course, because they've been ordered to by their mums. There are as many reasons for dating online as there are people who do it. But with almost 8 million British people using dating websites in the past year, the question is no longer, 'Why would you date online?' The question is rather, 'Why wouldn't you?'[15]

For many people who take the plunge, online dating is a paradox: it promises a thousand and one adventures but it's as romantic as a soap dish; it's a gilded palace of possibility but as limited as a corner-shop; it puts you in the driver's seat without giving you a map. 'I guess I was a classic case; my marriage had imploded on February 14 – I'm not kidding, my ex-wife had always possessed a superb combination of timing and humour – but by August I felt that I was ready to try and meet someone new. I wanted to break out of my geographical zone, but without mooching around West End bars feeling like a creep, there was nowhere else I could go.' So thought 50-year-old furniture restorer **Charlie23** of West London, spurred on in the summer of 2008 to sign up to Guardian Soulmates.

In Southampton, 63-year-old **VintageRedhead** was determined to make a last-ditch attempt to find a man with whom 'to share the joys and sorrows of life', but her options were looking thin. 'There's not much else provided for people of my age group – speed-dating and singles clubs are generally for the young. And the social circles I moved around in, sparse as they were since I'd spent most of my life bringing up children, tended to be with long-term married couples or confirmed bachelors. Little chance of flirting there.' She was reluctant to try online dating, which seemed alien and strange: 'This was a taboo area for my generation, who are hardly used to the internet, let alone this overt method of "putting yourself forward" to the extent almost of showing off to gain notice, playing up your attributes to sell yourself.' But one day she put aside her misgivings, took a deep breath and uploaded a profile. Crunch time. 'One has to overcome shyness, mistrust, fear of failure or rejection, and sally forth.'

'North London bloke' **DaPopester**, 41, a self-employed telecoms engineer, had recently left the Big Smoke for a new life in rural Cambridgeshire. One year out of a relationship, he had bought and renovated half a farmhouse and was starting to keep chickens. He found the landscape bewitching, but too beautiful to enjoy alone: so he set about looking for someone to share it with him. He had never had a problem meeting women when he lived in London, but how to find someone here, marooned as he was in the Fens? 'I had all the reservations you could imagine about internet dating, but I couldn't see how I'd actually meet someone any other way.'

Even in a city of 8 million people, 'meeting someone' is by no means guaranteed. **DanE1**, a 30-year-old who works in publishing, had been single for a year and a half when a friend gave him a 'kick up the backside' and told him to start dating again. 'There was no agonising over the decision at all: I knew she was right.' Describing himself as a relaxed, rather than obsessive, social networker – 'I change my Facebook status once a month and I don't tweet' – he turned to the internet as the natural, intuitive solution to his boyfriend search. 'I do everything else online, so why not dating? People are happy finding a plumber on the internet, so why not a partner? And if your partner happens to be a plumber, you're laughing. Saves you a fortune.' It wasn't London's legendary inhospitality that was making it tough to share his love of 'really inappropriate humour', 'rugby' and 'good cider' with someone (see Profile, p. 55), but the differences that a few years had made to his life:

> When I first moved here, I used to go out more to parties and had a lot of acquaintances, but now I've grown out of the club scene. Most of my friends are straight and even though they say 'there's this fabulous guy I must introduce you', it never happens because everyone's so busy. Marriages, kids and getting older change how you socialise.

But, as **DanE1** adds, it's not just reaching the ripe old age of 30 that has changed things: 'It's a societal change. Twenty-year-olds are doing this too. The way we meet people is definitely changing. Online dating is more efficient but less romantic than older forms of meeting people and it's symptomatic of our lifestyles. We just don't operate within communities any more so it is difficult to meet people within your peer group.'

It was grief that led **Blushes**, a 41-year-old human resources manager, to the online dating fold. When her beloved brother died young, of a heart attack, it left her 'devastated, completely at a loss'. She was numb and unable to work. Her world shrank into tiny routines. Living alone in London, with most of her family in the Caribbean, she sought solace at her local church. The pastor said that she would be able to find a bereavement counsellor on the internet. His words were prophetic although possibly not in the way he'd anticipated.

These six people, like the 8 million others who set off on adventures in online dating last year, were leaping into the unknown, opening themselves to a world of excitement, possibility and risk. They were united by one desire: to act on their own account to change their lives.

The appeal of cyberdating is clear: it's the modern way of 'getting out more' – you can cast your net as wide as you like, at any time of day or night. And where else do you go? People used to join evening classes to make new friends. But as funding for adult education declines, there are fewer places to meet.[16] And salsa classes may not fit your bill: women sometimes outnumber men by 20 to one – and if you happen to be a tall girl, you could find yourself 'playing the boy'. An office romance then? Although one in five people marry a colleague, workplace affairs are frowned upon, and within three months, half of them are toast.[17] The local pub, bar or club? It takes time and money to go gallivanting on the off-chance your future love will be there. Britain has the highest percentage of people in the European Union working weekends and nights,[18] and 21 per cent of all families have no disposable income.[19] With the breakdown of community networks that would once have supplied us with partners, the chances of finding love in the way our parents did are slim. So people are turning to the online school of mate selection: a self-reliant, protestant-work-ethic, own-bootstraps kind of place where you do the matchmaking for yourself. It may be that or nothing: in the words of 67-year-old

Starling, who contributes to this book, 'you won't meet your partner by sitting at home watching telly'.

Summoned home to see the pop-up that had popped up on her mother's screen – the delectable (in her mother's opinion) Mr Right – **LadyAms** knew what she had to do. 'I refused to look at the screen of the computer, so I had a cup of tea and thought about him and cake for 20 minutes. After drinking all the tea in China and eating all the cakes in the house, I looked at his profile.' And she liked it. Rather a lot. He was a slim, 6ft 1in, funky-country kind of beau, with a penchant for tweed and waistcoats. The kinds of things a 24-year-old seamstress with untameable hair and 'stuck-in-a-timewarp-hippy' clothes ('this chick does not wear black!') can spot at 500 paces. **LadyAms** set up a profile, clicked on his picture and waited.

> After half an hour I checked my 'history' on the site to find that Mr Ben had checked me out. 'Mum! He's looked at my profile! Why the hell hasn't he sent me a message?!' I tried to send him a message. No can do. You have to pay £25. No way, I'm not doing that, I'm a successful 24-year-old, happy-go-lucky, bohemian goddess. I don't need to give anyone £25 to sort my love life out for me.

But, quick as a whip, **LadyAms** worked out how she could send Mr Ben a message. In a moment of inspiration, she changed the little headline under her username from *Why? Because you never know* to *Waiting for Mr Ben*. 'That caught his attention! He messaged me that night and I was happy to give Soulmates £25 because I had someone to chat to. I spent every night for a week on the internet talking to him. The beautiful thing about internet dating is that you can learn so much about someone before you actually meet.'

Online, **Charlie23** spread his net wide. He looked for women between the ages of 26 and 50, and responded quickly to any interest he received. After one woman said his first profile sounded 'too worthy', he ditched his carefully-scripted words and replaced them with one sentence: 'I'm up for it!' and 'a really well thought-out photo'. Short and sweet was to serve him well:

> It only took a few weeks for a really gorgeous person to come to me, and I moved with the speed of a striking rattlesnake. After three days we called one another and got on really well. Then we arranged a date at St Pancras station champagne bar and that was it. I consumed no alcohol during this period; I was in charge of all of my faculties so I was aware of what was happening, and never had a doubt. She was as she had described; she had beauty, warmth, soul and sexiness in abundance.

Caribbean-born **Blushes** started surfing the internet for bereavement counsellors. 'By a completely accidental, roundabout route, I ended up in the midst of the fascinating parallel world that is gay.com.' For 15 years, **Blushes** had been living a secret life, in which no one but a handful of her closest friends knew that she was gay. 'I was completely paranoid about people detecting my sexuality because of family and cultural pressures. In most of the Caribbean it is illegal to be gay – in Jamaica it can carry a long jail sentence – and since I still have close connections there, I'd just resigned myself to life in the closet.'

Having stumbled across gay.com while seeking chatrooms where she could discuss her grief, **Blushes** quickly made new friends in Canada and the US. 'The internet became an absorbing, passionate, playful diversion for me – a way of engaging intensely with people who were safely distant.' In the silent intensity of live messaging across the Atlantic, she explored her sexuality without fear of criticism or judgement. 'Realising the potential of being able to express the essence of my true being in a free, anonymous and safe medium like gay.com was like being struck by a thunderbolt,' she says.

> From being a complete internet virgin I became a suave and accomplished textual flirt: I traversed from gay.com to gaydargirls.co.uk and pinksofa.co.uk, chatting about ideas, current affairs and love. I started courting and seducing

women in the US, Canada and later the UK with words alone: in the beginning it was all virtual relationships and cybersex – I didn't meet anyone. But I had access to an enormous, supportive online community that was in sync with me politically, intellectually and sexually.

In Cambridgeshire, **DaPopester** had uploaded his profile. It was as truthful and unvarnished a picture of himself as he could portray in words, scrupulously under-egged:

As you get older you're not trying so hard to impress: you want people to like you as you. I tried to be honest in my profile and not big myself up. I wasn't going to say 'I'm into windsurfing' or something just because I'd done it once. I put down a little about moving out of London and said I was starting to keep chickens. I wrote, 'the worst it can be is a pleasant half-hour conversation. If you like what you read then drop me a line'.

It was the chickens that did it. Instantly warming to him when she read his profile, 36-year-old **SnowieMunro**, a drama teacher based in Lincolnshire, sent him a message. She took him exactly at his word, and dropped him that line. Just the one. It said, 'I liked what I read'. Having spent hours crafting emails to other men that didn't receive replies, she was keen to try a new tack. Ironically, she'd sent her electronic billet-doux to the most prolific letter-writer in Christendom: he teased back with an 'I see I'm just worth five words!' and an epistolary courtship was born. Online dating had removed the embarrassment of going up to someone at a bar: 'I didn't feel I'd done any approaching,' says **DaPopester**. 'I'd just put what I had to say out there and she had come up to me, and said "I like that."'

Logging onto the website from her home by the sea, **VintageRedhead** was enjoying a new lease of life. Where she had not been able to find any men before, now they were flocking to her: 'The internet made dating a hundred per cent easier for me. There was no way I could have met so many people with the underlying intention of a relationship, especially being a woman over 60.' She discovered the pleasures of a virtual space 'where one can dare be oneself and cyberflirt', and spent many pleasant hours 'wining and dining, walking and talking', with people who came up in her local searches. All very fine and dandy, but she hadn't met anyone with whom to share her life. Clicking on the website, she changed the distance settings:

> I decided to look further afield in an area I fancied – Devon. For years, I'd had a picture from a magazine pinned above my computer of a thatched cottage dream home, so I thought I'd indulge my fancy and find someone who lived in one. My membership was about to expire and I'd been thinking of taking a break from the site for a while, so I was just playing about really, browsing one Sunday evening with a glass of wine and a vivid imagination. And there he was: oh my, what a lovely sight! My idea of a very handsome man, with a charming smile and beautiful clear eyes that looked straight into you. And he lived in a thatched cottage in a village in Devon! So I couldn't resist and, despite thinking he looked too good for the likes of me, I sent off my 'I'm interested in you' heavy hint and waited with bated breath.

She soon had her reply. 'I'm interested in you too.' They followed up swiftly with a phone call: 'After all, why wait – at our age there's no time to lose!'

Blushes was certainly getting out and about. She gradually felt confident enough to arrange real-world meetings with women she had been chatting to on the North American sites. For three years she had a long-distance relationship with a lecturer at the University of California – visiting her there, in New York, Boston and Paris: 'I've never done so much travelling in my life!' But eventually it came to an end, and she closed down her account. As she left, she realised that something in her had changed. She had overcome her grief. Her life had been transformed by relationships with people she had never met – as well as those she had. 'Up to three years after I first clicked on gay.com, I still felt guilty that I had come to terms with my brother's death by going on a thrilling and intense sexual odyssey. But ultimately it provided me with the best bereavement counselling I ever had.'

After a week communicating online, **LadyAms** was eager to meet the delightful Mr Ben:

> He had a broken foot due to a snowboarding accident, so I drove 45 minutes to his house for our first date. We went to four different restaurants that night and they were all fully-booked. It should have been embarrassing but it wasn't – it was hilarious. Needless to say, I never made it to San Fran. Now I'm off to Africa with Mr Ben. I'm a very lucky girl. We're going to travel Africa together, build a house, get married, buy fish and drink tea. How brilliant is that?!

VintageRedhead arranged to meet the man with beautiful eyes. They went for romance all the way: Dorchester, in Hardy country, halfway between their homes. 'It was the last Sunday in March, the day the clocks changed. The sun shone and the day sparkled. Our meeting couldn't have had a more auspicious beginning.' It was love at first sight. Looking into each other's eyes they knew that 'we'd be each other's futures, that we'd found the real, one and only soulmate'. **VintageRedhead** visited his Dartmoor cottage at the first available moment. Instinctively, she knew it was right. After that, she visited every weekend, and has recently moved there for good. They now celebrate a happiness and love that was forged in the most unexpected way: 'Life is utter heaven. We are both OAPs feeling like teenagers again!'

DaPopester met **SnowieMunro** for their first date by the sea on the Lincolnshire coast (see p. 151). He had researched a Plan B in case they didn't get on – there was a petrified forest nearby that he thought he could explore. But there was no need: Plan A was just fine. That one meeting 'changed my life'. He realised he had met 'the woman I could only dream about'. And for her part, **SnowieMunro** knew she had found someone who appreciated her poetic soul. He wrote her eight letters in as many weeks. Several months later, he and she, and her six-year-old son, are happily ensconced in the farmhouse, sharing the Fens and those matchmaking hens. **DaPopester's** life has changed in unimaginable ways:

This whole experience has blown my socks off. I have not felt like this in any relationship I've been in before. I never expected this. We've both been very upfront about each other's pasts. It feels very honest, very true. As both of us were completely honest right from the beginning, that honesty has carried forward into the relationship.

Looking for love online turned out to be 'the best thing I've ever done, bar none'.

Charlie23 and his date became lovers, and it rekindled his ability to love: 'We agreed on so much, we loved the same things and as she showed me new areas of London I had scarcely seen, I showed her my life and we loved one another.' But after an extraordinary time together, their relationship ran out of juice. 'Maybe it was too soon. My divorce was still happening and it was painful and a distraction. Our children argued, as children do, and cracks began to show. Around a year after we had met we broke up.'

He thinks of online dating as a challenge: by allowing you to meet people who are outside your matrix of friends, family or work, it suggests you can step out of your past life, with nothing holding you back. 'If one really has the courage to change and take on new friends and new geography, then it works.' In the end it proved a change too far, but he has no regrets:

I know that my experience has been so utterly wonderful; there were no nasty surprises and we were both aware enough to cope with the difficult times. But I needed to meet her, I needed to be loved and be able to love. I needed to have a wild wonderful time, a sexy free unbounded time, and I did and so did she. I certainly don't regret a moment. It's so sad that we didn't make it, but we gave it a good shot and had a lot of fun trying to get all the way.

DanE1 has now dated online for a year. He's made friends, had a brief relationship and a number of memorable dates – but has yet to meet the man with whom he wants to settle down. He marvels at the internet's capacity to cut across geography, ethnicity and class: 'People are interacting and having sex outside their community. If I was dating 50 years ago I would have stayed in Ipswich. I would have been dating boring white middle-class people. Now your choice is endless.' But, inspired by the example of his parents, who have been together for 35 years, **DanE1** is confident that the internet will help him find a love that lasts:

> Ultimately as a gay man I can go onto **Gaydar** – if I want to be spanked by a Chinese drag queen I can find someone to do that. But the romantic in me says that there are only very few people I can fall in love with. However great the choice is, there will still only be one or two people who you want to spend the rest of your life with – I'm channelling romcoms here – and that's where the internet comes in handy.

Relaxed and optimistic, he's sure that 'even if it doesn't work out with the first few people, somewhere along the line it will. As Maria says in *The Sound of Music*: "When the Lord closes a door, somewhere he opens a window."'

Not everyone who dates online finds a soulmate. But many cyberdaters describe other rewards. Some people journey to wild and unfamiliar places, like **AliceInWonderland**, who, in her late 30s, travelled out of one sexual identity and into another; **SoSueMe**, who took the plunge – '55, overweight, disabled, never married, 10 years since my boyfriend had died. Definitely time to move on' – and rediscovered her sexual self; **NomDePlume**, whose list of solitary freedoms (see p. 33), shows why a single life can be richer than a coupledom of compromise; **Ultraviolet**, who found not the transcendent love she'd anticipated, but a new country that 'burned its way directly into my heart', and **Marie_Mint**, who emerged from a marriage that had gnawed at her self-esteem into an exuberant adventure of sex, laughter, conversation and friendship that leaves her 'amazed'.

For all these cyberdating evangelists, there are plenty of dissenters too: people such as **Meg87**, 50, who subscribed to Guardian Soulmates for a month yet received no replies to her emails and no dates, which she puts down to 'a lack of gentlemanly decency': 'I would never advise anyone to carry out online dating, as the disappointments could push people who are insecure right to the edge.' The nay-sayers have a point when they list the reasons not to do it: the liars, chancers and players you might meet; the cost of the membership and the dates themselves; the time and emotional energy it takes; the harsh truths you might learn about yourself without even meeting a mate. Why, in the name of all things holy, would you put yourself through all this? According to a study by dating website parship.co.uk, one in three dates 'ends in disaster'.[20] That's a skyful of emotional turbulence for very short odds.

And it's not only that it can be soul-destroying. Many people, like textile designer **Emroselane**, 58, find the odd inside-out routine of online dating – find out about someone first, meet them later – an anaemic stand-in for traditional courtship: 'I want someone to appear out of nowhere in my real life and sweep me off my feet. I'm an old romantic. I have that longing for doing it the old way – meeting someone and there's the chemistry – because I know the rules, I know the game.'

Romance happens so differently in the online world. The preliminaries of browsing for a partner on a website can seem clunky and strange: but the magic only happens *after* people are brought together, and bringing people together is what the internet can do well. Beyond the hype, online dating is just a mechanised introduction service, with bells on. It's not a cure for existential angst, a balm for shattered hearts, or a keyboard shortcut to lifelong love. But as 45-year-old London-based project manager **Freudianslip** says, 'I didn't go online thinking "I'm going to find the love of my life". But, as the technology's here, I feel I'm not going to leave it to other forms of meeting people alone.'

Every second, millions of messages of desire are coursing through the fibre optic cables that tunnel through the ground and snake along the ocean floors, enabling love affairs that cross continents, putting girdles round the earth. But this weirdly unromantic romantic system is perhaps at its most brilliant, and most poignant, where it works far closer to home. As **letter_spaghetti**, 28, discovered, the internet has the power to bring together people who – in another lifetime, when such things existed – would have been connected through their community:

My subscription had run out and I was planning on having a break from the world of online dating. However – I got a message from a very attractive and charming Irish man, so I was persuaded to sign up again. After a few emails, we decided to meet up and go to a gig in north London. Before the gig, we went for a drink in a little pub. Sitting outside, we were throwing back the usual first date questions. I asked him where he lived.

'Battersea', he responded.

Me: 'Oh, I live in Battersea as well!'

Him: 'Where in Battersea?'

I told him the name of the road that I lived on and his jaw dropped and he asked,

'What house number?'

Me: '75'

His jaw dropped even further and he said, 'I live at 76!'

I didn't believe him at first, but after a fantastic date, we took a taxi home and it was true, he lived directly across the street from me. We had both been living in our houses for two years and had never seen each other.

Who said saddo?:
The stories

Alias: **Annie611** | *Age:* **28** | *F* | ♀♂ | **match.com**

Like many Londoners, I found it hard to meet like-minded singletons. My colleagues in the charity sector are utterly lovely but utterly undateable: mostly female, gay male or firmly coupled-up, while our few single straight men have the sex appeal of a Care Bear. My friends had gallantly but unsuccessfully matched me to their eligible acquaintances, and all they had left were those too deviant to recommend to me or those too sweet-natured to recommend me to. So I tried internet dating, and it was fantastic, introducing me to all kinds of people I wouldn't normally have met and to all kinds of places as my dates took me to their favourite haunts.

For a while I had the time of my life. But it changed the way I dated. Out went exclusivity and considerateness; in came multiple-dating and a harder edge, as I judged and dismissed and was judged and dismissed. I dated all sorts of people to learn what really ticked my boxes. But when those dates asked me what my hobbies were, I didn't have anything to say, because saying, 'Well, dating really. You know ... you ... anyone ...' doesn't go down well.

Eventually I tired of the disappointment of going on a bad date, the disappointment of discovering I was someone else's bad date, the games I played badly and the same questions over and over. So after a while I closed my account, went on holiday, took up a course and restarted some of the things that had made single life more fulfilling. And, fulfilled, I unexpectedly fell in love. I didn't meet him through online dating, but online dating gave me so much clarity about what I was looking for that I knew it as soon as I saw it.

Alias: **Charlie23** | *Age:* **50** | *M* | ♀♂ | **Guardian Soulmates**

Internet dating was so simple to start and really easy to maintain. I loved it. It proved that I could go out on my own merits, meet people and start a meaningful relationship from scratch.

Alias: **PlusOne** | *Age:* **39** | *F* | ♀♂ | **Guardian Soulmates**

Internet dating is a chance to be clear about what you want. I didn't want a short man, although I'm only 5ft 4in tall. I didn't want a Tory-voting, card-carrying racist. I wanted a 'nice' guy with a bit of a glint in his eye. I wanted someone fun, naughty, flirty and, above all, honest. And that's what I got!

Alias: **Marie_Mint** | *Age:* **49** | *F* | ♀♂ | **Guardian Soulmates**

I tried online dating in the spirit of hope over experience but mainly because my 11-year-old son told me to. He could see how unhappy I was and wanted his smiling mum back. I was aware of my baggage, still spilling out of its suitcase, and knew I was emotionally raw. However, I was sick of listening to other women moaning and groaning about their lot and their errant husbands, and I thought 'What have I got to lose?'

I enjoyed writing the profile as I'm gobby and didn't take it terribly seriously. I had thought that my dating and flirting skills were dead and felt like an awkward teenager again. I went on my first date terrified. Then much to my surprise, I took to it like a duck to water. I love Soulmates because it has none of the leery winking or feeling of being a prostitute in a window as did another site I tried.

Take the risk, trust your instincts and judgement and be open to adventure. Practise assertiveness skills and saying 'no' kindly. Beware of those who overuse the word 'tactile'. Don't keep putting GSOH, lol or :-) in your profile – they are intensely irritating – and don't overdo the value of red wine, open log fires and scuba-diving. Above all, be honest and open. I am frankly amazed at the power that online dating has had in my life.

Alias: **sparklehorse** | *Age:* **29** | F | ♀♂ | **Guardian Soulmates**

I was 29 when I signed up. I had a close group of friends, and I always saw the same people every Saturday night. I'd have a nice time with them, but they were all in couples and no one new ever came into the group. I'm not the sort of person who would meet anyone at a bar, probably because I'd be enjoying myself with my friends. Sometimes you feel 'Am I losing the ability to chat to people?' My friends did try and introduce me to people, but there's always a responsibility there. If you were going out with someone your friend had introduced you to, you'd have a responsibility to be nice to them or make sure you responded politely. And if you didn't like them, you had to make up excuses when your friends asked you about it to avoid hurting their feelings. Some of the people were so unsuitable! It's amazing who people think you'd get on with. You're left thinking, 'Why did you think I'd get on with *him*?' They are just trying to think of anyone they know who is single!

It's natural that our generation dates online – we do everything else online. If you think of your grandparents, they used to go to dances – that's how they did it in their day. It's better to be in control of finding someone yourself – you are your own matchmaker.

I started online dating with no expectations except to have some fun. I didn't think I was going to meet the love of my life on a dating website, and I've never even had a romantic image of meeting 'the one' anyway. In reality, I think there are probably lots of people who any of us could be with, it's just about whose company you enjoy.

I only had about 15 dates because I met Leon when I had been on the site for a couple of months. I was sure of him quickly. We're both honest about how we're feeling and thinking, and it just felt easy and normal from the beginning. He asked me to marry him while we were away in Prague.

It's strange – if I hadn't met him, would I have met someone else? Yes, I think so. I think there's more than one person who each of us could live with.

———————

Alias: **SaucyPedant** | *Age:* **44** | *F* | ♀♂ | **Guardian Soulmates/match.com**

After a divorce and then a relationship with a 'friend' who was happy for me to cook for him and sleep with him but wouldn't call me his girlfriend, I decided that I needed a new man. Living in a country town and working in a predominantly female environment made it hard to meet new people, so I embarked on internet dating.

I've had varying degrees of success. Several one-date-only experiences like the man who spent the whole evening telling me about a trip to Venezuela, yet managed to make it so boring that I went to the loo for a bit of light relief. Or the one who kissed me and actually bruised my tonsils with his tongue. There were also a few two-or-three-date guys. Like the one who took me to the supermarket then back to his place where he cooked egg on toast, which we ate in front of the TV.

I have had a couple of longer term relationships. One nice guy. We went to Southport and Slovenia together but didn't quite find the chemistry. Then there was Ben. He promised me the world. Put my Valentine card on his shelf next to the one from his ex. Had active profiles on several dating websites, but I only dumped him when I found out he'd been seeing another internet date, despite having been with me for 10 months. That was a year ago, and I've dipped my toe back in the water a couple of times. Most recently with a man who thought that serving day-old prawn curry on a table laden with newspapers, a compost bin and a dog's hairbrush was a romantic dinner.

Every time, I say 'Never again!' But here I am, still single. Maybe I'll just have another peep.

Alias: **charmedlife** | *Age:* **34** | F | ♀♂ | **match.com**

My family is crazy: they set me up! They would try anything to get rid of me, which is how I ended up on an online dating site. Because I come from a half-Italian South American, macho family, I knew that being single past the age of 25 was going to raise some hackles, but I decided not to care and not to notice the figurine of St Anthony of Padua hanging upside down so that my auntie could claim the 'miracle' of my finding somebody. (Apparently, you have to put it upside down, recite three Hail Marys and pray to find somebody to love. I do not know if it works, but it gives you loads to talk about when you're comparing your weird family with other people's).

So, when my older sister gave me a free six-month trial at match.com, I agreed, not only because it sounded interesting but also because it was free. And hey presto, with a couple of photos and some description of my personality, I did get, like a million replies. OK, not a million – more like 2,086 (not that I counted them) – and I did meet lovely, interesting and attractive people, but I also met some ... hmmm ... 'interesting' ones. Like John, who sounded so nice on his profile, being a librarian and doing a PhD in English literature. He had a nice sense of humour and was writing a book about the history of calligraphy, or something like that, but by the second email he had created an email address ILoveCharmedLife@hotmail.com and sent me a video of him masturbating (in his mother's bedroom because her computer had the camera) together with the message, 'I hope you don't mind.' As far as I could remember the last thing I posted on our chat was 'Talk to you soon!' (Apparently, that is the exact translation of 'I want to see you wanking on video, asap' in weirdo).

To be fair, John was the only *bad* experience, because in general the rest of my dates were great. I really liked many of those guys, and I still keep in touch with some of them. I went to the wedding of one of them last winter. In the end, I married one of my dates too, and yes, we are really happy, all thanks to online dating, even if my auntie says that it was down to St Anthony.

I think it's fantastic that there is a choice like this to find friends, lovers or a potential partner. It's like having a bank of men (or women) to choose from. It's great!

Alias: **SoSueMe** | *Age:* **56** | *F* | ♀♂ | **datingdirect.co.uk**

Well, there I was: 55, overweight, disabled and never married. It was 10 years since my boyfriend had died. Definitely time to move on.

It's been liberating for me as a disabled woman because I can be out every night of the week and still not actually meet a man. Having said that, I am quite picky – no football shirts, no dodgy pictures, no smoking and no facial hair.

Always follow the rules, meet in a public place, and if there's the faintest whiff of mad-axeman tendencies, make your excuses and leave. I always give the guy's home or mobile numbers to a couple of girlfriends and tell the date: 'If you're planning to murder me, you won't get away with it because my friends have your phone numbers.'

One website simply does not have enough members. This is not just my experience – a girlfriend 20 years younger than me found the same thing. The site suggested that I widen my search criteria to include anyone with a pulse north of the equator. I live in Manchester. I don't think so.

Another site revealed stacks of men wanting to meet me for an LTR (long-term relationship). What they were really after, of course, was an ONS (one-night stand). Be careful out there, but do have fun. You definitely have to be ruthless in deleting the time-wasters and sometimes playing them at their own game. As Jo Brand said, 'What's the best way to a man's heart? Through his top pocket with a Stanley knife.'

Alias: **Lorimer** | *Age:* **47** | M | ♂♀ | **Guardian Soulmates**

Here's a working definition of irony. I had no interest in dating. My long-term relationship had just ended, and I still lived, platonically, with my ex, Ally, and our kids. I wasn't as lost and upset as she was and had already decided on some independence and self-sufficiency. I'm happy enough alone, why not let the dust settle and enjoy a little, well, me-time? Except Ally, who's kind and concerned, kept asking when I was going to start online dating. She'd already begun; I'd grown accustomed to her tapping away until late, saying who-knew-what to who-knew-who. It registered as odd, but I had no complaints or difficulties.

Ally is persistent and knows me well. She said my slightly reclusive tendencies might, 18 months on, leave me melancholy and left behind, with just TV, wine and sofa for company, while she cantered sociably through her new-made life. So I relented and joined her on Soulmates. Candidly, I'm better at writing than I am at dazzling strangers with my small talk or sexual charisma. Online dating was a way, maybe, to find someone who'd accept how I looked because they'd already grown to like me. (Not that I think I'm an utter gargoyle, but neither would I have featured on the site's rotating gallery of its most toothsome and ornamental subscribers.)

Sorry, yes: the irony. Turned out that Ally wasn't ready, despite her talk of making new connections. And I – not looking, not bothered – started a relationship (a fantastic, still-thriving relationship) with the first woman from the site I met. Actually, it's not ironic. Maybe in a few years I'll call it that. It was upsetting, stressful and tumultuous, especially for Ally. Make sure you're ready and be careful what you wish for.

Alias: **NomDePlume** | *Age:* **47** | *F* | ♀♂ | **Guardian Soulmates**

It's time to fess up. It's tidier than fessing down. Although cunningly disguised as a friend of a friend of a person quite likely to be a friend, I met him on the internet.

I know. But everyone's doing it. All the friends of friends of people one is quite likely to know. It has real advantages over real life. Things like:

- We all know why we're here. It's possible to talk to his/her photograph without ever having had the painful experience of having a photograph given to you as a token of love and then just being left with the token when the photographee has wandered off.
- We can pretend to be better/wittier/saner/realer/less menopausal people without the real better/wittier/saner/realer people actually finding out that you're sitting there having a hot flush.
- There is no one to ask if you are really better/wittier/saner/realer. (Soulmates haven't cottoned on to the whole reference thing, which is the usual requirement of the matchmaker.)
- It's nothing to do with one's mother's conception of who a nice boy/girl would be.
- It's possible to judge people on purely spurious bases – like the quality of their punctuation, whether they're capable of making it through an entire form-filling process and how they look in a photograph obviously taken in a moment of desperation as they came to the bit in the form where asked to upload a photo (hence the Lion King pyjamas).

Alias: **HappyGoLucky** | *Age:* **29** | *F* | ♀♂ | **Plentymorefish**

When I was away doing voluntary work in Africa I met this guy, Paul, who was running one of the projects, and I completely and utterly fell in love with him. Things with Paul were great, but he had to live up on camp, which was often almost impossible to get to, so being together was really hard work. In the end I realised that I had to leave, even though it was so painful. The last thing I wanted to do was to come back to London. When I got home, I cried for about six months, really struggling to get over him.

Shortly after that I started internet dating and soon met somebody on Plentymorefish. We saw each other for six months. It was a strange relationship: I never met his friends and family, and he never met mine. We just hooked up and spent time together at a time when I was still broken-hearted about Paul. I knew it wouldn't last a long time, but it was fun and really helped me realise there were other men out there. I never would have started talking to him if we'd met any other way – he was not my 'type' – but he made me laugh on the internet. I was attracted to his cheeky grin in his profile photo. We got on really well and had some fun times together. He was very supportive when I was going for job interviews, and I was there for him when he was having a hard time. It was convenient and mutually beneficial in a really friendly way.

It was a total internet thing. Part of the reason it worked so well was that we had no mutual friends: we moved in completely different circles and did completely different things.

When I left his flat for the last time we just said goodbye as usual, yet I somehow knew we would never see each other again. I knew the relationship had run its course, and I didn't make any effort to track him down and he didn't call me. It was quite bizarre, but it had served its purpose: it helped me to get over Paul.

Alias: **TamsyQQ** | *Age:* **50** | *F* | ♀♂ | **Guardian Soulmates**

I was heading for 50 and at a big turning point in my life. After a family bereavement I was in freefall. I was no longer a carer, I'd moved house, and I'd changed job. It was an enormous loss of identity. Everything in my life was in flux. The person I had always put first wasn't there to put first, and I thought it would be nice to meet someone. I was strangely afraid of becoming too selfish with no one to create a bit of give and take.

It had to be Soulmates and no other in terms of politics, education-level and just the sense that most of my real-life friends are *Guardian*- or *Independent*-reading people and it's the most likely place for me to find someone that I would be *simpatico* with.

I spent a while lurking around before joining up, looking at both men in my age group and women in my age group – assessing the competition as well as the potential 'soulmates'. There were some men who'd been up there for a while, and it's a bit like houses that have been on the market for a long time and haven't sold. You think 'What's wrong with them?' So many of the women, in particular, talked about how happy they were with their lives. It's shorthand for 'I'm not a bitch from hell with a ton of baggage'. But it begs the question 'Why not stay single, then?'

I'm actually pretty OK on my own too, but I thought it would be nice to do some of that dating stuff and see what happened. When you spend time with couples, you remember what it's like to be a couple. I found myself wondering whether that's completely over for me or could I have another stab at it?

Alias: **NemoPut** | *Age:* **37** | *F* | ♀♂ | **Guardian Soulmates**

I found online dating a refreshing change from drunken chat-ups in bars. Typically, the community of singles online seems to share the same values and objectives, and while there are definitely 'players' and lifelong commitment-phobes on the web, the majority of people are full of integrity, humour and intelligence. Some people treat online dating like a sweetshop romance, moving from one date to another and always looking around the corner for the next best thing, but if you suss out the players, it's a life-affirming and positive experience.

I dated online on and off and didn't set myself unrealistic expectations or have clearly defined views, like a shopping list, and that's my best advice for anyone thinking of trying it. That and being proactive about communicating with people and not expecting all contact to be a one-way street: men are just as much in need of affirmation as women.

Alias: **RedAdmiral** | *Age:* **72** | *M* | ♀♂ | **Guardian Soulmates**

At the age of 68 I had been single and celibate for too long, and I thought that online would be the way to solve my problem. It wasn't hard to get started, writing a profile and so on, but I did realise that it isn't easy to be objective about oneself. Self-deception is easy to slip into. It is necessary to put yourself forward as attractively as possible but one has to refrain from gilding the lily too much.

If one has loved and lost (no matter what the circumstances), scarring does occur inside, and the capacity to love and be loved is jeopardised. Having said that, however, hope rises in the human breast.

It also depends on how comfortable you are in your own company. Too many years on one's own isn't ideal if you hope to share again. I'm now 72 and don't think it's going to happen for me, but I'm not bitter. I look around and think there is so much to be positive about: no regrets.

Alias: **MZEE** | *Age:* **83** | *M* | ♀♂ | **Guardian Soulmates**

1. One can be precise and, one hopes, accurate about oneself.

2. One can safely assume that one's correspondent is also seeking a soulmate, so there should be no misunderstandings about one's intentions.

3. However many friends and acquaintances one might have, the problem remains: who would be amenable to a romantic approach?

4. Seeking a partner, or even a friend, online – if the system is used sensibly and honestly – is an efficient use of available technology.

Alias: **Ms_E** | *Age:* **34** | *F* | ♀♂ | **Guardian Soulmates**

I have been on roughly 40 internet dates over about five years. I've had some amazing ones – been convinced I have met 'the one', fallen head over heels in lust within an hour and been planning babies by dessert. I've also had some corkers: Big Fat Stuart springs to mind (he was morbidly obese but had posted a photo of himself from 10 years ago). Sex Pest Pete too. I've met men who've lied about their height. (Why? How did they think I wouldn't find out?). I've met bald, cross-eyed, sausage-lipped men with massive boils on their heads who've tried to stick their tongue down my neck within 10 minutes. Overall, though, my experience has been positive.

You can't do it continuously. I join a site for a month, arrange about four dates, see them all and leave it for a while. You can't email someone for too long because you build up too many hopes and expectations, but if you're too quick you might find yourself on a date with a lunatic. But what else am I going to do? I'm 34 and I'm past pulling blokes in pubs and clubs. I wouldn't have any dates at all if it wasn't for the internet. And yes, I have been to a match.com wedding, and I still remain hopeful that one day, when I least feel like dragging myself out for a drink in Soho, I'll actually meet the one I've been looking for. I've had a couple of near misses; he can't be that far away now.

Alias: **Daisy_Daisy** | *Age:* **39** | *F* | ♀♂ | **match.com**

Looking for your soulmate, whether in real life or online, is like looking for a tiny needle in a seemingly impenetrable haystack. The search can be exhilarating and demoralising in equal measure. Having exhausted conventional means and having an address book full of wonderful couples and fabulous unattached girlfriends but not a single encumbrance-free man, I needed to take positive action in my search for enduring love.

The best advice I can give to new online daters is to enjoy the experience, not to take it too seriously or the rejections too personally, and to make sure you have industrial quantities of salt readily available until you really know someone.

Alias: **Saes** | *Age:* **55** | *M* | ♀♂ | **Guardian Soulmates**

I started online dating simply because once one hits the big five-0 it gets increasingly difficult to meet suitable potential life partners. I'd already tried salsa classes, watercolour classes and Welsh classes, and I'd made some good friends, but no one who hit my spot. My first site was Soulmates, and I did find a lovely lady with whom I had happy times over almost a year, but it didn't work out in the long term.

Since then I've tried a range of sites and found that you get what you pay for (the sites, that is – not the ladies!). I'd encourage anyone thinking about internet dating to stop pussy-footing about with toes in the water – just jump in and swim with the tide!

Alias: **AllyT** | *Age:* **41** | *F* | ♀♂ | **Guardian Soulmates**

My workmate coaxed me into it. She seemed to be having so much fun. Some weeks she went on three or four lunch dates with different men. My curiosity aroused, she showed me their photos and I had to admit that some of them looked rather good and had decent jobs and interesting hobbies. It certainly wasn't the freak show that I had imagined. It also appealed to my sense of efficiency – being able to scan through lots of potential mates and screen out the unsuitable ones. The joy of knowing that someone liked children or wanted their own instead of having to ask the awkward question on the first, second or third date was fantastic.

It was practical, too: I was a single mother working full-time in a demanding job, and I didn't have time or energy to go out a few nights a week and 'meet people'. I would advise people to give it a try. I have met some very genuine and lovely people online, even though none developed into a relationship. I would also say be honest and open and always give people a chance. Even if things don't work out romantically, you may make a new friend or gain a funny story with which to regale your friends.

Alias: **BrownEyesBlue** | *Age:* **46** | *M* | ♀♂ | **Guardian Soulmates**

Dating online made me feel very self-conscious. I hated the idea: I felt I'd curl up and die if my workmates saw my profile or if someone tried to wind me up. I was a man in my mid-40s with two long-term relationships behind me who had decided to give up and throw myself into work, watching *Match of the Day* and finishing the things I wanted to get through in my life. But my friend badgered me into it; and in three weeks' time, my girlfriend, her foster son and I will be celebrating a year together.

Alias: **Yorks_star** | *Age:* **26** | *F* | ♀♂ | **Guardian Soulmates**

It all began over a few drinks with my housemate, who, I must admit, I'd had a little bit of a crush on. Although he hadn't yet met 'the one', he was a great advocate of Soulmates. He'd met some interesting people and could always be relied upon for a comedy story.

I think in my mind there'd always been a bit of a stigma attached to internet dating, but after chatting with a few other friends it turned out that most of them had dabbled in online dating at some time or other, so I figured it wouldn't hurt to give it a go. After all, past university, where do you meet people? It isn't always appropriate to date people from work. Most of my friends are already in relationships, and I'm past the stage of 'going out on the pull' and hoping to meet people in bars. To be honest, I never really enjoyed that, and on the few occasions I'd let friends persuade me, it was as painful as I'd predicted.

Alias: **Gromlin** | *Age:* **30** | *M* | ♂♂ | **Guardian Soulmates**

Without a badge on me, people cannot tell that I am gay. I'm not the media stereotype, so how do other gay men identify me as a potential date? They cannot. And so, as someone who does not parade his sexuality and does not appear 'obviously' homosexual, I am forced to use the world of online dating sites. Simples.

Alias: **_eh** | *Age:* **25** | *F* | ♀♂ | **match.com**

Nearly two years ago I finished a very long relationship which took me from my teenage years into my early 20s. I found that meeting people once I was back on the shelf was considerably harder than it was when I was at school. This combined with the fact that I worked in a female-dominated environment, and the only men I ever met while I was out were the drunk ones who wanted to take me home at the end of the night.

So, after a few glasses of wine on a lonely winter's evening, I decided to join the throng of solitary hearts online. It wasn't difficult to get talking to people, and within a few hours I'd received my first message. Within a few weeks I had arranged and been on the first of many dates. The whole experience did make dating a lot easier for me. I would probably never have approached a 'real-life' man if I'd liked the look of him, but I could do it online, and online rejection was easier to take. I went from having no idea at all about the world of adult dating to meeting and dating men from all walks of life and having fun – most of the time – doing it.

Alias: **Idina** | *Age:* **54** | *F* | ♀♂ | **Guardian Soulmates**

Online dating was recommended by a younger flatmate who'd had some success. However, there are fewer men than women on many internet sites, and middle-aged men often have unrealistic expectations of their appeal to younger women, leaving women their own age on the online shelf or dating pensioners almost as old as their fathers. I have done much better dating men my own age in the 'real' world.

Alias: **LadyLongLegs** | *Age:* **54** | *F* | ♀♂ | **match.com**

Reality check for me: I was over 50 years old, divorced and with a limited social circle. It became a question of hanging about in pubs or clubs, going on Saga holidays or relying on friends as matchmakers, none of which was really my scene. I decided that I had to take the plunge and make changes in my life. Having been practically a child bride and totally out of touch with the thrills and spills of the dating game, something told me that the only way, given my limited circle, was to throw in my lot with the world of internet dating.

There are lots of drawbacks, including the fact that some guys appear really interesting online or on the telephone but, when I meet them, I spend the whole time thinking: 'How can I make my excuses and get the hell out of here without being rude – or else risk being bored to death?'

To anyone considering online dating I would say go for it, enjoy it, don't take it seriously and make notes, because, at the very least, you'll dine out on tales of your adventures. I know that without the internet I would never have met such a wide range of people or had anything like the interesting times that I have had. I've had the experience of a lifetime. It has been a journey of discovery about myself, not forgetting all that I have learned about men – enough, in fact, to rewrite *On the Origin of Species*.

Alias: **UltraViolet** | *Age:* **34** | *F* | ♀♂ | **Guardian Soulmates**

When I was a little girl I used to love a Grimm fairytale where a servant girl had to outsmart a witch before she could win her prince. The climactic task set to her was to search through a room filled with precious, ornate rings in search of a plain gold band. The only catch, as she soon discovered, was that the plain ring lay trapped in the beak of a bird, trapped in a cage, trapped in the bitter clutches of the witch.

The second I set eyes on Tim, I felt as though he was my plain gold band. The only catch, as I instantly discovered, was that smart, witty, keen-eyed Tim lived in Auckland, New Zealand, several thousand miles away from my home in the Isle of Man. Of course, his inaccessibility was also an essential part of his appeal; that's the way it goes with romantics.

We sustained our mutual enchantment with an epic correspondence, which, as the months went by, drifted clean away from its moorings in reality. Our email courtship became an end in itself – a creative challenge, a delicious flight from the threat of disappointment, a seemingly endless courtship with possibility itself.

In time, however, gravity took hold. As strangers without the resources to meet more than once or twice a year, we couldn't meet the emotional demands we had begun to place on each other.

Tim had placed in my hands an unexpected gift. I realised not only that I wanted to travel but that it was the romance of a journey I'd craved all along. Several months later, I went to New Zealand. Naturally, we had to meet, but when we did so, both pairs of feet stayed firmly on the ground. The country, however, burned its way directly into my heart, and of my time in North and South Islands, I have nothing but lovely memories and the lingering sense of possibility.

Alias: **AudreyB** | *Age:* **38** | *F* | ♀♂ | **Guardian Soulmates**

The first time I signed on to a dating website was a few years ago, soon after my marriage of 10 years had come to an end. If stepping back into the dating world after a long relationship was uncomfortable, putting myself on an online dating website was terrifying. Unsure of what to write on my initial profile, I failed to mention that I was, at the time, separated, with two lovely children. First lesson learned: always be honest and not ashamed about your past. I read much literature on 'how to' date correctly, and I spoke with other women. We had our own rules about who we would respond to and who we wouldn't. Anyone who wrote one sentence as an initial email would not get a response. Similarly, too long an email was off-putting. And so on. Talk about being closed-minded and having high expectations! I wanted a man to tick every box: he had to be over 6ft tall and have dark hair and a good job and so on. And let's not forget that elusive spark I was seeking. Unless it was present within the first five minutes, a man would more than likely be ruled out in my mind as a potential match. At some point I began to wonder why he had to meet all these requirements.

Over the past few years I've met a lot of men. There was the much older man who taught me to look at my 10-year marriage not as a failure, but as a success. The much younger man who taught me to be proud of my daughters, my greatest achievements. The man who taught me to play games – and made me want to stop. The man who laughed with me and kissed me like no one else before, and then showed me I had to let him go, lovingly. I have listened to my heart, my head, my body. And sometimes unknowingly, I haven't listened to any of these. I've met men with whom there has been an instant, electrifying attraction – dangerous, exciting and oh so intoxicating. I've been on dates I couldn't wait to leave, but for no other reason than a lack of connection – deathly silences filling the air with morgue-like connotations. And I've had dates with lovely, pleasant men, who enriched a couple of hours of my life. With each date, I began to feel more confident. I began to gain a sense of what I was really looking for in a partner ... and what I wasn't.

Learning to accept rejection and trust that it wasn't meant to be were other big lessons for me. Recently I've found myself wondering what would have happened if I had continued to see the nice man I met when I was still on my quest for perfection? What if you meet someone with whom you get along very well, but don't feel that initial spark? I have begun to realise that what I'm seeking will perhaps not reveal itself on a first or second date. What I'm now seeking is more lasting. A friendship and a mutual liking of each other, not just that initial spark.

As I was browsing profiles some time back, I saw a man I had met online two years ago. We had had two enjoyable dates before I told him I didn't feel a spark, and we lost touch. We renewed our email contact and found that both had been in long-term relationships since, and both were recently back online. I asked him if he was interested in meeting up. I am learning not to expect the man to make all the moves and am assuming responsibility for what and who I would like in my life ... while, of course, letting go of the outcome!

We met for our third date two years after our second, and I immediately felt comfortable with him. It did not feel as if a gulf of time had passed between us. We walked and walked. We spoke of life and love. We ate food and drank tea. We both agreed how much more relaxed we were in each other's company. He is someone I would like to get to know better: he interests me and we laugh together. Is he my soulmate? I don't know. At the least, I feel I have found a good friend.

This is no great story of love found. On reflection, though, perhaps it is. Through all my experiences, all the dates I've been on, I have rediscovered more of myself: my likes and dislikes, and whom I choose to let into my life. The qualities I value and seek in another are qualities I wish to enhance in myself. While seeking a mate, I have become reacquainted with my own soul.

Alias: **NomDePlume** | *Age:* **47** | *F* | ♀♂ | **Guardian Soulmates**

It's my birthday. I got an email. It said:

> Here's wishing you a very happy birthday! Let's hope that this is the year when you find that someone special at Guardian Soulmates.
>
> Warmest regards,
>
> The Guardian Soulmates Support Team

This, I believe, was a cruel and heartless thing to do. After all, it stands to reason that if one is a member (albeit lapsed) of Guardian Soulmates (other dating sites are available) then there is a strongish likelihood that one is spending one's birthday alone.

Without one's soulmate. So rubbing it in and being the only birthday email one might receive is just a tad insensitive. I am, however, not downhearted, grey, drab or slightly cheerless. For I have discovered many truths of being single, things that only single people can do just because they are single. Here are some of them:

Burst into loud and tuneless song any time of the day or night.

Dance naked in the kitchen without giving the impression one wants sex.

Talk to friendly inanimate objects.

Kiss friendly inanimate objects.

Shout at not friendly inanimate objects.

Dance clothed in the kitchen without giving the impression one wants sex.

Give the impression one wants sex without the danger of offending.

See the world through rose-tinted glasses.

Fantasise about Prince Charming.

Wear glass slippers.

Use words like itsy, didums and zipadeedoodah.

Be happy without anyone thinking one is crazy.

Be crazy without anyone thinking one is crazy.

Be without anyone wondering why.

Wonder about being without anyone wondering where their clean pants are.

Not wash pants.

Not wear knickers.

Sleep in trees.

So, to the Guardian Soulmates Support Team I'd like to say 'sod off'. Because – and this is a fact – only single people can live their lives as stars in musicals; when they marry they have to leave immediately. Or the musical ends.

Zipadeedoodah!

Which website to choose?

So, you're a time-poor metrosexual hurtling towards a significant birthday. You're a love-minded ruralite tired of scouring the hedgerows for a soulmate. You have stood by as your treacherous best friend ditched the complicities of singledom to join the smug-marrieds. Watched ruefully as the last eligible person in a 100-mile radius was snapped up. Tried pointlessly to factor some Spanish classes into your 60-hour-working-week plus three-hour-commute. Whether you have been pulled, kicking and screaming, into the online future, or have glided in on rollerblades, you have some decisions to make. Which website to plump for? How do you choose from a smorgasbord that offers you everything, in dating terms, from ash-rolled goat's cheese to curled-up ham? How do you know that TrystsOnTap is to be trusted, that MailAMate is not mendacious or GrabaShag is your bag?

Your online cup certainly overfloweth. Among the 820 sites Hitwise estimates to exist in the UK, there are the generalists like Match and PlentyofFish and the specialists like Guardian Soulmates, Christian Cafe and Gaydar, which appeal to people with a shared sensibility, credo or liking for a freshly-waxed torso. As Mark Brooks, editor of OnlinePersonalsWatch.com notes, membership in many general sites is falling while the specialist sites rise, particular in the gay, ethno-cultural and religious dating categories – such as JDate (for Jewish singles), AsianPeopleMeet and Manhunt (for gay men).[21] There are niches within niches – you only have to ask. Muddy Matches for the Barbour set, DatingBBW for the voluptuous (BBW is an 80s acronym for big, beautiful women), GreenSingles for the eco-minded and PlatonicPartners for celibates. There's dating for geeks, dating for goths, dating for yoga bunnies and dating for druids. There are sites that match you to people by your personality or your taste in cult sci-fi. And there are websites you can't enter if you try: fewer than one in eight British men and three in 20 British women who have applied have been accepted to the looks-obsessed BeautifulPeople.com, which only admits newbies if enough members of the opposite sex vote them in.

Most sites are self-certified: you don't ask for, or receive, a reference. But a hugely popular home-grown site, Sarah Beeny's MySingleFriend, has cleverly adopted the traditional 'friendship obligation' – the onus on couples to match-make for their single friends – and integrated it into a site that asks people to upload profiles and 'references' on their friends' behalf.

There are a few things to look out for if you're thinking of entering this brave new world: is it geared to long-term relationships or to one-night stands? Is there a vigilant customer service team who will filter out the likes of Bigamist99? And will they answer their phone in less than a month? Just as there's no point in advertising your love of Biblical exegesis on a swingers' site, it is a good idea to take advantage of a website's trial membership to assess whether it hosts, in a nutshell, enough people you like who would like someone like you. Bear in mind that the declared numbers of members may not all be paid up – many profiles are inactive as people let their subscriptions lapse without removing their page. And sites have their own cultures, which change over time – majority interests that may represent a hidden bias against you. That doesn't mean you don't stand a chance on that site, but it may be worth spreading your bets. The website match.com recently surveyed a sample of over 11,000 users, a large proportion of them in the 25-34 age range, and found that the majority of heterosexual men who expressed a preference were looking for blonde women with an average figure.[22] So if you're dark and curvaceous, you may not find yourself becoming Miss Popularity on the site.

HappyGoLucky is a 29-year-old performance coordinator based in London who has used a number of different websites, and received entirely different responses according to which one she chose: 'Within a few weeks of me and my friend both doing each other's profiles for MySingleFriend, she started to get loads of interest, and I was really chuffed for her. But I still haven't even had one date from them! I'm very cynical about why. I'm no stick insect, as I say in my profile, and, to be quite honest, I think guys on the conventional websites are looking for your typical slim model-type girl with long blonde hair. On internet sites I always tick the box for "curvy" or "a few extra pounds" and I think it puts blokes off. I do really find that they look at me and just discount me. I went on another site called DatingBBW.com – Big Beautiful Women – for fuller-figured ladies. I didn't tell any of my friends that I'd signed up because I was embarrassed – it's like announcing: "I'm going on fat dates", and I knew my friends would think I was being silly, but everyone's got their hang-ups, haven't they? The profiles have a fairly limited focus: it's basically "man seeking woman" and his star sign, which I don't give a shit about – I'm never going to look at someone and say "Omigod, he's a Virgo – we must get married!" But I got quite a lot of attention and guys winking at me, which felt quite good.'

Guardian Soulmates has an average age of 38 and a half, and a gender balance that is roughly even – 56 per cent female and 44 per cent male (generally-speaking, fee-paying 'relationship' sites tend to have more women than men, while free and no-strings-sex sites tend to number markedly more men than women). And while only 58 per cent of Soulmates users actually read the *Guardian*, 80 per cent of them value the connection to the paper. For 30-year-old Londoner **DanE1**, who works in publishing, 'It was always going to be Soulmates because I'm a real intellectual snob. I really don't care where people are from or what they do or anything about them at all as long as they have a brain. My dating experiences in the past before I went on Soulmates, and also my friends' experiences on other dating sites, made me think I might have problems and might have to filter out a lot of people where I would know from the start it wasn't going to work. With Soulmates I knew that, apart from anything else, I'd be able to go on a date and at least have a decent conversation – even though they might be pigeon fanciers or into fetishism. That's not to say I'm looking for a university professor – *I* wouldn't be able to keep up with *him*. I'm looking for someone who has a brain and ambitions and thinks about the world.'

For **Mmmm**, a 33-year-old woman who works as an education officer in a London theatre, it had to be MySingleFriend: 'I chose the site because I felt uncomfortable "selling" myself. It was so much fun writing my friend's profile – we made an evening of it, with dinner, wine, a laptop and lots of laughs. I didn't make suggestions while she wrote my profile, but giggled a lot while she was writing it – it was really interesting to hear what she thought about me. I had got to a point where I'd met "friends of friends", and the people I was meeting through work were all the "wrong kind of man" for me – actors who always put themselves and their careers first – so internet dating was a way of widening my network. I dated about eight people in total over a year, but did have multiple dates (up to three times) with some people. I was quite shallow when it came to "favouriting" people – I was very much led by their photos.' **Mmmm** met her current partner on the site – who happened to be someone she had already met six years before in the real world setting of a friend's wedding, when she had sat next to him. 'I recognised Pete when I saw him on there, but couldn't remember where from, so I favourited him and he got straight back in touch with me, having recognised me too. I liked that it said on his wall, "I now feel that I'm in a position to continue to spoil my daughter and another special someone": this attracted me as he was more than happy to talk about his daughter on his profile, rather than not mentioning children, as many people tend to, even when it is mentioned in the stats at the top of the profile.'

London-based project coordinator, **Freudianslip**, 45, opted for GaydarGirls over Soulmates, her second choice: 'I associate GaydarGirls with anonymity and a lack of seriousness, whereas I associate Soulmates with seriousness. I've also seen a lot of my exes on Soulmates so I've steered clear of it for that reason too. I've been using GaydarGirls on and off for a while, partly for its chat function.' GaydarGirls' chatroom layout enables written conversation in a social networking style as well as dating, blurring the boundaries between friendship, romance and community-building. 'Sunday evenings and Monday evenings are the peak times for GaydarGirls: about 400 can be online in central London alone. Not only in London: there are lots in Brighton and Manchester. You can search by city to see who's online. But it's not just about friendship – as one friend of mine says, "I'm not here for cake recipes!" Some people are clear about just wanting a sexual relationship and others clear about wanting friends. On GaydarGirls you can now put down your sexual preferences, which *can* be too much information! It's a real signal of a move in a GaydarBoys orientation – people hooking up for sex – noticeably different from how it was when I first went online four years ago. GaydarGirls has changed the women's scene: about 10 years ago, before Gaydar, things were more ghettoised – there were the Islington lesbians and the south London lesbians and the Forest Gate lesbians, and there wouldn't be much cross-pollination. Since GaydarGirls, that ghettoisation has diminished. But the biggest difference I've noticed is that professional lesbians who would have mixed less in the bar scene and bar culture are now mixing more. I was always a barfly so I knew a lot of the clubbing girls but now I know a lot of the professional lesbians too.'

This softening of the boundaries between dating and friendship is becoming widespread. Social networking sites such as Facebook and MySpace have taken a wedge out of the online dating pie. In the US, according to web-traffic monitor ComScore, the number of people visiting dedicated dating websites in December 2007 was down 10 per cent on the previous year. But according to Brooks, that does not necessarily mean a drop: it's simply that the lookie-loos – those curious window-shoppers – have gone away.[23]

And the future? There's a wild new development in online screening that will shortly be coming to a laptop near you: using Second Life-style web-based avatars, as pioneered by a company called Omnidate.com, people will be able to go on 'virtual dates' in advance of real dates.[24] This will happen at the interface of, yes, dating and gaming: the technology will allow people to visit a simulated environment, such as an online art gallery, and interact with the other person via their avatars to see whether they like each other enough to brave a real date. It's achingly postmodern: a kind of pre-date date – a preamble to a preamble to an amble to a relationship.

Social networking sites will gradually take on more dating functions. Free sites, such as plentyoffish.com and OkCupid.com, will grow and grow. And as the general sites become harder to search meaningfully because they are simply so chock-full, niche websites will take over the world, as like-minded people club together. One can only hope that they won't all be looking for their mirror-images: how boring that would be.

Let's hear it for oppositesattract.com.

Chapter 2:
How to sell yourself in 500 words

Self-marketing for the cyberage

It can feel like the worst job application in the world. Few others could come close, whether it's to become director general of MI5 or voice of the Speaking Clock. Applying for the post of lover, best friend, chef, personal trainer and gardener-cum-handmaiden to the love of your life is tough. Especially when you don't know who she or he is.

To enter the dating pool you have to create a 'profile', your resumé in cyberspace. But how do you sell your talents, dreams, passions and baggage to a stranger in the proverbial '500 words or less'? 'Just be yourself,' say the websites. But which self? And how exactly to be it?

The profile is a strange animal with mismatching feet: a CV crossed with a pop-up survey and a love poem. From one angle it's an honest, authentic summary of Planet You. From another, it is a sales pitch in a crowded market, a brazen act of self-marketing, a shameless strut in your glad-rags on the world's high street. A lot hangs on your ability to use language in a way that is both sincere and seductive: as one commentator put it, 'composition matters – it gets you laid'.[25] With little more than a short piece of prose, you will attempt to dazzle, amuse and entice your lovers-in-waiting. So what if the entire history of sexuality has relied, until now, on chemistry, physical attraction, and pairs of *homo sapiens* being close enough to lick the pheromones off each other? The first step in online dating is a monastic communion between a writer and a reader.

'You have to be aware of the limitations of words, but you can be witty, appealing and very true in your writing,' says **sugar_hiccup**, a 41-year-old woman who joined Guardian Soulmates after moving from London to Brighton. She was hoping to meet new friends for gigs, galleries and walks; and perhaps a new girlfriend. 'I'd be lying if I said I wasn't hoping to find someone lovely,' she says. Her profile took a number of rewrites:

> I spent a long time, if I'm embarrassingly honest, trying to be witty. I was quite sarcastic as well, though I probably didn't give a full list of what a glass-half-empty bugger I can be. I thought honesty was important. One or two people messaged me and said 'Oh! You sound quite scary'. But I don't suffer fools – I didn't want people to think I'm really lovely: I'm opinionated! I think that being quite warts-and-all about yourself is the best strategy. Ultimately you want to attract the people who will like you as you really are.

For the dating novice, your first brain-tickler is to choose a username – your online pseudonym. Actors and musicians from Michael Shalhoub to Anna Bullock (that's Omar Sharif and Tina Turner to you and me) have been doing this for years – re-baptising themselves with spangly new aliases that separate them from lives more ordinary. With the internet, we can all rebrand. The web is one big, non-stop Mardi Gras: a giant masked ball where, under the disguise of a username, you can shop, banter, cruise or have a whirl on the dating dancefloor without anyone finding out.

Your name is ideally a little piece of you. Some actual recent aliases from dating sites show the range: from splendid daftness (**LoveCrumb**, **2leggedtree**) and droll anti-sell (**grumpy_old_git**, **SlightlyDishevelled**) to boy-next-door simplicity (**DanE1**) and literary innuendo (**john_thomas**).

'Usernames are important,' says **sugar_hiccup**. 'I probably hadn't realised how much when I started. I would advise people to think really carefully about how they want to appear. Anything new agey and any spiritual names really left me cold. Even though I'm really into yoga! A name like **shakti123** would immediately put me off because I'd think someone would be going on about *The Secret*.' Wanting a name that was 'a little bit cryptic, abstract and random', she hunted through her iTunes and found Sugar Hiccup, the name of a Cocteau Twins song. 'The Cocteau Twins weren't a passion for me – I just wanted some randomness to it.' No chance. 'One woman in Eastbourne said she appreciated the allusion to the Cocteau Twins, while another in London said: "What a stupid name!"' The one thing you can guarantee is that every word you write on a dating website will be read, analysed and read again by hordes of singletons on a nocturnal browse; and that everything will be taken to be deliberate. But is **OysterCatcher** random ornithology or *double entendre*? Is **mariposa** (*butterfly* in Spanish) poetic or fey? Does **Joe_the_Plumber** evoke on-the-nail political satire or Scandinavian porn? Or is he just a guy who mends U-bends for a living?

You can use almost any word or phrase as a username providing it's not too long. With a few caveats: names involving sixes or nines together are to be avoided, even if you were born in the year of the Moon landing. Ditto names that belong in the subject line of Viagra spam – unless you wish to be besieged by sex addicts. Next, you need a headline, the phrase that sits just below your *nom de plume*. Think of it as your own special jingle, the 'Because you're worth it' of the personal ads. It can span from whimsy ('yesterday tomorrow and in between') to wry self-deprecation ('I'm not bad. I'm just drawn that way'), ruminative quote ('Had we but world enough and time ...') to sweet come-on ('Pint?'). A good choice of name can even help you filter out unsuitables, as 45-year-old **Freudianslip**, who uses gaydargirls.com, discovered: 'The headline underneath my username is "Guardian Reader". Someone had a complete rant at me, challenging "why I would define myself by a newspaper?". She obviously had no sense of humour and couldn't see the self-irony. I wrote back and gave as good as I got!'

Your first foray into profile writing will inevitably lead you to paint yourself in adjectives. But adjectives are slippery things: the more you use, the less they mean. People will struggle to visualise a chain of abstract qualifiers ('I'm talented, forgiving, generous, funny, sensitive, hedonistic, creative, original and loving'). Best to follow the inverse proportion rule with adjectives: use fewer, mean more. Take a leaf out of the Hollywood scriptwriter's bible and 'show, don't tell'. Instead of *saying* you are funny, *be* funny. Instead of *saying* you're hard to please, set them an amusing quiz. Evoke concrete images in people's minds. These two examples could refer to the same person, but which is the more interesting to read?

1) I'm a good listener with a wide circle of friends and a great sense of humour, and enjoy eating out as much as a candlelit dinner at home with a bottle of red.

or

2) My friends include a busker, a comic book artist, a Dusty Springfield impersonator, four Siberian goats, two girls who can juggle, one girl who can juggle goats, a family of organic farmers and a baby. I have been known to chew a Mezcal worm, love the smell of fresh rosemary and can cook a mean kangaroo but would never touch a happy one.

Whatever you think of the second one, at least it's not bland.

'It's difficult to know what to say,' says **sugar_hiccup**, 'but I find insipid profiles like "my friends say I'm a good listener" really off-putting. I would advise people to be really, really honest and to think about the people they want to attract. Don't go for the insipid stuff: all of our friends would say we're kind.'

Being precise about yourself at the start will spare you the tedious grind of so many unsuitable dates later on. For **DanE1**, 30, ('that's my name and my postcode, though I often get asked if I'm Danish'), who has dated online for a year, 'Mediocrity is a terrible turnoff. A lot of sites have a whiff of desperation about them because people are very generic in what they say – they won't pin themselves down. The classic is "I like going out and staying in." Well I like going out and I like staying in with a bottle of wine and a movie as well. Everyone does. But there are more exciting things you can say about yourself.' On a dating site with a million users, you need to work to make your individuality come across. So you love movies? Would that be *10* by Blake Edwards or *Ten* by Abbas Kiarostami?

What attracts and what repels people is the million pound question. In a recent analysis of 4,767 profiles on its website by dating juggernaut match.com, the top turn-off for men was sarcasm (followed by piercing, tattoos, assertiveness and power), while sarcasm was women's third most hated quality in a man (after long hair and piercing, and just above tattoos). But over on Guardian Soulmates, 35-year-old **SlightlyDishevelled** actively *sought out* men who could appreciate the joys of this particular brand of irony – 'Avoiding all the joyless dullards who cited sarcasm as being unattractive, I stumbled across **Spike418**, who had possibly the worst profile I've ever seen – three sentences at best & no photo' (see p. 226). She has recently celebrated over three years of hedonistic happiness with him. For **sugar_hiccup**, turn-offs were 'subtle things: the use of LOL in a profile would make me think, "You are probably not my cup of tea"'. For other people, absent apostrophes or errant exclamation marks are deal-breakers. For those of a critical disposition, sloppy grammar shows an insensitivity to detail that could manifest itself in equally troubling ways during a relationship: absent underwear, errant personal hygiene – who knows what horrors? London teacher **sparklehorse**, 29, who met her future husband on Guardian Soulmates after being on the site for a few months, says:

> I'm really critical about writing. Bad punctuation and poor spelling are an instant turn-off. If I noticed someone's email was badly written, I'd look more closely at their profile. Some of them were really colloquial and it made me think, 'do you talk like that?' Were they wide boys, or worse, were they putting it on for effect – which would have been even more annoying.

During her months online, **sugar_hiccup** became adept at spotting people she might have a chance of liking in person: 'I was drawn to witty, quirky profiles, such as a woman in London who was very attractive: she was a bit arrogant in her profile, but I thought, "She's telling it like it is". She wrote about her ideal match: "They've got to know their Dries van Noten from their Dotty Ps," and I liked the challenge. She was just being herself and not trying too hard to make everyone like her.' Similarly for **DanE1**, precision is good:

> What really drives you? You want to climb Everest or you like singing opera? I don't care if you're burningly passionate about breeding frogs, but put it out there and stand by it. I like the unique combinations: 'I'm a computer nerd but I also like playing water polo and I rap in my spare time.' There was a really good-looking guy I came across who said: 'You have to know that a major part of my life is bird-watching and I have photos of every bird I have ever seen.' Of course, you might find that you're having a picnic and he's eyeing up the pigeons and not you, but I like the fact that he felt he could write that.

But beware: for some people, there is such a thing as too much originality. 'If a profile was too witty it put me off,' says **sparklehorse**. 'It was annoying to see someone trying too hard.' You can be too obscure, too particular. One man who referred in his profile to his 'terpsichorean writhings' (an allusion to his two left feet), on the grounds that it would filter out any woman lacking either a classical education or the curiosity to reach for a dictionary, did not fare well in cyberworld: nobody reached.

SJP123, a 28-year-old movie-buff who teaches disabled students, feels the simple list is the way to go when it comes to writing profiles, an elegant way of telegraphing your distinctiveness to others. Her own list juxtaposes her hero, Noam Chomsky, with Shuggie Otis, cats, art galleries, sleeping late, Chilean merlot and an indiscriminate appetite for food of any kind 'apart from endangered species and tripe', while her handful of dislikes includes 'Happy Hardcore (worst music ever!)' and 'Israel's continued breach of Palestinians' human rights'. Half English and half German, she grew up in Yorkshire, studied film in Edinburgh and came down to London four years ago seeking a wider film culture. As she says in her profile, 'If you're not put off by my geographical and biological heritage then there are still lots of reasons to keep reading'. Fresh and forthright, she announces that 'in a man I like a challenge, someone who interests me, who I can share some common ground with. However, as open-minded as I am, there are a few variables that I will not negotiate on, which would be racism, homophobia and devout Christianity'. She has had some good feedback about her profile: 'Some of the comments I've had from guys have been positive. The fact that I mentioned Shuggy Otis has been a hit with the men because not a lot of women are into funk.' But she worries that her stance might scare some men off: 'My fear is that maybe my profile's too intimidating for guys, that maybe I sound too much like a woman who knows her own mind. I'm debating whether I should just dumb it down a bit. I'm not domineering at all – it's just that there are things I won't compromise on.' However, the signs are that, far from shunning her up-front attitude, guys are drawn to it: her profile spent many weeks on the website's list of the 200 most popular profiles, which is calculated using an algorithm that displays those that are both favourited and messaged most often by other members.

For **sugar_hiccup**, there is no point in hiding your light under a bushel, or indeed worrying about who you might be putting off. 'I told myself I shouldn't be shy to be a bit cocky about myself – you have to get that across.' Her profile (see p. 53) trumpets a brilliantly eccentric repertoire of skills: 'I can do a headstand, cook a great meal, freakishly wriggle my tummy muscles, know the word for monitor lizard in Thai ...' She is adamant that the more honestly people use the tools offered by cyberdating, the better their chances of meeting 'someone lovely ... you should just put that you really want to have children if you do. When people hardly put anything at all you have to wonder why they're on there.'

When you have translated yourself into a small box of text on a computer screen, your next challenge awaits: describing your partner-to-be. Well? What *do* you want? If you're looking for a fellow traveller on your life's journey, you need to map out some of the places you might visit and project a fleeting image of what life with you is like, as did **DanE1** (see p. 55).

Your 'preferences' allow you to refine the image of your desired partner even further, using drop-down multiple-choice boxes. The information you provide allows the dating website's computer program to shortlist potential mates for you by matching your 'attributes wanted' to other people's 'attributes possessed'. Most websites have a one-way match facility (they suggest people who meet your criteria) and a few offer a 'double-match' (they tell you and your shortlisted candidates how well you meet each other's criteria). This standardised format also allows people to search for others by category, whether hobbies, religion, body-type, activity or distance from their homes. So specific is it that you sometimes feel you are not so much seeking your own true love as designing your own pizza, as you order up a slim Sikh with a sailboat, a canoeing Quaker in Consett or a Latvian couch-potato.

What to put in and what to leave out? Be too prescriptive and you might unwittingly be giving out the wrong signals. Does it suggest to others that you're racist if you don't put 'any' under ethnic preference? Does excluding particular body-shapes make you shallow? 'I was quite careful about smoking,' says **sugar_hiccup**:

> I wouldn't want a partner who smoked but I have friends who smoke occasionally and I wouldn't want to exclude those kinds of people. I put that it was 'moderately important' to me that someone didn't feel the need to drink every night. I'm half Maltese and was brought up in the Middle East. It doesn't put me off if someone's first language isn't English – I feel I could communicate in other languages with them. I decided that the only thing I wouldn't be able to handle is someone who is actively religious.

This prescriptiveness has a drawback: as many critics have pointed out, despite online dating's power to take people out of their existing sphere, it often merely entrenches their habitual choices, excluding exactly the kind of people they might love. 'I could see that it was kind of useful to have the tick-boxes, but it was so reductive', says **TamsyQQ**, 50, a vivacious Yorkshire-based screenwriter who dated online for a brief stint before deleting her profile:

> I would be reading people's profiles and finding them interesting but then scrolling to the bottom and thinking 'Oh, Church of England'. I would see that box ticked and it would conjure a whole different person. This is where the online business is so different from meeting someone in person, where chemistry comes first and you might not know this kind of information until much later. I wrote a whole thing on my profile about exactly what I was looking for, and ticked all the boxes. Then I looked at what I'd put down and thought, 'This isn't actually like anyone I've ever been out with!'

sugar_hiccup agrees that there's a danger of excluding people who might suit you. Indeed, she could easily have missed meeting her beloved **WolfWhistle**, the woman she is planning to marry: although **WolfWhistle** was a 95 per cent match for her, **sugar_hiccup** was only a 65 per cent match in return, partly because she is two inches shorter than **WolfWhistle**'s preferred height.

TamsyQQ found the experience of writing a profile intriguing but problematic: 'Online dating makes you examine yourself. I didn't want to describe myself as having been a carer in my profile. The very word "carer" is unsexy. I *was* a carer but I didn't see myself in that word, and that's a prejudice in me. It's one of the really interesting things about online dating – the prejudices it throws up. You see other people's and you see your own.' She found that she was subjecting people to a highly judgemental screening process:

> There were one or two people living quite close by me – lonely widowers not out painting the town red – but I looked at the photos and thought, 'I don't really want to fill your life'. My response was what I imagine people's responses would have been to me had I described myself as a 'carer'. It suggests you have a big hole in your life that needs filling. This is why I've come off Soulmates: I can't bear my own prejudices!

These dilemmas are alien to **sparklehorse**, who thinks profiles function as little more than a vetting procedure: 'I think people can put too much emphasis on writing their profiles. My approach is quite simple. I figured that most people would do what I do – look at the pictures first, look at their interests and then read the blurb just to check the person isn't weird, and if they're normal, arrange to meet. It's at the meeting that you can really tell.' And **Freudianslip** has found that a telegrammatic directness can produce the best profile of all. She used to write expansively about her likes and dislikes, but has recently whittled her profile down into a veritable miniature of the form: 'My profile's very sparse at the moment,' she smiles. 'Under "About Me" it just says one word: "Super". Under "What I'm looking for" all I've written is "Someone who makes me laugh". I used to go into lots of detail about what food I like, but I'm finding that this new profile is working for me just fine. I'm meeting lots of people who make me laugh.'

As for photographs, what's best: to see or not to see? While many people prefer to conceal their photos until a dialogue has been established, men who don't show their faces on their profiles get just a quarter of the responses of those with photos, while women's photoless profiles only pull in a sixth of the response of those with them.[26] Most of us are primarily visual creatures who will only investigate further if we are drawn to an image. 'I would never go for someone who didn't have a picture – not that I'm looking for Brad Pitt, but I think pictures tell you a lot about someone,' says 29-year-old performance coordinator **HappyGoLucky**, who admits that a poorly-considered selection of photos will determine her attitude to the person:

So many blokes who are registered online are unbelievably shit – they put pictures of themselves with their ex-girlfriends, or in a group so you don't know which one he is! I think you can look so different from one photo to the next, so I like it when people have a few pictures and each one shows a different aspect of them – say an outdoorsy photo of them walking the dog or flying a kite, and one that shows them in their everyday life: photos that show their personality as well as their face.

> I also like to see a full-length picture. I can't be doing with skinny men and I don't like blokes with skinny legs in particular, so I like to know what's going on there!

There are a few photographic howlers to avoid: the ridiculously large house or vehicle in the background; pictures that are so blurred and badly-lit you might as well be a squeeze-action mop as a hot date; a frame-filling photo of your face or body that makes you look as though God created you in widescreen. So make sure you enlist someone with at least one eye and no grudge to take your picture. The rule of thumb in choosing your photos is only to use pictures you would be happy showing on television, as you have absolutely no control over who will see them once they go online. Your main profile image should be a head-and-shoulders shot of you, and only you. It sounds obvious to say that it should be well-lit and in focus but you'd be surprised ... It must also be decent. All websites that promote relationships – as opposed to no-strings sex – will have strict rules about material that is risqué or liable to offend their users. Most importantly, your pictures should be as truthful as they can be. **HappyGoLucky** is clear about the need for honesty:

> I deliberately don't go for the photos that show me looking ultra-glamorous, because that's not me. I don't wear little dresses and I never wear make-up. When I choose photos, I try to keep it real. It's me volunteering on the building site in Namibia, or me with friends at the pub having a drink. What's the point of putting out this image and when you meet up the guy says, 'Where's the girl from the profile?'

If there's no photo on someone's profile, should you be worried? Not necessarily. It is possible that the online dater in question is married or has some other small detail to hide, but there are many other reasons why people might want a degree of discretion. **Emroselane**, 58, once had a stalker and is therefore reluctant to be identified publicly as single; as a TV presenter, **sugar_hiccup** chose to remain anonymous until she had struck up a dialogue with someone, after which she was happy to email photos – 'I'm a pretty open person: once I've got chatting, I'm not there to hide, I'm there to meet someone'. **Freudianslip** chooses not to have a photo up. Although she has no issues with people knowing she is gay, she is very clear about guarding her privacy: '*Everybody* is on Soulmates or Gaydar: I don't want people seeing me on there and thinking they know about me.' She also doesn't want her looks to become the sole rationale for a date. 'I would rather people didn't make assumptions or decisions about me based on my appearance, as in "Oh you've got blonde hair and you're quite good-looking – would you like to go on a date?" It's too superficial. I like to think people will have a conversation with me before they form judgements about how I look.'

Once you have condensed your messy life into a tidy profile and subjected it to the rigours of peer review (i.e. your friends pointing out everything you've got wrong – 'Yes yes, of *course* you're a massively talented, misunderstood genius, but you've forgotten to mention you're a good laugh, have a dress-sense that predates the fall of the Berlin Wall and are horrifying at karaoke'), all that remains is to upload it, an act which invokes emotions in a ratio of two parts excitement to one part terror. Leaving this cipher of yourself in the ether is an act of blind faith, a love-song into the void akin to those NASA experiments to find life in Outer Space. You are sending your crackly radio signal into the deep, dark, scary unknown, at the risk of looking very foolish indeed. But with luck, perseverance and a prevailing wind, one day you'll enjoy the mystic moment when the universe signals back.

And sends you a reply.

SAMPLE PROFILE: sugar_hiccup, 41, F, ♀♀

Why should you get to know sugar_hiccup?

I can do a headstand, can cook a great meal, freakishly wriggle my tummy muscles, know the word for monitor lizard in Thai, bear no resemblance to the image with grey, Farah Fawcett flicks ...

Potential partner prescriptiveness aside, I'm new-ish to Brighton/Hove so looking for friends to do stuff with – gigs, movies, dog walks, coffee ...

That said ...

I'm a complex mass of contradictions (cocky/instrospective, city life/wilderness, eat healthily/love crisps, Radio 4/Radio 1/ ClassicFM, silly/serious, adventurous/homely, compassionate/ judgmental, independent – perhaps too much so –/love good company ...), but self-aware with it, deeply analytical and not as hedonistic as I aspire to be although very cheeky. I have, like you, undesirable qualities, with no dropdown options, interspersed amongst loads of desirable ones. Lists is the best we can get online, given that I may tick all your boxes but somehow fail you.

My top values: probably integrity, authenticity and passion. That's a bit too serious isn't it?!

Work – varied: health, media, write books etc. And now doing a master's.

Looks – feminine but boyish, Mediterranean, slim, keep pretty fit ...

I'm open to a wonderfully wide range of things – inspire me to expand beyond crochet and stamp collecting. Although I'm not desperate to visit Scandinavia (I am, in fact, a reptile) and will only ever go into McDonalds to use the loo.

And I don't really collect stamps, although I do have a set from Uganda and one from Burma (discuss). And a treasured collection of echinoderms which dates back to the mid-70s.

Ideal match:
I'm hard to impress. In an ideal world … in addition to being fiercely bright, fit, worldly, outgoing, sensuous, successful at something, unpretentious, curious, silly, open, analytical, sensitive, creative, confident, you have a great smile, inspiring eyes, love urban life and slow time by the sea/outdoors, going to see live music, are into food. I walk my dog twice a day, rain or shine, so if you're into that, great.

I'm up for meeting new friends in the Brighon/Hove area as I haven't lived here long. So seeking like-minded souls for coffee, gigs, walks, movies, getting up to tricks, browsing the shop at the dump … Hence the 'let's see what happens'.

Girls who can only have fun by getting smashed, couch potatoes, anyone who really thinks I'd bring a relative on a date – I'm not your type.

SAMPLE PROFILE : DanE1, 30, M, ♂♂

Why should you get to know DanE1?

I like to laugh, generally at myself. I'm always up for meeting new people and doing new things. Well, except for dogging. Or morris dancing.

I'm a bit of a film geek and I write and direct my own stuff on the side. I'm passionate about what I do and I like guys who have a passion too.

Likes:

Plays and films that make me think
Good cider
Really inappropriate humour
Rugby
Comedy accents
Baked goods

Dislikes:

Cider hangovers
Football
Boris Johnson
Skinny jeans
Country music
Socks

I think that covers the important bits. If you want to know more, or you want to try and persuade me that Boris Johnson is more likeable than an almond croissant, drop me a line.

Ideal match:

I suppose I'm looking for a guy who doesn't take themselves too seriously but knows what he wants.

Someone who likes to have their own space and is happy for

me to have mine; has travelled a bit (not just to Sitges) and wants to do more; has got something to say; is generally a bit scruffy but scrubs up well; and is equally happy in old man pubs and poncey bars.

Oh, and they must like semi-colons. I used a lot in that sentence. Come on, don't be shy.

How to sell yourself in 500 words:
The stories

Alias: **SaucyPedant** | *Age:* **44** | *F* | ♀♂ | **Guardian Soulmates**

Time for a change of profile, I think. But how to write the perfect profile? 'Cute, bubbly 44-year-old …' Hang on a minute. Cute makes me sound stupid. Bubbly makes me sound fat. Should I tell the truth about my age? Most men my age seem to be looking for 25- to 35-year-olds.

Oh I'm fed up with this dating lark.

What am I actually looking for? 'I'm looking for a man who can cope with a bitter, cynical, fiercely intelligent woman. Scared? Well stop reading now. This is a challenge, and only the hardy-hearted need continue.' Ha ha. That'll scare the ones who can't spell. Like Gary from Huddersfield: 'i,m kined and have a sence of humor.' I don't care how kind you are, if you can't even use a capital letter correctly what future do we have? And how can you expect a man who can't find an apostrophe on a computer keyboard to have any more success finding a clitoris???

And why do I get attention from 68-year-olds from Morocco when I think it's quite reasonable to hope to meet someone of a similar age within a 30-mile radius of my home? Why? Where are all the single 40- to 50-ish blokes in my area? I sometimes think I have a force field that deflects all the nice ones at about 20 miles. And the only thing more powerful than the force field is the huge wanker-magnet on the top of my head that sucks them in. And they think they are such catches!

The one thing that's sure to put me off is the old text-speak. Especially 'LOL'. Isn't it supposed to be an indication that one implies a humorous slant in what one has written? Like Nigel from Nottingham: 'I'm 46 lol and I work for the local council lol.' What in the name of all things holy is remotely funny about any of that?

Right, must get back to this profile. What sort of partner am I looking for? 'So ... don't wink at me if you haven't got a photo, if you can't use an apostrophe or even a capital letter properly, if you can't spell, if you live over 50 miles away, if you're looking for "friends first" (I have lots of friends, thanks and I don't need any more!), if you have text speak as part of your username (like Lover 4 U) and if you say LOL even when you have not said anything funny.'

I'm getting jaded by this internet dating world.

I've met a few people. Lovely, sweet, handsome Ben, who went out with me for six months and even told me that he loved me, until I found that he was still advertising himself as available on at least three different websites. Gorgeous, funny Matt, who went out with me until his ex found out and then decided that maybe she would leave her husband for him after all. Or David, who had such a good relationship with *his* ex that she helped him choose dates from the website and was in the habit of phoning him at all times of day and night with vegetable emergencies. Then there were the weirdoes. The ones who weren't totally honest about things like their height or age.

Why am I still here?

Maybe I should make my profile so prickly that only someone as cynical as me about the whole thing will reply! 'So ... don't contact me if you plan to continue using dating websites even if you start going out with me (it has happened!), if you're under 5ft 8in (I like to wear heels), if you're still 'best friends' with your ex or if you look like someone's hit your face with a frying pan.'

I'm not that scary really. I just want an honest, decent man who I fancy the pants off and who can make me laugh like a drain. Is that too much to ask for? I suppose I'd better say something positive. 'You may contact me if you're clever, funny and good at hugs, if you like eating out and long walks in the country, and if you want to help me finish the *Observer* crossword in bed on a Sunday morning. (I can do it by myself but I need someone else to fetch the paper and make the tea).' That's a good bit. I sound fit, clever and worldly, yet there's an underlying hint so he won't be shocked when I want to lie around in bed all day eating toast.

Right, I've probably put off about 99 per cent of the male population now. 'If you've got this far reading this I'll tell you I'm not really that bitter or cynical. I just want to meet a man who will be my lover, best friend and partner through life. If you're still not scared, then write to me. I dare you!' Then again, I don't want 99 per cent of the male population. Cynical, bitter, jaded, twisted serial internet dater that I am, I'm still looking for 'the one'.

Alias: **Lorimer** | *Age:* **47** | *M* | ♀♂ | **Guardian Soulmates**

I'd say don't be afraid to reveal quirks, foibles or unreasonable dislikes. Reading endless profiles is like looking at a paint-colour swatch in a DIY store: there are page after page of oblongs of colours so similar that it's hard to tell a Snowfall from a Tiramisu from a Toasted Almond. In such a context, with profiles appearing and disappearing before your reddening eyes, the reader – or this one, at least – looks for a detail, an observation, an outburst, an opinion, for anything to snag the attention.

Of course, we all like to be liked; we're all painfully aware of smiling our photo smile, of cutting our nails and not wearing the wine-flecked shirt. And it's the same with our words. You love the sea. You love animals. You love laughing and your family. You love your friends. You love the cinema, theatre, reading, eating out and eating in, long walks and long talks. (And you don't just love watching DVDs, you love *curling up* to watch DVDs. I read so many profiles written by devoted curler-uppers I began hallucinating rubber-limbed women spirally arranged on sofas all over the UK.) Oh, and you love travelling, relaxing, exploring and (on the *Guardian* site, at least) you probably love camping as well. Given that there will be many reasons – geography, looks, aspirations, politics, whatever –

for people not to be attracted to your profile, the business of trying to make yourself universally likeable is not only doomed to failure but pragmatically flawed too. You risk sounding so bland that you're practically transparent.

An early favourite of mine was a woman who'd updated her 'What I'm looking for' to refer to nightmare dates she'd already endured. She mustered impressive vitriol about stinginess, road rage, being pawed on a first date and, on a second, being pestered for anal sex. I thought it was laugh-out-loud funny but, more importantly, in getting away from a list of things she loved she gave an idea of what she might really be like. And what people might really be like isn't always clear from a profile.

So, practically, I'd say don't worry too much about putting people off. If you hate camping, say so. If you think there's something a bit wrong in the head with people who fetishise fancy cars, admit it. If you've never made the interval of a play without falling asleep, confess. (If you can spin 50 words out of being scolded for snoring at the RSC, so much the better.) Thing is, if someone's put off by your Shakespeare-snoozing (or your aversion to camping or fancy cars) then they're not really for you anyway, are they?

In the end, people know that what they're reading is a prepared line, a refashioned, highly modulated version of you. The 'real you' is, arguably, pretty subjective and illusory anyway, but whatever it is, it probably doesn't exist on a website's profile. What do you look like when, hung-over, you get up for a wee in the night, stub your toe on the bed and hop around, swearing? What do you say on the hard-shoulder of the sleet-lashed M5 at two o'clock on a February morning when you've got a car that's gone pop and an AA membership you forgot to renew? These are probably more telling indicators of the 'real you' than any form of words you've agonised over on a dating site. But the 'real you' will have to wait; there's no shame in acknowledging that the online you is merely a device and a promotional tool.

Personally, my profile probably alienated the overly optimistic (I was politely caustic about relentlessly glass-half-full people) as well as those who described themselves as a little bit ker-ay-zee and bonkers. Going out of your way to narrow the field down is not the same as having an inflatedly high opinion of yourself; it's just common sense. One woman I quite liked the sound and look of told anyone with facial hair (like me) not to bother. I was a pretty plausible-sounding match for someone else who categorically refused to correspond with men less than 6ft tall. If you pretend to be something you're not – even if it's something you wish you were – the pretence will haunt you and cling to you like a fart in a lift. Imagine all the nervous energy of a first date, then factor in the extra pressure of maintaining a web-based fiction: the stapled-on happy-face smile, the insatiable curiosity for antique shops or extreme sports, the yearning to learn the bassoon. Something's going to give: you could easily implode into a quivering heap of exhaustion and panic even before the first coffee's cooled. And then you'll never know what you might be missing.

Alias: **Miss_Conduct** | *Age:* **30** | *F* | **Bisexual** | **Guardian Soulmates**

My advice to new online daters: there are thousands of people on here, so try to say something *different*. Here are a few of my favourite extracts from a selection of real Soulmates profiles:

I want to wear your face as a mask.
I believe the mix-tape to be the highest form of courtship.
I'm 27 and determined not to die alone.
Despite what some people may think, I *do not* work as a model for the over-50s knitwear department at Marks & Spencer.
I am the illegitimate love child of Ken Dodd and one of the founding members of Hot Gossip.

Alias: **Emroselane** | *Age:* **58** | *F* | ♀♂ | **Guardian Soulmates**

If you change your profile too often you're going to look vain, self-obsessed and desperate, but if you get it wrong at first, put it right soon. My first mistake was with the privacy settings. In my paranoia about 'going public' as an online dater, I made myself totally hidden – not just my photo, as intended, but my profile too, which was unintended. I was acting even shyer than I felt. When I realised I'd gone completely invisible, I took the opportunity to revise my profile. My first version described a few selected but unadorned things about me. When I read it again, I couldn't see why anyone would be interested and I didn't really recognise myself in it. I needed to make the profile express something about me, rather than just saying it. It's not what you say, it's the way that you say it. My second attempt was a little more crafted.

By this time I realised there are two things guaranteed to attract 'passing trade'. One is a decent photo – that is, not one taken by you at arm's length unless you have abnormally long arms (in which case you should probably warn people in your profile) and not an out-of-focus black and white shot, because that suggests missing persons or the recently deceased. The other is finding a 'hook' in the opening words, the ones that pop up to lure the browsing punter into clicking through to your full profile. (Oh no, did I just say hooker, punter and passing trade in the same mouthful? Oh no, did I just say mouthful as well?)

I had a problem going public with my photo, not because I'm particularly hideous, but because I once had a stalker, which made me more cautious. This left me with just a few pop-up words to make my mark. I no longer have a copy of my profile, but I believe it began something like, 'I hope we can make each other laugh – but not at first sight.' Light, but heartfelt.

I explored other profiles in my age range before writing my own, and some interesting patterns emerged. As a 58-year-old woman when I joined Soulmates, I pitched myself at men a few years older and younger than me, an approach I thought was realistic. This was pretty much the norm in other women's profiles too. But it seemed many men had different ideas and were looking for women 10 to 15 years younger than themselves. Women their own age, all these gorgeous 'new 50s and 60s' didn't even feature in their desired range. Call me Germaine, but I was furious with half my ageing, unreconstructed potential soulmates before I even got my profile on screen. Not a good start.

So, beyond the opening line, what comes next? Here's where it gets tricky. One of the big unspoken questions, at least for a newbie like me, is 'What brings you to an online dating website?' and I struggled with how to address this question in my own profile. The truth is I had been a mother and carer for a long time, and I came to online dating after the death of my son. Not immediately after, but in retrospect it was still too soon. If I was totally honest, even with myself, my profile would have said: 'There is a huge aching hole in my life where my son should be, and I'd like you to stand with me on the edge of this pit and just understand.' This is not what people put in their dating profiles.

The art of writing a profile is like being good at small talk at dinner parties. Its function is 'getting to know you' without actually getting to know you very much at all. It's more 'getting to know whether I'd like to get to know you', and the sadnesses, struggles and triumphs that actually shape our lives are reserved for sharing at a later stage, if and when you get there.

I wrote instead about how I spend my time. In the 50+ age group there are coded ways of declaring yourself upbeat and active. Salsa dancing, sailing, mountain-climbing and travelling to far-flung, exotic destinations feature prominently, and I found my personal versions of these to express my own (genuine) sense of being young for my age. Add in the odd flirtatious touch, and a 'guilty secret' to hint at intimacy (while giving nothing much away). I did a pretty good job.

I wasn't dishonest, but if it was a pie chart I reckon my profile would represent about 15 per cent of me. Perhaps that's true of all profiles – they are the 15 per cent we begin with, just something to go on, a conversation starter. I shied away from any advances that were made to me, and after a while realised that online dating wasn't for me at this time. Two years down the line, would I do it again? Maybe, but next time I'd ask a couple of friends to help out with the profile and cheer me on.

Alias: **Starling** | *Age:* **67** | *F* | ♀♂ | **Guardian Soulmates**

Answer truthfully and fully without revealing who you are to strangers, so that the other has an idea of how you are different from all the rest – if they don't want you, you probably don't want them either.

Don't bother with those who answer 'any' to too many questions – they are too lazy to look carefully.

Don't be put off by a few red Xs – we don't all want mirror images of ourselves.

Take no notice of those friends who tell you that you are 'brave' (by which they probably mean 'foolish'): you won't meet your partner by sitting at home watching telly.

Take it as fun, an adventure, a step into the unknown and nothing irreversible, and enjoy yourself.

Alias: **Charlie23** | *Age:* **50** | *M* | ♀♂ | **Guardian Soulmates**

My advice for a newcomer to internet dating? Really work on your photo! Don't use daft shots to show what a lot of 'fun' you are. Keep your profile simple and be honest. My best line? I love kissing.

Alias: **CC** | *Age:* **33** | *F* | ♀♂ | **mysinglefriend.co.uk**

Watch out for photos in which the subject is hiding something – teeth, one side of their face, an arm ... Ask politely if they have any more photos you could see before you agree to meet because they currently look very serious/one-sided. Also, check for their height. They could look great but turn out to be much shorter than you thought.

Alias: **Daisy_Daisy** | *Age:* **39** | *F* | ♀♂ | **datingdirect.co.uk**

Online profilers would have us believe that there is an astonishing (and entirely disproportionate to the real world) number of men who are 'very attractive', 'earning £150,000 plus' and spending their weekends in such impressive pursuits as skydiving, scaling mountains and fighting sabre-toothed tigers before breakfast, while going to the gym five times a week to make sure that they remain at the height of physical perfection and holding down hugely successful jobs. One wonders when they have time to write their profiles, let alone reply to their overflowing inboxes.

Assuming, for a moment, that such profiles are genuine and unembellished, I have often wondered why the photographs accompanying them rarely bear any resemblance to the written assertions of rugged good looks (or to the men themselves, should online flirtation progress to a meeting in the flesh).

Disappointing though it was to acknowledge that many profiles owe more to artistic licence than reality, I moved on to the next category. These men couldn't be further removed from the Alpha male mould: a sorry collection of lonely individuals looking for a new mate, or should that be a female-shaped sticking plaster to fix their broken hearts, which have been so cruelly shattered by their evil exes? No, no, no! Playing the role of the fourth emergency service is not what we're looking for in a relationship. Guys, take note: please put yourselves back together before diving into the dating pool. No one else can do it for you.

There is another category that should be handled with extreme care, particularly if your future plans involve babies and cosy togetherness. Online dating appears to attract a huge number of men in their late 40s and 50s who, when confronted with a multi-choice list of questions including whether or not they would like children, reply, 'Yes, someday'. So when? When they retire? When they are too old to play with them? When someone tricks them into it?

Alias: **spirograph** | *Age:* **31** | *M* | ♀♂ | **Guardian Soulmates**

Women's profiles break down into a few broad categories. There are those who are quite happy being single thanks, but thought they'd give this a try anyway. Not quite the actions of a contented singleton, but let's not talk about that. Practically everyone claims to be fun-loving, as opposed, presumably, to disliking fun and preferring to swear at traffic lights. The majority also claim to enjoy going out and staying in, so they're really covering all the bases. They don't usually mention how they feel about the point between leaving the house and arriving at their destination – presumably they can take it or leave it.

Women on dating websites seem to have little idea what they want when it comes to filling in the 'ideal guy' parts. On the face of it, they all seem to want someone 'that they can have a laugh with', who is 'up for some adventures' and 'knows their own mind' – characteristics so hopelessly vague that you could, at a stretch, apply them to virtually anyone bar the odd hermit and maybe Harold Shipman. Hardly anyone ever mentions looks, except half-jokingly. This is disingenuous. Even though women are less interested in looks than men, to suggest that it isn't a factor is so staggeringly wide of the mark that it beggars belief. Yes, one or two people might see past baldness, obesity and chronic halitosis if you're a Really Great Guy™, but not many. People would do better to be honest. Everyone states humour as their number one requirement, but if that was even remotely true Charlie Brooker would be fighting women off with a pointy stick.

Online dating reinforces the reality that we all know but often choose not to recognise because it is so spirit-crushingly terrible: in the majority of cases, the people who will be interested in you are not the same people you will be interested in. In real life some guys punch well above their weight by virtue of being witty. Online, this is utterly useless since having to come up with endless funny emails is both exhausting and generally fruitless. You'd be better off looking like Brad Pitt and being as thick as a whale omelette. That's the reality of online dating.

Alias: **foxglove** | *Age:* **36** | *F* | ♀♂ | **match.com**

When I created my profile I gave my job as an investment consultant and added my hobbies and the colour of my eyes. It is true that some of my details were different from the typical profile – including the fact that I had been an acrobat and trained in a circus as a trapeze volant artist for a few months – but I never thought they would trigger the sort of kinky fantasies in potential suitors that they did. I was avalanched with emails from men wanting to 'make the best use' of my skills. One guy from Manchester sent me an enthusiastic email in which he explained that, since he worked for a company that made ejectable seats, we could have a great time together – him driving and me testing the ejectables. Another one from Spain, despite his broken English, got his message across very clearly: 'I have a good proposal to you that we can meet and know better and go to hotel for spend the night and make love all the night. I am a very romantic, I don't ask for any obligations for you.'

I immediately deleted my profile, changed my username and started all over again. This time there was no mention of acrobatic or fancy stuff, and the picture I used was of me wearing sunglasses.

Alias: **snowstorm** | *Age:* **65** | *F* | ♀♂ | **Guardian Soulmates**

(Written by snowstorm's daughter)

It's the sense of time passing that gets me. I can't help feeling that my mother is going to waste. She's gorgeous, she's funny, she's bright and she's complicated. It seems such a shame that a stunning, bilingual, musical, solvent 65-year-old woman, who looks 15 years younger, is up for things and has just retired from a job at the top of her profession, should be alone. She won't have this time again. But underneath her polished exterior is a person who is hopelessly shy and frightened of rejection.

So I'm determined to find her a playmate, someone to go to exhibitions and films with – and if they fall in love, so much the better. Every weekend for the past few years I have cruised through Soulmates on her behalf. Today I'm even carrying a folded-up page of the *Guardian* classifieds in my purse. There's a man I've circled in red who has cropped up a number of times over the past few months. (dear God – is there something wrong with him?!). He says he is a romantic doctor. I'm visualising someone on the spectrum from cello-playing neurologist to agony uncle. His ad is not straining to be original; in fact it's not original at all. But he sounds nice. He lives south of the river in London.

Last weekend his ad jumped out at me again. I said to my mother that she should call his voicemail and have a chat with him. 'You could go to the Festival Hall together ...'

But when I called her to check, she said: 'I'm dreading you asking!'

'Did you leave a message?' I asked.

'No,' she said, 'I'm not ready.'

Drastic measures may need to be taken. I'm plucking up the courage to call him myself and say, 'I know this is not really orthodox, but I'm calling on behalf of my mother.' It might sound barking, but when

I was in London yesterday I almost called him and said, 'Why don't you just nip down to the South Bank and meet me and I can tell you all about my mother?'

It's a minor triumph when I finally manage to manoeuvre my mother to look at Soulmates online. I get her sitting at the computer with me while I cajole her to describe herself. But the profile she writes is scarily intense: all about world politics, child protection, famine in the global south and playing the piano at midnight. I try to soften it, but she keeps saying, 'That's not me!' Writing the profile is like deconstructing my mother. She's coming across as armour-plated, but actually she's not – she's like jelly inside. She wants to meet an interesting, loving, aware person, someone who is socially responsible and has left-wing leanings, a man of her own age or a bit older. But 65 is a difficult age for a woman on a dating website. Even the men of 75 are still looking for 20-year-olds.

Conscious that I have her attention and not knowing how big this window of optimism will be, I search for men within a 20-mile radius of where she lives. A guy comes up who has all the right attributes. He looks good, he's intelligent, he used to lecture in social studies (her field), he's culturally compatible with her, and they read the same kind of books.

'He sounds perfect!' I enthuse.

But we read on with mounting horror. The next lines are as incongruous as hearing a whoopee cushion at a harpsichord recital or finding porn in the middle of your home movies. In his extended profile he describes his perfect partner as a woman with such exaggeratedly large breasts that she has, throughout her life, suffered mortifying embarrassment at their size. He says that lovely, attractive, intelligent women who are perfectly compatible in every other way but not in possession of busts so abnormally huge as to have given them a lifelong complex should not bother applying. Having been thinking, 'He sounds really nice and interesting', we swiftly move on to 'What a *bastard*!' He might as well have had a strap-line saying: 'Humungous breasts wanted' or 'Wet-nurse required for mother-fixation.' I can't see women advertising for men with the slogan 'Big penises only need apply'.

That ad has changed my mother's view of her chances of finding a partner down this particular route, and I can quite understand her reluctance to leave a message on Romantic Doctor's voicemail.

Alias: **Loopyloo** | *Age:* **25** | *F* | ♀♂ | **Guardian Soulmates**

Browsing other people's profile before consigning my own to the Soulmates server involved a variety of emotions, all rather judgemental. Feelings of my own inadequacy in the face of the witty repartee of others were combined with surprise at some of the grammatical oddities and textspeak I encountered in supposedly adult profiles. Take, for example, the chap who on first inspection looked like my kind of person. His interests were music, reading, walking and camping. Marriage material? Possibly. And then I read on and discovered that apart from reading and walking, another of his hobbies is 'farting'. That sounds like fun ... not.

How was I going to make *my* profile strike the right tone? Although in real life I am, of course, sophisticated, interesting and not desperately socially miscalibrated, I didn't want to come across online as, well ... a twat. To describe myself as 'very attractive' might get me done under the Trade Descriptions Act. And when it came to 'in my own words', I chose my 'likes' and 'dislikes' quite carefully. If I'd have told potential dates that I like sitting in my pyjamas eating tinned prunes out of the can I would hardly have painted a picture of myself as the dynamic and sexual woman that I so clearly am. Am I?

But something other than desperation must have emerged from my profile because, after a week of Soulmates subscription, I have two dates on the cards and am participating in numerous online conversations. One is with a lovely chap who'd written a poem, an 'ode' to online dating, if you will, in the 'in his words' section. It didn't comprise the usual 'I am interested in, I like, I think', and it seems to me that taking such a step spoke volumes about him, although only time will tell if he likes reading, walking or, indeed, farting.

Alias: **Upgrade** | *Age:* **50** | *M* | ♀♂ | **Guardian Soulmates**

Crap dating profiles are all alike, but every great dating profile is great in its own special way. I think it was Tolstoy that said that.

There is no rule for how to do a good one, just a heap of ways to get it wrong. Most problems are based on a simple failure to remember what is bad in real life. Selling yourself is not the same as boasting, standing up for yourself is not the same as being aggressive, using a line Julius Caesar thought was old hat is tiresome, and so on. So here are my 10 Simple Don't-Go-There Clichés:

1. Announcing how awful it is to be (a) single and (b) reduced to being on a dating site.
Every person who reads your profile is (a) single and (b) on a dating site. We don't want to be told we're a bunch of pathetic saddoes or that you intend to lie about how we met.

2. Taglines about Mr Darcy.
Whether it's Elizabeth Bennet or Bridget Jones he's linked with, no matter, because you are at least the spazillionth person to mention it, and everyone was bored after reading three.

3. Taglines based on mottos, like *carpe diem*.
Trying to disarm the pretension and lack of imagination by changing it to 'let's carpe the jolly old diem!' or whatever will not work.

4. My friends/children/gay best pal/the kids in my primary school class say ...
I don't know them, and I don't care what they think of you.

5. Things you should never say about yourself.
I'll decide if you're funny, sexy, gorgeous or good company, not you.
If you are feisty, sassy or outspoken or you stand up against injustice,
that's great. But if you choose to say so, to strangers, I will think you
are a mardy, obnoxious, arrogant loudmouth who can't keep her
mouth shut or her nose out of other people's business.

6. I want someone who'll send my buttons flying when she rips my
    shirt open, not someone who'll sew them back on.
Qualities I would hugely value in a mum, sister, best friend or the
head housekeeper of a hotel I'm thinking of staying at are unlikely to
be the ones that make me ache to 'favourite' you on a dating site.

7. Modesty is just as irritating as boasting.
Down-to-earth, ordinary and not-too-hideous are only a slip of the
pen away from dull, lifeless and plain. There's a perilously slender
path between doing yourself down and boasting, but you have to
find a way to tread it. Similarly, if you see fit to proclaim that you are
'not some long-legged buxom blonde bimbo who'll dress to please
and giggle at all your mannish jokes', you're also telling me you are
'not very nice'. And no, I don't 'feel threatened by a woman with her
own career, money and opinions'; but I feel impelled to move along
from any profile that suggests I might be.

8. Meta profiles.
Save me from another, 'I'm not usually lost for words but ...' or 'Oh,
is this not eBay, then?' or 'Considering I sell stuff for a living I'm
finding it amazingly hard to sell myself LOL' or 'I'll come back to this
later. Damn, not enough words. Is that enough words? Erm, OK,
three more then ... there, that's it' or 'I'm not here to see how many
fans I can get' or 'Does anybody actually read this bit? Aren't you just
looking at my photo?'

9. Lists of things you are *not* looking for in a man.
The bitter unshopping list of your wicked ex-husband's crimes or of
all the freaks and weirdoes you've dated before – who is that going
to weed out? 'Emotionally retarded mummy's boys' are not going to
decide not to contact you because you ask them not to, any more

than liars are going to choose not to lie to you. And as for middle-aged men who'll try and get off with your daughter – they're looking at girls 20 years younger than you, so there's no point addressing them in your profile.

10. If you absolutely must have pet photos, be in there too but don't be kissing them.

And be in those pictures of landscapes and rivers and of the metal sculptures on Crosby beach. If you must have other people in your photo, make sure I can tell which is you, and don't be so crazy as to include those hotter girlfriends who show more cleavage than you do, or be draped around a guy. If you're stalking a wild animal in your pictures or skiing or climbing a mountain or riding a camel or standing by your posh car, know that everyone will laugh at you and move on. There is not one rule for men and one for women.

11. Lists.

Avoid them. Just kidding, lists are great. They lead the eye on, they're almost impossible to stop reading, and they're fun.

Alias: **NomDePlume** | *Age:* **47** | *F* | ♀♂ | **Guardian Soulmates**

I'm testing internet dating sites. For a number of days, weeks or possibly millennia I have been exhibiting my profile on a plethora of sites. And in the interest of fairness, equality and non-prejudicialness I have been reading other people's profiles. Men's. And this is what I've learned:

All men are sincere, fun-loving and honest.
Many men ride motorbikes and believe this to be sexy, attractive and cute.
All men have a good sense of humour.
Most men have travelled a lot, thus forgetting to have a proper relationship.

Men who have travelled a lot are prone to list all the countries, beaches and small tributaries they have visited.

A large number of men are too shy/ugly/famous to put up their pictures.

A significant proportion of men don't believe in spelling, punctuation or words.

Men are as bad as women about putting up photos that were taken 20 years ago.

Some men lie about their age but forget to put up photos taken 20 years ago.

Yet others put up photos but don't let people see them, which is very mysterious and disturbing.

People use acronyms I don't understand. GSOH.

Some men have taken pretension on to a greater plane than one might have thought possible or even probable.

Some men are very cute.

The cute ones are out of my league.

And since there has been a lot of interest in 'How to tell if a man fancies you' and since the internet dating way of being is *de rigueur* among singletons these days, I have also investigated how to tell if a man fancies you on an internet dating site.

Here's how it works: they wink at you.

Childish, I know. ;-)

Profiles for the fainthearted
– a brainstorming technique

Make a list of:

Five things that make you feel light-hearted (e.g. baking meringues, eating sushi, snowboarding, dancing to Motown)

Five things you love doing on a regular basis and when (e.g. making fresh hollandaise for eggs benedict, cooking to early Talking Heads at full blast, swimming outdoors at dusk)

Five unusual things you know (e.g. which plants are safe to eat in a forest, the Sanskrit alphabet, the best Ethiopian restaurant in Swansea)

Five surprising things you can do (e.g. build a house, play finger-piano, serve tennis at 105mph, sing the nuns' harmonies from *The Sound of Music*)

Five beautiful things that move you to tears (e.g. the sound of Anfield singing 'You'll Never Walk Alone', the light in East Anglia, your grandmother's lasagne)

Five very different types of people or personalities you enjoy (e.g. rude comedians, extravagant foodies, people who write beautiful letters, posh types who are sticklers for quality)

Five things you would like to share with someone you love (e.g. play music on the beach, learn to tango, ride horses across the Sahara, wear 30s clobber to Glyndebourne, camp in a bluebell wood)

When you've come up with your best answers, choose two or three from each section, combine them in no particular order, and see what you've got. Allow a few well-behaved adjectives back into the mix and there you have it: the basis for a portrait of the superb peculiarity that is you.

Chapter 3:
From cybercourtship to real life

Flirting your way from email to facemail

_____

As soon as you upload your profile to a dating website, your freshly-minted alter ego steps into the virtual ballroom, and it is only a matter of time before the virtual you is asked for a make-believe dance. You, the real flesh and blood you, might be sitting at your computer in a threadbare tracksuit you no longer even let the postman see, with your feet buried in furry animal slippers. But your online self is a suited-and-booted charmer in black dress or white tie.

The genius of online dating is that it offers a simulacrum of the classic real-world seduction sequence that most of us know by heart: you go to a party; you clap eyes on someone who, for whatever reason (electrifying charisma? implausible oddness?), quickens your heartbeat. Said person notices the blowtorches of lust in your stare; you turn away shyly; you turn back; the lovely one shoots you a grin like a heat-seeking missile; you look down; and then a third party comes over and says those magic words, 'My friend would like to buy you a pint'. This standardised, averaged-out human mating ritual, with its trade of glances and come-ons, of teasing and reciprocation, is now a computer program. The techies at Date Central have rewritten flirtation in binary code.

You might find the regular members swarming to you like bees to a honeypot, especially if the site showcases its new members, dish-of-the-day style. And you'll be able to see exactly who's been making eyes at you: if you are logged in, every act of browsing people's profiles leaves a trail, so that you can click on your admirers' pictures and browse them in return. 'You have a new fan,' says the website, your new best friend, sending you messages to lift your spirits and passing on your admirers' 'winks'. Like eBay, where sellers are awarded achievement 'certificates' by automated software, or Facebook, where people can take comfort in their huge tallies of 'friends', online dating sites use deep affirmation strategies to smooth your progress in dateworld. They cuddle and confirm you, stroke you and feed your ego. So you have fans now? You've been favourited? You heartbreaker, you.

To receive a message that you are wanted can – despite any natural taste for irony you might have – be fabulous. If you have been single, or in a stale relationship, or grieving, or lacking in confidence, then to be told, even by an automated message, that you have a fan, could be the sweetest thing you have heard all day – or year. You get that flutter in the solar plexus. You're in the swim. Back in the loop. On the world's radar. For a mad minute it doesn't even seem to matter *who* has messaged you, it's the sheer glorious fact of it that counts.

Then you get a grip. It's not quite as rosy as you thought. **DanE1** says, 'I'd describe the initial experience as exhilaration followed very swiftly by disappointment. The expectation is "I've set up this profile and instantly Prince Charming will walk into my life and send me a message", which is bollocks'. One contributor referred to the spate of responses she received on first signing up as a 'false summer' – a moment of miraculously intense popularity that was never to be repeated. As 31-year-old **Spirograph** cautions, 'At first, you'll probably get a flurry of activity because you're new – fresh meat – but mostly from people you'd cross the street to avoid'. Younger women, in particular, complain of being 'ogled' by older men. **2leggedtree**, 21, found it deeply disconcerting: 'I think it's a bit of a strange notion anyway, being able to see who has "viewed you". But sometimes it's really old men in their 50s, which I find really disturbing as some of them are older than my Dad.'

But nestled among the people who don't ring your bell will be some who do ... or could do. You can click on their profiles or send them a wink, adding your equivalent of the raised eyebrow to the virtual courtship dance. In the democratic world of online dating, everyone – male or female, shy or bold – has the same ability to make the first move. Although **LoveCrumb**, 28, a self-employed design consultant who has been dating guys on Guardian Soulmates on and off for several years, rarely favourites men or writes introductory emails, she finds that 'sometimes simply viewing a man's profile might encourage him to look back at yours, and in this way internet dating seems similar to the way women might "drop hints" to attract the interest of men in real life'.

The first message is the trickiest. **sugar_hiccup** recommends referring to the website's profile-match results to make a simple, no-pressure statement: 'The computer seems to think we have something in common. So hello', followed by a brief but friendly comment that shows you've read their profile. But don't hold your breath. Like the majority of first messages, yours may never get a reply.

The dating website OkCupid.com tried to understand why. Analysing over 500,000 first contacts made through the site, they discovered that men and women preferred entirely different kinds of messages.[27] Women, both gay and straight, generally responded better to somewhat longer messages, while men, regardless of their sexual orientation, generally preferred messages that cut to the chase. The study even analysed how using particular words affected the reply rate: Netspeak, bad grammar, and bad spelling predictably had a low response – *ur*, *u*, *wat*, *wont*. The exceptions to the rule were expressions of amusement: *haha* had a 45 per cent reply rate (as opposed to *hehe*, which only got 33 per cent – it is thought to sound a little evil). Words like *gorgeous*, *beautiful*, *hot* and *sexy* fared badly in a first email – evidently making the recipient feel uncomfortable. Guys who were slightly self-deprecating in their messages, using words such as *awkward*, *sorry*, *apologise* and *probably*, did well with women. And atheists apparently had more fun: dropping the very word *atheist* got a better response than mentioning the word *Christian*. Or the word *God*, which in a first message, did not go down well.

Bright and breezy is the way to go for functional emails that inch people closer to the real-world meeting as soon as possible. But there are plenty of people who are suckers for a more literary flirtation, who want to be seduced with words. For them, courting via the internet is not the means to an end, but an intensely enjoyable end in itself. Hand-written letters may now be a quaint anachronism for most people, but the romantic inner selves that used to invest in writing and reading them still crave their seductive magic. Online dating has ushered in a renaissance in written courtship. 'At this point in their short history, online personals are long on wit and charm, the breeding ground for a reinvigorated epistolary tradition. For now, the literate have the run of the place.'[28]

Cybercourtship is simply old-fashioned wooing on Ritalin – as creative, inventive and full of uncertainty's sweet sorrow as courtship ever was – but faster, more clandestine and more promiscuous. It can be addictive. 'Experimental studies show that the more anonymous a person feels, the more they will disclose sexually. People will give out four times more personal information when only using text, rather than speaking on the telephone or face-to-face.' One-to-one communion with a stranger via your computer can be as erotic and illicit as an affair: a thrilling secret you connect to in the dark of night.

For **Blushes**, 41, 'the internet became an absorbing, passionate, playful diversion for me – a way of engaging intensely with people while hiding my fragility'. She quickly 'learned the trade' of live chat: 'you learned to be short, sharp and succinct – and to type quickly because people were waiting to hear what you had to say.' This witty, flirtatious and sometimes sexual banter can be intoxicating. There are a lot of romantics online, courting each other, enjoying the bittersweet pleasures of erotic fantasies that are craved for yet permanently out of reach. The technologies create a hypnotic experience of desire lived at one remove, always mediated – by email, by mobile text, by instant message or by Skype. Before you know it, casual messages are escalating into hot dispatches and your life has become a breathless rush for the inbox.

Toolatetostopnow, 50, fell in love online with a man based abroad. Once she'd tasted the pleasure of this desire that wants but can't have, it cascaded into an obsession. She dedicated her waking hours to feeding their mutual appetite for contact, like a one-person, 24-hour, rolling news station:

> From a cheeky first email from me – 'nice scenery' (his profile photo was in front of the Colosseum in Rome) – we had rapidly moved to lengthy, daily emails chronicling our lives and our passions, and from there to video-calling so that we could chat live and see each other. Every conversation seemed to confirm our mutual interests, but of far greater impact was the sexual chemistry and the increasing desire to open up to each other. All the way along the line we matched each other in romance, in intimacy, in our commitment to our time together. The exchanges became ever more unrestrained, and as we talked late into the night, finding it unbearable to let each other go, we took our respective computers into bed to increase the intimacy. We were obsessed. We spent six hours at a time online together, sometimes even briefly falling asleep then waking and starting again.

Online intimacy can become potent and charged; yet its poignancy is that, even with live video, your lover is effectively a hologram. And with textual courtship alone, there is even more room to fantasise about a person that you hardly know. Your paramour is still little more than their literary output.

Because of the internet's propensity towards the unreal, many online daters follow one cardinal rule: meet face-to-face after the second email. It prevents you from projecting your dreams onto someone who doesn't exist outside your imagination. 'I felt the internet was a gateway to a meeting rather than the meeting itself. I didn't want to be excited by a message without knowing whether I would be excited by the person: you can pick things up from internet communication that aren't necessarily there,' says **sugar_hiccup**.

DanE1 is equally cautious about the discrepancies between online and offline rapport:

> I like to meet someone really quickly. I can't work in two dimensions. It's as much about photos as writing – the whole is always more than the sum of its parts. I like to get that reality jump out of the way as soon as possible, so I know this person and how I feel when I'm around them – if they fidget or have nasty yellow teeth – I like to have the whole package there as soon as possible. I presume that people are the same as me and they think, 'I've got that profile information – I can't make any further judgement until I've met them'. I'd rather do that than send endless messages back and forth, which is a very disjointed way of communicating. It's never a conversation – it's two sets of monologues.

For the romantics who immerse themselves in cybercourtship, 'real life' often falls disappointingly short. In her heartbreakingly poignant tale of how she and her lover met, **Toolatetostopnow** describes how they were unable to make the 'reality jump' from online to offline, 'each not able to overcome the obstacles that would have turned the fantasy into a permanent reality'. Her first vision of the lover she had courted so passionately online marked the precise moment where fantasy and reality collided. Her words echo the deflation people feel when they see film actors in the flesh: he was so much smaller than she had expected.

The irony for **sugar_hiccup**, however, despite her rule not to engage in a long correspondence, was that the woman she eventually fell for was the one she had courted most elaborately online.

From cybercourtship to real life:
The stories

There are all kinds of reasons for people to be standing at railway stations, and mine had all the elements of a romantic black and white film, with the exception of Rachmaninov playing over the Tannoy. I was waiting at Darlington's Victorian railway station for the Edinburgh to London service and counting off the seconds until the arrival of the man I'd been exchanging letters, and falling in love with, for the previous seven weeks. You hear about seconds seeming to last for minutes, and for the first time I understood what that meant.

Unlike most stories, ours began on page 21. It was there that CJ saw me for the first time and 'instinctively knew' that he'd found a kindred spirit. I'd joined the site some months earlier but had forgotten about it until I started receiving his messages. I liked it that after the short paragraph in his first letter he finished with 'Hi'. Something about it struck a chord and still does when I read it now. We generated something like 300 messages in a week, and they weren't short messages – we must have talked about everything from carrot cake to the meaning of life. Our time was night time. When my children had gone to bed, we'd camp out at our laptops, where we progressed from our long emails to that first, nervous but full of laughter phone call, then webcams combined with phone calls. We were totally reliant on technology and frequently confounded by its unpredictability – we had no choice because CJ was in Scotland, 327 miles away from me. Seven-hour conversations became the norm. We'd talk through the night, and at five o'clock in the morning, curled up on our respective sofas, we'd say 'goodnight and good morning' and see in the dawn together, apart.

Weeks began to pass, and we recognised that we were falling in love. We've since tried to work out when this happened and how we knew. CJ's explanation was, 'Put it this way, as soon as I saw your picture,

I was already falling in love – it couldn't have happened any other way.' We'd both been married before but had never felt anything like this. We called it a 'love tsunami'. But still we were hundreds of miles apart, frustrated by lack of money and time. CJ was a student and I was a single parent on a tight budget with a strict routine and the only one of us who could drive. The nights of wishing we could somehow fold a map and magically bring two points together became harder to bear. But finally, the perfect answer: my best friend was getting married in Darlington, and we could afford the funds to meet halfway between where we lived.

At last the day rolled around, and there I stood, telling myself not to be nervous but just to enjoy the moment. Still, my hands were shaking (unbeknown to me), which is why, he later told me, one of the first things he did was to take my hands in his. I must have looked at every single face in the crowd and watched every train in and out. Then I heard the arrival announcement and my heart gathered speed. The train was a long Intercity one, and as the doors slid open there was a chaos of people getting on and off. Would CJ spot the clock and me hyperventilating beneath it?

I couldn't see him. The platform cleared, and the only people remaining were at the far end, where someone was talking animatedly to two guards. I knew it was CJ and decided to abandon the clock. He'd spotted me and as I got nearer, he began to turn … You know those romantic moments where the hero and heroine run towards one another in slow motion? Well, CJ began running. He ran towards me, and I could feel myself smiling. Then I realised that he wasn't going to stop when he ran past me at an impressive speed shouting, 'I've got to get my luggage off the train!'

We had to wait for an hour for the train to get to York and for station staff to find his bag and put it on the next train back. That was fine, though – we held hands and kissed and hugged and generally embarrassed everyone else in the coffee shop for the entire hour.

That was over a year ago. We've managed to spend more time together than apart in that time, with CJ making more low-budget, soul-destroyingly long coach journeys and stop-overs in cold cities in the wee small hours than he no doubt cares to remember. But we've finally managed to conquer the space–time continuum and fold the map: CJ has moved to England. I'm delighted to say that the webcams are quietly gathering dust in a corner somewhere.

Alias: **Freudianslip** | *Age:* **45** | *F* | ♀♀ | **gaydargirls.com**

Although I was based in London, I was temporarily relocated to Paris. In advance of going away a friend suggested we use Gaydar to chat. I'd recently bought a new laptop, and this seemed a good solution in case I got homesick for queer company. I created my profile and started chatting to my friend – it felt good to be in touch when phone calls were still so expensive.

Then I started receiving messages from someone else. She was younger than me, and her profile, like mine, didn't contain a photo. Her messages were sparse and funny; not overwritten or overly explanatory. She didn't try too hard. A lack of exclamation marks made her sound dry. Slowly she became the reason I logged on, not my friends, who found themselves waiting an uncharacteristically long time for responses.

She divulged little about herself, yet it felt as if she knew me. Before long, small rituals were created – I'd pour a glass of wine as she had a beer. We would ask each other, 'Can I get you another drink?' which placed us almost in the same room – a strange reciprocity of experience, which belied the reality of being miles apart. If I was slow to reply to messages she suggested that I tell others I was chatting to to 'fuck off' so I could focus on her alone. I was half aware of the absurdity of the situation, but I had come to so enjoy the experience that I was willing to accept it at face value. We made no commitments, nor did we speak about the nature of our developing friendship.

One Monday I logged on after work as usual. Our chat picked up where it left off. I mentioned I was getting a glass of wine. When I returned she asked if I would like to go for a drink on Friday. I replied 'yes', accepting her playful but unrealistic request. When she asked 'which bar?' I stopped short. She explained she'd booked a flight to Paris and wondered if I wanted to meet for a drink. If not, she was happy to amuse herself. It was confusing and exciting at the same time. I still didn't know what she looked like. I was under no obligation to meet her but I'd started to develop a connection with her, even on a superficial level, and curiosity alone made the meeting inevitable. But beside that there was the gesture – the bravery, the foolishness. It made me feel incredibly special.

Friday came. We recognised each other quickly and got a pint. We were both nervous. I was trying to work out if she was how I'd imagined her, until I realised I hadn't imagined her at all in a physical sense. She was attractive, but I wasn't necessarily attracted to her. I forget the details of that night – I just remember looking at her and trying to work out what I felt. I walked her to her hotel and then went home. I can't remember if we kissed.

The next day we met again, visiting various gay bars. This time we ended up back at her hotel – the proximity, the fun, the spontaneity of the weekend had seduced me. We slept together in that first unfamiliar way you're not sure you have actually enjoyed. I think she kept most of her clothes on. We got up the next day, flushed with sex and stale alcohol and had breakfast. Later, we left the hotel into a grey, cold March Sunday, and had one last drink before she left.

I didn't know how to feel. We loosely discussed meeting in London on my return, but I assumed we'd continue to write online as before. We did continue to write, but there was a drop in intensity. I assumed we'd see each other again, and she must have been uncomfortable with this as she withdrew, which I didn't understand. I had to acknowledge that I'd formed expectations that weren't going to be realised. My pride wouldn't allow me to have these discussions with her, however, so I tried to play it cool. I told her I was flying back to London for a day and asked if she wanted to meet. She didn't give me an answer until the day. We met in a London park, had sex, went for a drink, went to her place, had sex and the next day I went back to Paris.

Again the coolness took over. This continued on and off. I'd withdraw, and she would ask me to spend time with her. Then I'd be set down until she wanted to see me again. She never accepted my suggestions to hang out, never stayed at my house.

In between times I met other girls and was able to form relationships. I eventually recognised that, although I really liked her and the sexual chemistry was amazing, I wanted more. And to give myself the best opportunity to find it, I had to get her out of my life.

Alias: **HappyGoLucky** | *Age:* **29** | *F* | ♀♂ | **mysinglefriend.co.uk and others**

When I read Mike's profile I said to myself: 'Omigod, you are everything I'm looking for in a bloke!' He had just one picture, but he looked really sweet – a little bit cheeky. He was tall, dark, a bit rough around the edges but quite good-looking and well-built. He was Irish and was studying to be a nurse. We had loads in common: we both enjoyed travelling, music, film and lots more besides. He winked at me, I winked back and we got some email banter going. He was very flattering and told me I was gorgeous, so I thought, 'Well done you! You're all right!' I thought it was too good to be true, but my friends said, 'Don't be ridiculous. It does happen.'

As Mike wasn't making a move about meeting up, I asked him if he'd like to get together. We set up a date for a few weeks later, and I asked him to name a place.

'Pimlico,' he said. I was living in Herne Hill at the time, and he was on the other side of London, so it was quite a trek, but it sounded intriguing.

'At five o'clock,' he added. A bit early for me, but he seemed to have something planned. I got quite excited in the build-up to the date, and nearer the time I asked what he had in mind.

'Nothing,' he replied.

'Oh.'

'What do *you* want to do?' he asked.

'Do you know Pimlico?'

'No. I just thought it was somewhere to meet.'

Oh. Right. I said that maybe we should go somewhere that at least one of us was familiar with and suggested the South Bank, near Waterloo, which I know like the back of my hand. So I arrived at the rendezvous at the agreed time. No sign of him. He texted to say he was there, but I couldn't find him. It turned out that he'd gone to the wrong place. This doesn't look good, I thought. He can't follow simple directions!

As soon as I laid eyes on him, I wanted to run away. I instantly knew things weren't going to be great. Bizarrely, straight after we'd met, he started walking really quickly in the opposite direction.

'Where are you going?' I asked.

'I don't know,' he said.

I guessed he was just nervous, so I steered us towards the National Film Theatre, thinking we could either go to the café or the bar. 'What do you fancy?' I asked.

'I don't mind,' he said.

'Well I'd like a glass of wine, so let's go to the bar,' I said. We went to a table in the bar, and it was clear he wasn't going to get the drinks in.

I'm not someone who expects to be paid for, but usually, on a date, the guy likes to offer you the first drink.

'I'll go to the bar then,' I said, 'what would you like?'

'No, nothing. I'm fine,' he said.

'Are you sure? I'm going to have a glass of wine.'

'Oh, I'll have a glass of water,' he yielded. 'But just tap water.' When I came back to the table with a large glass of wine for me and a bottle of mineral water for him, he tried to give me the money for the water. I told him I could stand him a drink. Then he piped up with: 'One thing you should know about me is that I'm really tight with money.'

I made that glass of wine last two hours. During that time we chatted about all the things we had in common, and I realised that we did each one differently. My idea of travelling was to pack everything up and go to Africa for a few months and do voluntary work. His was travelling around Europe on a shoestring, saving money by staying in youth hostels – despite being the same age as me – and not even sending a postcard to his mum to save on the stamp. And that admirable nurse's training of his: it turned out that he was only doing it to get a Green Card to get to America.

And then there was Ireland. 'Do you go back very often?' I asked.

'No, I don't really go back,' he said.

'You must miss your friends though?'

'I don't really have friends,' he revealed. 'I'm a bit of a loner.'

Great thing to announce on a date! At 7.30 the date came to an abrupt end. I had finished my drink and really didn't want to get another so I asked what he wanted to do.

'I should probably get home,' he said, 'I've got an early start tomorrow.'

'Oh!' I said. 'OK!' It was probably the most enthusiastic I'd been all evening.

When I reread his emails I realised that he hadn't been dishonest at all: he was exactly the person he'd claimed to be. We did have lots in common, and at no point on the date had we struggled for conversation. I had simply read into his emails exactly what I had wanted.

Alias: **Miss_Conduct** | *Age:* **30** | *F* | **Bisexual** | **Guardian Soulmates**

Online flirting can be hazardous when you live in a small – or even medium-sized – town. You never know when someone you see on screen might turn up in the flesh or vice versa. Here's what happened to me ...

I was at the doctor's with a seven-day itch. The over-the-counter ointments hadn't worked, and it was time for professional intervention. Although I'd requested a female doctor, when Pete appeared (they used first names here, to put you at ease before getting personal with your privates) I was so sick of waiting that I conceded to let an unknown male inspect my ailing genitalia. He turned out to be kind, unassuming and incredibly gentle. And he couldn't find anything noticeably wrong with my nether regions.

'It all looks very healthy,' he smiled, emerging from the blue 'modesty-covering' paper that bedecked my lower half. Nevertheless, swabs were taken, and I was packed off with some cream and an industrial-size bag of free condoms. The whole experience was so painless and comfortable that I resolved to ask specifically for him should venereal disease ever strike again.

Four days later my symptoms had disappeared, and the tests had all proved negative. Itch-free and uncontaminated, I was ready to hit the dating world once more. But the only new profiles to grace my screen sounded dull and uninspiring: 'Let's meet for a movie, wine and good conversation.' Let's not. Then, a very sweet message appeared in my inbox from a guy who referred to himself simply as 'P', saying he also liked poetry, psychology and photography and would I like to meet up in the pub? I decided to give his profile a closer look. He sounded funny, thoughtful and interesting and wasn't bad-looking either. But something about his photo niggled me. He looked just a little too familiar. I checked his age – 37 – and then his height – 5ft 9in. Then, finally, his profession – medical/dental/veterinary. A hot sensation crept up my neck and ears, as I realised with 99.9 per cent certainty what was going on here. I'd just been asked out by my gynaecologist.

For a few days I ignored the email; then curiosity got the better of me. I wrote back: 'Hello P, Thanks for the message. I think we have already met. Last week. Do you know what I'm referring to, perchance? MC.'

To which he replied: 'Gosh, no idea. Can you enlighten me?'

Then I wrote: 'Well, do you often find potential dates on the examining table? If this was a genuine case of not recognising me, then fair enough, but if not, I'm not sure how appropriate it is you contacting me on here. Not that I had a bad experience – I thought you were extremely professional and caring. I just didn't expect to hear from you again – unless I had chlamydia. MC. PS Symptoms all cleared up now.'

And his final message was: 'Oops, so sorry, genuine case of not recognising you.'

No more contact. I'll never know whether he truly didn't recognise me or whether he was just saying that to save face – and his job. Though to be fair, it wasn't really my head and shoulders he'd been focusing on in the consulting room. All I can say is, thank goodness things hadn't happened the other way round: 'Oh hello, haven't we chatted on Guardian Soulmates before? Now if you'd like to just remove your undergarments and pop your legs in the stirrups ...' That would definitely have caused a nasty outbreak of redness and discomfort.

Alias: **NomDePlume** | *Age:* **47** | *F* | ♀♂ | **Guardian Soulmates**

They say that money can't buy happiness, but where's the empirical evidence for this? Strangely, when I google 'money can't buy happiness' it turns out that there are a number of scientific studies that appear to demonstrate just that. However, never one to be put off by evidence, fact, science or the truth, I have decided that money will buy me happiness and have done it again.

Subscribed to Guardian Soulmates. Th is time it's going to be different. This time I'm not going to sit there and hope that my well-worded (wordy anyway) profile and glamorous picture will bring the Soulmates flooding in. Or trickling in. Nor am I going to believe that simply ticking 'any' for all the boxes in 'my ideal mate' will attract Mr Right. Or that adding all the cute guys who are way out of my league to My Favourites will mysteriously make them in my league.

This time I'm being proactive. I'm taking control. I'm actually emailing people. I have a technique. This is what I do. I find a man I fancy. Or a man. I carefully read what he's written. I then craft a cunningly worded sentence or two to say how interesting and sexy he sounds. Examples include:

'You sound interesting'

'You look nice'

'I've read your profile'

And 'I fancy you.'

I then craft a cunningly worded sentence or two that lets them know just how interesting and sexy I am. Examples include:

'I have written a load of bollocks on my profile'

'I can catch a ping-pong ball on my nose'

'I know how to read'

And 'My shoulders match.'

Then, finally, and this is the important part, I craft a cunningly worded question so they can answer my email without the awkwardness of not knowing what to say. Examples include:

'How do you come to be living in Iceland/London/the World?'

'Why have you put up that appalling photograph?'

'Can you direct me to the Caves of Redemption?'

And 'How?'

So far three people have replied. One of them didn't have a subscription yet, one of them had let their subscription lapse, and the other was the man who emailed me last time. And they say money can't buy happiness. Pah!

Alias: **Gromlin** | *Age:* **30** | *M* | ♂♂ | **Guardian Soulmates**

To find a guy so close to where I lived was great, especially when he was 'tall, dark and handsome'. I was impressed by his profile content – there were some nice pictures there, and he looked like a fresh, clean, well-kept guy, clearly physically fit. And he was articulate about his passions, passions I felt I shared. It is so hard for me to find someone that ticks the right boxes. What am I looking for? Security for one thing – guys never seem to have very much of that going on, they're always looking over their shoulder. Intellect, again, is so important. When you find yourself getting excited over the discovery of a new fundamental particle, you need someone who can at least appreciate that excitement, right? Then there are morals. I need to be with someone who has a keen sense of morality.

This guy was ticking all the right boxes. I sent him a short message, and a day later had an email from him, short and sweet. He said he worked in a job where he was exposed to the great outdoors and made positive comments about my photos. Great! After this message a real conversation started. I could feel we were bouncing off one another with witty retorts and remarks. The banter was developing and so, too, was my interest in him. And my hope: maybe I had finally met a guy with the brains, looks and stability I so wanted in a partner. I quickly moved to suggesting that we might meet for a drink.

Over the course of the evening we had a great laugh. We both quickly discovered that we had a very non-PC sense of humour, and I really tapped into that. As the evening drew to a close, we decided to say our farewells. Impressed with the conversation and interaction, I suggested that we should arrange to do something again. He agreed. Awesome!

However, after that night the complexities of internet communication spelled trouble for us both. It would seem that both of us took our attempts to 'play it cool' as a sign of a lack of interest. After a few short messages in which I attempted to explain what had happened – that we had spoiled the 'magic' – we mutually decided that it would probably be best if we left things there. Such is text-based communication. What a real shame.

Alias: **Toolatetostopnow** | *Age:* **50** | *F* | ♀♂ | **toyboywarehouse.com**

That day my new lover played his first – and last – practical joke on me.

I was at my desk when a text came through, and I instantly recognised the familiar number. A brief, seemingly unfinished message from him, saying that his boss says he has to be at a meeting with an important client tomorrow morning so he will not be able to come. I am instantly distracted from all else, completely bereft. How can he mean this, how can this happen, how can I be so unlucky?

This date – set four weeks earlier and anticipated with increasing fervour by both of us – was for his flight from Barcelona to his first meeting with me and 48 hours together. The moment of setting that date was an especially precious one in our brief history when, during an instant messaging conversation about the possibility of meeting when we could both actually find a weekend free, he simultaneously sent me an email confirmation of the flight he had just booked online while we were talking. That moment changed everything for me. He was turning our remote, virtual relationship into something real. He was turning words into action, he was decisive and he believed in the possibility of us. From that point on I was going to fall in love with him.

But it was the day before he was due to fly, and I was losing my dream. I texted him back: 'What are we going to do? I can't bear this. Your boss is a bastard.' No answer. Minutes later I was searching every airline for alternative flights for him, and then alternative flights for me to him – hang the cost! There were so many options to search. I was living in Birmingham with several airports within an easy drive, and even at his end there was a choice of two.

Then, at last, half an hour later, the answer came through in a text from him. He had negotiated with his boss, who had agreed that he would buy him a later flight that day, so he would arrive only two hours later than previously planned. Somehow what he had meant to send me in two immediately consecutive texts had come through with this agonising gap in between.

So there I was, driving to East Midlands airport to meet and kiss and make love to the man I had fallen in love with over the previous six weeks. From a cheeky first email from me – 'nice scenery' (his profile photo was in front of the Colosseum in Rome) – we had rapidly moved to lengthy, daily emails chronicling our lives and our passions, and from there to video-calling so that we could chat live and see each other. Every conversation seemed to confirm our mutual interests, but of far greater impact was the sexual chemistry and the increasing desire to open up to each other. All the way along the line we matched each other in romance, in intimacy, in our commitment to our time together. The exchanges became ever more unrestrained, and as we talked late into the night, finding it unbearable to let each other go, we took our respective computers into bed to increase the intimacy. We were obsessed. We spent six hours at a time online together, sometimes even briefly falling asleep, then waking and starting again.

Until a couple of nights before he came to visit me, like boxers before a match, we refused to allow ourselves this intense contact in order to save our energies for the real thing. All the barriers were down. Four weeks before he had, in a gentlemanly fashion, booked his hotel room for the weekend as he did not want to presume to stay in my house, let alone my bed. Now it was beyond any shred of doubt that the hotel room was to be a shared one and that our online passion was to be realised physically and indulged from morning to night of our precious 48 hours.

So how strange it was when he finally came through the arrivals door at the airport. I only had a few seconds to take in the sight of him before he would see me too. He was smaller of frame than I had thought, and so young-looking, like a boy (emphasising all the more our 13-year age difference). He made his way towards me ... We had promised to greet each other as boyfriend and girlfriend coming back together after a separation, rather than as two people who have never met before, and immediately to take each other in our arms and kiss like lovers. We did.

We had our 48 hours of promised love-making, with a little sightseeing and eating out on the side. It was extraordinary, strange, beautiful and very, very loving ... and then it was over. With tears at the airport, we said goodbye, knowing that it had been the most spectacular, wonderful fantasy, but each not able to overcome the obstacles that would have turned the fantasy into a permanent reality.

I had a rule that I would always suggest meeting someone after the second email. I felt the internet was a gateway to a meeting rather than the meeting itself. I didn't want to be excited by a message without knowing whether I would be excited by the person: you can pick things up from internet communication that aren't necessarily there.

It was summer, and I had just split up with my girlfriend of five years. I thought, 'A little bit of interest might be good for me,' and signed up for gaydargirls.co.uk, which has a reputation for being more upfront than some websites. I was quite shocked at how sexual it was, and I found that there were people there who *live* in cyberspace. There was a beautiful photo on one profile – a back view of a naked woman with a guitar. I sent this woman a message saying: 'Do you play the guitar?'. But she said the photo wasn't of her: it was someone else and she just happened to like it. That was weird enough, but it got weirder.

I wrote to her saying: 'I'm not really into pursuing a cybermessaging relationship. Presumably you, like me, are quite normal and have a social life.' She wrote back and said: 'No, I'm quite lonely, and I don't have any friends.' It might sound harsh, but I felt I wasn't there to be social services, so I stopped corresponding.

When I went online the second time I had just moved to Brighton and didn't know anyone. I thought Soulmates would be a good route to meet new friends, although I'd be lying if I said I wasn't hoping to meet someone lovely.

I started a correspondence with a woman who didn't have a photo up, and there was something about the tone of our emails that made my ears prick up. Now I'd be the first person to give a friend a shake and say, 'Don't get hung up on emails', but Lucy was hugely busy writing her PhD so we couldn't meet for a long time. Her previous relationship had ended, but she was in that awful situation where she was still living with her ex. I resigned myself to the idea that I wasn't going to meet her straight away.

She impressed me. She's really into cooking, she has an allotment and knows all about plants, she's a doctor, and she's far better read than I will ever be. There was the tangible stuff we definitely had in common – shared values in terms of health and the outdoors – but there was also a gentleness to her that drew me in. I found myself thinking of things that would delight her. I watched a kooky musical documentary about people living along the M1 and thought, 'I bet Lucy would enjoy this film.' I saw a gardening show about the movement to get 'flower rivers' flowing in England by creating the tiniest connective bits between different patches of flowers and thought, 'Lucy would love this.'

We had this charm thing between us. She would tell me about her walks on the Sussex Downs with her dog: about the beautiful mists or a patch of wild orchids on a particular hill she went to. I looked on the internet to find where on the South Downs wild orchids grew and found the exact place: Newtimber Hill, just behind Hove. I'd never been there before, but I started going, like some weird stalker, just to be close to her. I sent her a picture of a rare Twayblade orchid.

We were courting each other by email. It went against everything I'd said. I felt, 'I can't stop thinking about this Lucy person yet I've never even met her.' I was becoming obsessed with someone I hardly knew. Yet our emails weren't erotic – there was nothing smutty, sexy or flirtatious in them. We were asking lots of questions, and what we found was a genuine meeting of minds. We were falling for each other.

The tension and the build-up and the way she was filling my thoughts were so intense that I wanted to meet her as soon as possible. But just before we'd planned to hook up, a month after we first messaged each other, she told me she couldn't come. She had met her ex that day and told her about me, and the ex had 'had a meltdown'. Lucy said she would completely understand if I didn't believe her and please to trust her when she said she was allergic to lesbian high drama, but out of respect for the ex she had to sort it out before she and I met.

We finally met a little while later. I had seen her photos and didn't actually think she was very attractive – one was of her on Kilimanjaro suffering from altitude sickness – but I found her overwhelmingly attractive in real life. We were both so nervous and awkward on that first date. I felt a complete dork. It was weird because there seemed so much at stake. I don't normally feel so much so soon. I texted a friend just after we'd said goodbye for the first time: 'Just met Lucy. Oh no – I like!'

What we had been drawn to was some made-up profile – words written on a screen – but we both got an accurate essence of the other through those words. We are fantastically compatible – formed for each other. Lucy is my ideal in so many ways and unquestionably my partner for life. We took our profiles down that week. I thought, 'I don't need this any more'.

Alias: **Kandinsky** | *Age:* **45** | *F* | ♀♂ | **Guardian Soulmates**

I set strict criteria for my first foray into internet dating: must live within 20 miles, no kids, and I definitely need to see a picture. So what was it about him that made me click 'OK' when I found that he lived more than 60 miles away, had children and there was no picture? It was the honesty of his age range – purely and simply. A middle-aged man who wanted a middle-aged woman. Shock! This man was even prepared to consider a woman older than himself. I'm a very young middle-aged woman, but apparently too old for most men of my age, who want a 20-something date, but perfect (apparently) for men in their 60s.

We started corresponding, then emailing, then finally talking over the phone. Then the photo arrived, and although the kitchen cabinets in the photo were very unpleasant, he had lovely smiley eyes and deep laughter lines. Yippee! And the kitchen cabinets weren't his!

Unfortunately, he'd ruptured his Achilles tendon so was unable to drive to our big date, and I had to drive to him – more than 60 miles away. This was (a) the truth or (b) a big, big lie. Could he not drive? Didn't he own a car? Had he been banned for some reason? Was the air-cast boot hiding an electronic tag? All these questions went through my mind.

In the end it was the truth, and he's been telling the truth ever since.

———————————————

Alias: **NomDePlume** | *Age:* **47** | *F* | ♀♂ | **match.com**

I've fallen off the wagon. Yes, for some whole weeks I stayed off internet dating. But somehow, possibly without my knowledge, I've signed up to match.com.

It's not that I had anything against Soulmates, they were fine, cute and moderately dandy. It's just that, well, if I signed up to that one again then all my ex-dates would see that I was back, and it would be revealed just how really sad, terminally foolish and obsessed I am. Also my friend, whom I met through Soulmates, would realise that all my swearing off internet dating and swearing on being single was a complete, utter and overwhelming sham.

The problem seems to be that it might be addictive. Like any good drug it is the promise of some high that is better than some low or medium elevation. Just click on this man and your life will be better.

This time, however, I have it all under control. I've got it sussed. No more disappointingly unanswered emails, winks, nudges or adding to favourites. Rejection is not on the agenda. There will be no more lying in bed at night wondering why WhiteKnight34 hasn't contacted me, why HeavenGuy11 doesn't want to have sex with me, or why Wnaker26 hasn't proposed yet. I have a cunning and infallible plan. This is it: I won't email anyone, or wink at them, or nudge them, or poke them in the bollocks. It will be like coffee. The smell will be better than the tasting. For I am simply a voyeur. I will read the profiles but not touch the keyboard. I will fantasise but not indulge.

I am not addicted.

Chapter 4:
Playing the field

Pick-ups and let-downs in dateworld

You've got to kiss a lot of frogs: this is the first commandment of online dating. And the more of these amphibious snogs you have, the greater your chance of finding your princess or prince. It's the scratchcard approach to love: you've got to be in it to win it. Online dating is a numbers game – and clearly the dating companies have the teeniest vested interest in reminding you of that, as their own numbers would hardly stack up if everyone found their ideal partner on the first date. But the statistics suggest that, if you stick at it – and some people really roll their sleeves up and graft at it like a full-time job – you have a one in five chance of striking relationship gold.[29] And if you don't get lucky, you can at least have fun.

'Dating' is a very un-British idea. This American brand of courting – of light, non-committal one-on-ones with as many people as you can manage, while weighing up their relative merits – brings a new kind of romance to our shores. We're used to a different courtship ritual entirely: a more rapid pairing-off, a quick funnelling into monogamy, which has been called 'the British adolescent school of relationship formation':

Namely, go to a party, down some drinks, make eye contact with a person you fancy, proceed to kissing and often much more, wake up the next morning to find that you have magically become one half of a couple, then spend the following weeks,

months, and sometimes years, discovering whether you have
anything whatsoever in common.[30]

Maybe it's not surprising that we've taken to this new import in such
a big way. Of the 18 million first dates in Britain last year, two thirds
were catalysed by the internet.[31]

Wait. British people, en masse, making appointments to be genial to
strangers? Twelve million times in a year? Surely not. This is not the
guarded, hostile-to-people-we-don't-know Britain we thought we lived
in. Online dating seems to have triggered an outbreak of sociability. It
is not visible to the naked eye – online daters don't wear purple roses
to identify each other in public – but every night of the week, at pubs,
restaurants and bars, some of the customers will be couples on their
first internet date. Twelve million of these first cyberdates per annum
add up to around six couples per month for every single one of the
90,000 eateries and watering-holes in the country.

It is nothing short of a craze, on the scale of the early 20th-century
dating revolution in the United States when, for the first time, young
men and women started to meet each other outside the home,
replacing the earlier convention of a male admirer 'calling' on a young
woman with her parents' express permission. As Theodore Zeldin
describes in *A Brief History of Humanity*, by the 1920s, 'most of the
youth of America was obsessed with dating, which surveys showed
to take more time than any activity apart from schooling'. The word
'dating' originated in street slang and was first used in 1896. It was
the working class, who were 'not corseted by the fear of meeting social
inferiors', who showed the middle class how to date. Dating was how
you learned about life, other people and the workings of the world.
Until about 1945, 'the aim in dating was to go out with as many
people as possible: the more sought after one was the better. There
was less talk of love now. The goal was to acquire self-confidence by
more certain means, namely by the number of dates one had'.[32]

Now Britain is swept up in a version of this extraordinary rage
for dating, with an updated creed that it is acceptable to explore,
flirt and have sex with a range of people before committing to a

particular one. Millions of British people are now playing the field on a scale previously unimaginable. With it there's an easy come, easy go attitude: as 25-year-old **_eh** says, 'If you go on one date with a man and it doesn't work out, it really doesn't matter as there will always be another waiting in your inbox'. **CC**, 30, advises other women to 'think of it like a job. If you're out of work you wouldn't just email one company for a dream job, you'd blanket your CV to everyone and see what comes back. Don't hang yourself up on one guy, date a few and keep your options open'. The Ohio-based *Woman's Home Companion* offered very similar advice on those 'options' in 1940: 'Never brush off a date, because he might come in handy for an off night.'[33]

This sense of being empowered by our 'options' is something we have come to expect in our comparethemarket.com culture. And while it may have a whiff of consumerism about it, the obligation-free format of internet dating has liberated people: straight women from the sense that in accepting a drink or dinner from a man they are somehow expected to pay 'in kind'; straight men from the spectre of connubial bondage as the price of a few nights of fun; gay women and men from dependency on relatively small groups of connected people to introduce them to partners; and older people of all persuasions and backgrounds from the idea that profound love, adventure and sexual passion are no longer on the cards when a marriage or long-term relationship ends.

For **Freudianslip**, 45, who re-subscribed to GaydarGirls.com after splitting up with her girlfriend of four years, it is exciting to have a virtual space in which to chat and flirt with people without investing in fantasies of a romantic future with them: 'I'm quite discerning and hard to please, and I know it's not going to be easy to find someone, even in the midst of this online dating sweetshop. What I do know is that I can have great fun online with people who are funny and intelligent and smart, with a lot of the heat and expectation held at bay.' As **sparklehorse**, 29, says:

> On my first Soulmates date I thought, 'this is really weird'.
> I felt a bit bad that I didn't like the guy, but he didn't contact

me afterwards so I thought, 'that's fine, he doesn't like me either!' After that, it was quite exciting. You never know who you're going to meet. It's interesting finding out about people you don't know – it's a nice way of spending an evening. It doesn't mean you have to get married!

But the non-committal aspect of online dating doesn't stop it from being taken seriously. Recent figures from the dating empire parship.co.uk show that the average length of a first date is over four hours, and people are spending around 12 hours arranging and preparing for it in advance. Of this prep time, 'pre-date communication' – emails, instant messaging, phonecalls, texts and Skyeping – takes five hours and 36 minutes on average: over 10 hours for almost a quarter (22 per cent) of women and 17 per cent of men, while similar numbers (22 per cent of both men and women) spend less than two hours on initial screening and setting up the date.[34]

A 'date' now encompasses everything from a flying visit to a leisurely stay, with only 2 per cent of first-daters ready to leave after a quick cup of coffee: 10 per cent spend less than two hours on their assignation. On average, men prefer to stretch a first date out to four hours 48 minutes, while women tend to prefer a maximum timeframe of four hours. And 'one in 10 men cite dates extending to over nine hours, while just 3 per cent of women claim to have prolonged the pleasure to that extent'. Dr Victoria Lukats, psychiatrist and resident dating expert at parship.co.uk, explains that:

The prominence of internet dating as a method of meeting people naturally leads to a slightly longer process, as it then becomes like the first meeting and first date rolled into one – most people need to feel fairly sure they're not wasting their time on a first date, so they want to get to know the person first. It takes time to do this as there's no short cut to a long-lasting relationship.[35]

There's a real sense that some people are applying themselves to the new role of self-matchmaker in a conscientious, almost professional way – embracing hedonism, sociability and sexual liberalism, yes, but with the accent on exercising their skills of discernment. Even though, according to match.com, 95 per cent of online daters from their sample of over 11,000 people are ostensibly looking for a long-term relationship, many people are in no hurry to commit. Around 62 per cent of women say they have become fussier in the past year about who they will date.[36]

Perhaps this simply reflects our modern obsession with 'shopping around' to get the best, obeying the command to Gocompare.com in the marketplace of available singles: if we've done our homework properly, we'll inevitably find the perfect one. But, as the sociologist Barry Schwartz has described in the context of shopping, the 'paradox of choice' is that endless variety is a poisoned chalice – the freedom of too many options causes mental meltdown, indecision, self-doubt and even distress.[37]

There is some evidence that online dating can also create a kind of 'Bluewater effect': the bewildering conveyor belts of singles whizzing before our eyes in the online dating malls can reduce our ability to choose. This brain overload was observed in a scientific study of online daters in Taiwan, who were presented with varying numbers of potential suitors for their online search requests. The more potential candidates the subjects were offered, the less time they spent evaluating each one. They simply became indiscriminate, opting for quantity over quality.[38]

LoveCrumb, a 28-year-old woman who has dated on and off for almost three years, believes that people develop different strategies for processing the vast quantities of information generated by online dating:

> I have sometimes felt a bit bombarded and overwhelmed and without the time to search for someone while I'm online, because of the traffic of profiles to read and emails to answer … A lot of the guys I've spoken to seem to use the search function a lot more frequently than women to find people they might like, and spend a lot longer generally online. The joke goes that men look at the photos and women go

straight to the words, but in all seriousness I think that women, for obvious reasons, need more assurance about the type of person they're speaking to online and might potentially meet – they're naturally more cautious. I think women spend more time assessing the content of men's profiles.

This constant assessing can overwhelm people. It can also hone their judgement to razor-sharpness, introducing an unwelcome insensitivity to their dealings with others: 'For a while I had the time of my life,' says 28-year-old **Annie611**, 'but it changed the way I dated. Out went exclusivity and considerateness; in came multiple-dating and a harder edge, as I judged and dismissed and was judged and dismissed.'

The numbers game entails a process of constant appraisal and rejection. The more you date, the more you will reject and be rejected. There's a big psychological risk here: online daters are effectively laying themselves open, again and again, to other people's criticism. Ironically, it can exacerbate the low self-esteem that motivated some people to go online in the first place. 'After initial rejection and the lack of mutual fireworks, I felt vulnerable and exposed. It seemed as if all the negative things my husband had said about me must be true,' says **Marie_Mint**, 49. **SJP123**, 29, was dismayed by the abrupt silence of a guy with whom she had spent an enjoyable evening:

You do take it personally. After our date we exchanged four or five emails and then all of a sudden he didn't reply. I wrote to him and said, 'Is it something I said?' If he'd sent me a message to explain, saying, 'Hey, I'm meeting up with someone', that would have been different. I could see that he was still on the site and I struggled with that. But in the end I realised I couldn't take it personally.

Rejection comes in many forms. There are the standing-ups and the messing-arounds; there are the snubs, as described vividly in 50-year-old **Upgrade**'s deadpan account of a date with a woman who treated him to a dozen varieties of rebuff (see p 111); and there is the physical disdain, like the barely-disguised contempt that **Ms_E**, 34, braved as she approached her date for the first time. 'As I walked up to him at the bar, I saw Neil clock me. I saw Neil's face drop like a lead balloon ... I don't believe there are many things that are more soul-destroying than seeing someone's negative reaction to you. It was awful.' There are the Dear John emails which 9 per cent of online daters send when they end a relationship,[39] such as the affable one **Mmmm**, 33, received from her short-term lover:

> While I had a fantastic time on our dates and we got on really well, I've met someone else via the site, and it seems like it might be heading in the direction of becoming exclusive, and I don't want to mess you about. Wishing you the best of luck for the future – from Pretty Tim ...

She received another that was altogether less pleasant:

> Hey,
>
> Said I'd be in touch, I've been a naughty boy, and been two timing – with another girl from the site, and think I need to come clean.
>
> All the best!

Rejection is tough in any context, but does it get easier the more of it you experience? **sugar_hiccup** thinks not: 'I'm not sure we ever get better at dating. We're all human, we all have egos and feelings, and we all feel incredibly uncomfortable about rejection.' Some people even react with aggression, as **KatieKat**, 34, found on leaving a date. The man she had met ran down the street 'shouting and cursing' after her because she didn't wish to stay for more than one drink. 'You actually get quite a clear sense of a person's temperament through how they handle rejection,' says **LoveCrumb**. 'There have definitely been a few cases where I've received tirades of abuse for not wanting to email or meet a man from the site, and I have felt validated in my decision by their reaction!'

One of the difficulties is that many people wrongly conclude that being turned down is a personal attack, a slight on their being that they didn't deserve. 'Not everyone takes rejection well. One guy sent me a message and I didn't respond,' says **DanE1**. 'Very soon after that he wrote again, saying "I can't believe you're so rude as not to bother replying". I didn't respond to that. I thought, "there are a lot of people here, and if I don't respond it probably means I'm not interested".' And perhaps the swankiness, the streamlined efficiency, of the emporia of online dating fosters an illusion that finding someone will be easy. 'One of the things people have to work through is that just because other people are there doesn't mean they're interested. I'm advertising my availability but I'm not making any promises as to that availability. This isn't Tesco.com: just because I'm on the shelf it doesn't mean that you can buy.'

Another difficulty is that, in the absence of an online dating etiquette book or a standardised Code of Conduct, people are making up protocol as they go along. While some people are wounded by email silence, others have accepted it as the short and sweet 'No thanks' of cyberspeak. London woman **Freudianslip** comments that 'the big decision is whether you respond to an initial approach. Sometimes I think it is better not to respond, if you're not sure, than to speak to someone and have to drop them later'.

In dating theory, if you widen your net – to borrow that well-worn fishing metaphor that crops up so often – you won't mind so much if one or two minnows swim away.[40] This is an obligation-free zone, after all. Some people have learned to build relationships without attachment. **LoveCrumb** notes that:

> On the site, conversations often start but get stalled or cut off because work, holidays, and other commitments interrupt or someone else catches the eye. It's pretty much accepted that people are usually talking to more than one person at once, so there's no need to take it too personally if an exchange ends or if there's a decision not to meet again after the first date. Being big-hearted about it has also meant I have kept a huge amount of ex-dates in my life as good friends.

Difficult as it is, the ability to accept rejection graciously, taking it on the chin, learning from it and moving on to amorous pastures new, is, in cyberland, not just a lofty philosophical ideal but an emotional necessity. Some people even come to appreciate the benefits of rejection, taking it as part of their emotional education. **MilesAway**, a 29-year-old corporate lawyer, tasted rejection after he started dating online last year. After being reprimanded at work for an affair with his assistant, a married woman, he came to the conclusion that 'sleeping my way through the women at my practice was starting to look cheesy'. He set 'really different parameters from usual' when he signed up. 'I've always been quite predictable I suppose – curvy blonde women who are younger than me and don't demand much. My sister had pulled me up for not having the courage to go out with someone who would challenge me. She said I was "going through women like Epsom Salts".'

Having messaged a woman he thought was his intellectual equal as well as being 'intimidatingly beautiful', he engaged in a series of 'quickie flirts' by email with her for a few weeks ...

> ... which is as much as I can manage ... I have the attention-span of a goldfish and I work my bollocks off, so someone has to be both direct and witty to chisel into my inbox. She was. Funny emails – two, three lines – clever little messages that made me laugh. When we met, I saw that was exactly how she talked – sparky, clever and sharp. Over dinner, the conversation motored along and I thought she was extremely good company. I kept looking at her wondering, 'How long can you keep this going?' I mean in the long-term. My great fear is that people will go off the boil and I'll lose interest and have to get out.

The next morning, however, she sent a polite thank you email in which she said she had enjoyed the evening but couldn't see it working, and she never contacted **MilesAway** again.

> It was quite a slap as she didn't say why, and although it might sound arrogant, it doesn't happen to me often. I didn't bother

writing, because at the time I didn't feel I needed to dignify it with a reply. I felt pathetically sorry for myself for five minutes.

Sympathy was not forthcoming from his sister.

She just told me to get over myself and that this was exactly what I needed! In the end that was right: it has been good for me to know the sting of rejection. You have to learn that you can't always get everything you want. She was only exercising her free will, and had every right to do that. Since then I've also been in the position of having to turn down someone who was great, but not for me, and I think I was kinder about it than I perhaps would have been otherwise.

For all the harshness of dating, there is a discernible new approach to rejection that is not bogged down by either guilt or scorn. People are learning how to adapt their emotional skills to accommodate the unique let-downs of the online world: how to get over rapid, unexplained rejection by strangers and how, in turn, to reject people they don't know, yet with whom they have communicated one-to-one.

'You can always be kind even if you decide you don't want to be with someone,' says **Freudianslip**. And there is a huge sensitivity, thoughtfulness and care evident in many people's exchanges: from 38-year-old **AudreyB**'s commitment to giving a response – 'otherwise it's like tumbleweed in the wind' – to 47-year-old **Lorimer**'s decision to act on his gut feeling that he should let one woman know about his growing interest in another.

It is refreshingly modern, direct and up-front: a new frankness in which people know where they stand, emotions are discussed, there is less fear of rejecting or being rejected, and there are new ways of saying, 'Thanks, but no thanks'. Sometimes it is so straightforward as to seem almost hilariously blunt: **Blushes** describes a direct, matter-of-fact, interaction she had with a woman, **Angelika**, she had been chatting to on pinksofa.co.uk. Having exchanged 'four sparky, interesting emails', they swapped phone numbers with a view to deciding over the phone where they were going to meet for their first date:

> Very early in the conversation I said to her, 'Can we meet somewhere that isn't obviously gay?' She said, 'Why, aren't you out?' I said, 'No, I'm not out at all – why, are you out?' She said, 'Yes, completely'. I said, 'Well, I am not the one for you then'. She replied, 'Thank you very much for your honesty', put the phone down, and I never heard another word from her!

Playing the field can bring a confusing variety of emotions. You can find messages that provoke anything from joyful sexual awakening to wall-crawling frustration vacuum-packed in your inbox on the same day, waiting to burst out at you when you log on. To keep your nerves from fraying and your sense of humour from straying there is an essential procedure that you must follow from time to time: log off. Do all the other things that you love – dancing, going out with friends, travelling, learning to sing. As **Ms_E** advises: 'You can't do it continuously. I join a site for a month, arrange about four dates, see them all and leave it for a while.' And it's good to choose a few people selectively rather than trying to vacuum up the entire internet. **DanE1** says, 'A friend of mine said to me "Never forget it's a numbers game – go on as many dates as possible". I saw where she was coming from but I'm too impatient and I don't have the time or the money to go on a different date every day of the week. I'd rather have a few really good dates with interesting people: quality not quantity.'

Despite all the emotional hazards of this new style of dating, this proactive, semi-professional pursuit of romance, most people find it worthwhile. **sparklehorse**'s approach and experiences – 14 great dates and she married the 15th – could make her the poster-child of cyberdating:

> Dating got easier to do, the more I did. You get used to chatting and asking people about themselves. I didn't worry if I didn't like them because I went with no expectations and

there was no obligation: I didn't contact them again if I wasn't interested in them. I felt that none of the guys I met had heavy expectations either. That's where it became really fun. I had a nice chat with almost everyone I met. I wasn't being dishonest. With internet dating you do have to be quite 'Yeah, whatever', because you don't know anything about them – you don't know who their friends are, or how they commit. I didn't want to get involved with anyone unless I was sure: there was no point in getting into a four-year relationship unless it was right. But I do know that it's when you're at your most relaxed that things happen.

For **Annie611**, things only happened after she had walked away from the cyberdating mall; yet they could not have happened without it.

Eventually I tired of the disappointment of going on a bad date, the disappointment of discovering I was someone else's bad date, the games I played badly and the same questions over and over. So after a while I closed down my account, went on holiday, took up a course and restarted some of the things that had made single life more fulfilling. And, fulfilled, I unexpectedly fell in love. I didn't meet him through online dating, but online dating gave me so much clarity about what I was looking for that I knew it as soon as I saw it. We moved in together last month.

Playing the field:
The stories

Alias: **Upgrade** | *Age:* **50** | **M** | ♀♂ | **Guardian Soulmates**

The woman with one ear, the one who's the image of a filmstar, the one who actually is a long-ago filmstar – you've come across all the dating site, erm, clichés. Like the university professor whose published book titles you don't understand and whose best friend back in the US is a 6ft 6in performance artist called Vaginal Davis.

(And yes, it is Vag for short.) You survived the woman who's snogged Jude Law and Mick Hucknall. And the American in her 50s who, like a 20-year-old, thought you'd be impressed that she knew an obscure little backstreet pub. And the tiny woman with the unfeasibly large chest, and the one who wore sweatpants for a year because her husband left home to be a gay, and the one who virulently rubbished JK Rowling with the total unironic conviction that teaching English to 12-year-olds qualifies her to dictate whether the spazillion-selling Harry Potter books are any good or not.

You were unfazed by meeting the woman who, entirely on her own initiative as an adolescent, dressed up in a posh frock to sing-and-dance 'I'm Just A Girl Who Can't Say No' to her bemused Guide troupe and leader to earn some badge no one ever goes for. And the one who thought a first date was the time to tell you she had her youngest kid after a one-night-stand endured to please her husband, and they couldn't go through with the plan to pass her off as their own because the baby was of mixed race.

So when a Supremely Normal-seeming woman got in touch, you liked it. Exciting and exotic are great, but normal must be good too, right? She seems far more 'down to earth' than the thousand women on Soulmates who say they are, but in fact come across as people who are only on secondment to The North, maybe from Primrose Hill. Undercover, testing a theory that it's possible to survive in a suburb with no Caffe Nero, where the *Guardian* is placed discreetly on a higher shelf in the newsagent's and people still eat red meat and non-organic veg.

Supremely Normal's been prevaricating for weeks, so when she suddenly wants to meet up you accept at very short notice. You bolt your dinner, hurriedly shower and change and run for the bus, all so that you can arrive on time at a bar convenient for her. In fact, it's five minutes' walk from her house. So it's a little surprising when she rings, already 10 minutes late, and says, 'Are you there? Oh good, get me a pint of lager, I'll be there in less than a quarter of an hour.' Nice. As though you'd be some kind of neurotic perfectionist if you thought anything less than 25 minutes late was excessive.

You have to say something, or your mouth will get away from you and sour things before they've started, by asking her why she's late. And Supremely Normal has no photo up, so you ask – lightly, you hope – if she thinks she'll recognise you. 'Oh don't worry, you'll know me – I'll be the one chaining a bike to the railings outside.' So she's coming from just around the corner by bike and still going to be late? Brilliant.

Eventually you sit down together. She doesn't really look at you, but you can tell she knows you're there by her relentless questioning. You accept that people often think 'showing an interest' is charming, maybe even alluring; but it's not meant to be the level of interest that the Gestapo showed in resistance fighters. Worse still, the conversation typically goes something like this:

> You: 'So I went to the pictures the other day with my son. We saw the new Indiana Jones and ate white Maltesers.'
>
> SN: 'What did you see?'
>
> You: 'Er, the new Indiana Jones.'
>
> SN: 'Who did you go with?'
>
> You: 'Well, my son ...'
>
> SN: 'What did you have to eat?'

Eventually she does this once too often, and you snap. 'I just told you that!' 'Oh, sorry,' she says; 'the music in here's too quiet, I can't hear you properly.' You resist the urge to say, 'How's the volume of music in here for you?' and instead suggest moving to a table that just became free outside.

Once you're out there, sure enough, she no longer asks you questions you've already answered. No, she concentrates so hard on making and smoking her roll-ups that she barely talks at all. And then, thankfully, it's time for your last bus. Well, small white lie –

time for your penultimate bus. But you'd rather suck the exhaust than stay here for another hour.

At regular intervals over the next few months Supremely Normal contacts you again, till you eventually write back and say, 'You obviously don't remember, but we have dated and, believe me, you had no wish to see me again.'

'Sorry,' she replies, unabashed, 'I suppose people all look the same on here after a bit.'

Alias: **Marie_Mint** | *Age:* **49** | *F* | ♀♂ | **Guardian Soulmates**

My adored husband left me for a woman who was 'everything you are not'. He left me, 'not the children', but did precious little to help bring them up. Life was working, keeping home, coping with abject missing and misery, and maintaining a smiling face amid crippling grief and adversity. Then my son said, 'Go on Soulmates mum. You're quite "fit" for someone old. Someone might fancy you.'

So, swallowing pride and many other doubts (especially about my wobbly bits), I did. Life started to change in unexpected and startling ways because of the men I met.

Mr Music. Promising, caring and effusive online. Charming on our date. Began to talk at length about his extensive iPod and CD collection but not about my beauty and charm. 'I hope it's not alphabetically ordered,' I quipped. Long pause. 'Why would that be a problem?' I was not filed under C for Chemistry.

Mr Tractor. Profile headline: 'Have Tractor, Need Shed.' Vintage farm vehicle enthusiast. Halting date in an art gallery and coffee shop. No revving of engines. Suffice to say his tractor was never to park in my shed.

Mr Divine. My best date mate. Great repartee and friendship. Told me I was funny and could write and made me feel worthwhile again. Online banter so good that I was wary of meeting. Reluctantly relinquished my mobile number with the request, 'Send me a dirty text, I've never had one.' He texted back, 'Switch your phone to vibrate' ... and off we went! A few hours later (speed was not of the essence as my predictive text skills were lacking) I felt thrilled and sheepish in equal measure. Met once in a bikers' café and had a snog in the sunshine, and he had trouble mounting his motorbike to return to work because of swelling in the trouser region. We are sexy-matey rather than lovey-dovey and have decided to be friends. I treasure him.

Mr Banker. Charming, self-aware, rich. Went out in his Jag for a classical concert and a meal. Had a touch of the transvestite about him, as if he was about to return home and change into a sequinned frock. No mutual marvelling.

Mr Pub. When on the verge of stopping my membership because failed dates were making me feel exposed and vulnerable, Mr Pub bounced in and out of my life like an enthusiastic labrador. Diamond Geezer with his own pub who called me 'F'ing gorgeous' and could not keep his hands off my squidgy bits (much to my surprised delight). Inexplicably vanished as quickly as he came(!) with the familiar phrase, 'You're really lovely, but goodbye.' Big sigh but lesson learned.

Mr Priceless Profile. My best, exquisitely funny friend. Talk, write and laugh to knicker-wetting degree daily. Never met, never will? Doesn't matter. Brilliant ranting Alf Garnett of a man with a soft heart under the gruff exterior. Has delighted me and my children exceedingly with his wit and wisdom. Idea of fun is to stand in a hailstorm with a metal bucket on his head.

Mr Sooty. So named by Mr PP (above) because his first name reminds him of the puppet and hands in unmentionable places. I adore Mr Sooty and he me. We met in a remote beach house in North Wales having communicated (rather steamily) online for only four days. The weekend was supposed to have been with Mr

Pub. I was a staggeringly unpromising 0 per cent match for him, but we took a deep breath and ignored horrified friends and took the risk. He arrived in a Porsche and was gorgeous, complex, funny and intriguing. Idyllic weekend of sunshine, sand dunes, dolphins, sunsets and stars. At the end he said: 'I have learned more about life, nature, poetry and contentment from you in 48 hours than in 49 years.' I cried and have been crying intermittently since, because our relationship is fraught with impossible practical barriers.

Mr Horny Hands. Current much-loved friend and lover. A gardener who is cultivating my happiness. Wooed me with a Flake, which he delivered to my doorstep on my birthday, riding 25 miles on his motorbike (I had told him about my walk in a local meadow like the girl in the advertisement). I tried to resist because of Mr Sooty but failed in my attempts, probably because we were in said meadow at the time of my rejection speech and ended up crushing the cornflowers instead.

Then there's the novelist after my 'fur-lined jewel box', the public school master after a spot of 'body-twitching passion' and the man I have desired and mailed since the very beginning but whose desired attributes I do not possess. I really do feel I have started to live again, and I am, frankly, amazed at the power that online dating has had in my life.

Alias: **2leggedtree** | *Age:* **21** | *F* | ♀♂ | **Guardian Soulmates**

There is no polite way of saying this: online dating feels a bit like shopping in the discount food section of a supermarket. You know that you could get a really great deal, but on the other hand you could get something quite reasonable that you wouldn't usually go for if it cost any more.

Alias: **KatieKat** | *Age:* **34** | *F* | ♀♂ | **match.com**

I don't remember his name. But on paper he looked good. We were interested in the same kind of things – travel, theatre, art, good food, current affairs. We both had the same taste in bars – not too hip, but cool and laid-back places away from the try-hard crowd.

We got drinks and proceeded to cover some of the ground carefully trodden in our emails. He was nice enough, but there wasn't a hint of a spark between us. The conversation fast ground to a halt.

Was it rude to apologise politely, thank him for a pleasant chat and leave? I hoped not. Was it rude for him to follow me into the street shouting and cursing because I hadn't stopped for another drink or given him a chance? I think so. Worse things happen.

Alias: **indigo_voyage** | *Age:* **44** | *F* | ♀♂ | **Guardian Soulmates**

It's 12:30pm and the tiredness or exhaustion that normally takes me into sleep hasn't quite yet arrived. I start to search the internet, looking for freebies, tenants for the spare room and a man. It's 2009, and the middle-class black woman has arrived!

Three years ago, when my nieces (who were all born with computers in their little hands) convinced me to seek a partner on the net, I was horrified. I was teaching in a further education college at the time and was terrified that friends, family, other lecturers and, especially, my students, would see my advertisement. I hadn't considered changing the name or my picture as that would be dishonest, and if the above did see the advert, well, they would think, 'She must be desperate!' I started to think they might be right.

As a black woman from a social science background, nothing in my life is straightforward. Most people go off and dye their hair, grow it, weave it, wear shorts and go off on impulsive holidays and think

117

little about 'what people think'. I, on the other hand, analyse the effects of racism, sexism, socialism and capitalism, the plight of single families and black teenagers, the media's over-representation of some things and under-representation of others. Dating on the internet was never going to be easy!

I decided to place my first advert with no picture. My nieces laughed, of course, for in their world of Facebook, blogs, Twitter and everything else, their whole lives are one big photo album. But I just couldn't do it. The simple advert with no picture brought little response, of course, apart from sex-crazed men who seemed to send out a standard response or from men who would commit to developing a further dialogue only if I sent a picture back.

I panicked and decided to rethink my approach. I sat and asked myself a few questions. What exactly was I looking for and why? I thought about past relationships and how the traits that most of those men had had were not what I wanted now. They were all that I knew, however, so I started to read more profiles and decided to place an ad with a smiling image of myself. More responses came, and I was on a roll! Black woman. Single. Needs TLC. Interested in men who enjoy healthy living, walks in the park and interesting conversations. I showed it to my cousin (male) who has been married to his teenage sweetheart forever, and he said 'Hmmm, it sounds as if you're looking for a husband!' And? Man, this was not going to be easy!

Now I am two years into the experience and have decided that I really *do* need to get out more. Experiences of love on the net hit hard and end hard. Within two conversations (virtual or real), I have gone from life-story declarations, to thinking this might be 'the one' and waking to texts, emails and voicemails that confirm 'This is *so* not "the one"!'.

Then, though I state that I am looking for a black man, white men insist on emailing me to tell me how much they love black women and would be able to give me all the things I've asked for and more, and my mind reverts to analysing racism, sexism and history ... Through internet dating, I have met men who offer great first dates that could not have been scripted if I tried: the music, food and ambience of the restaurants have been fantastic. However, the experience should have ended right there, for they then go for the character assassination of the ex-partner. Now, hold on sucker! This is a thinking woman here who is immediately saying, 'I need to hear that sista's side of the story,' so ... *next!*

He was shy at first but soon opened up, and we talked, had great physical chemistry and started making 'future plans'. My mobile and house phone bills confirmed that I had spoken to no one else for three months. We had clothes at each others' homes and were talking about a holiday away – a real 'couples holiday'. Then, like a puff of smoke, he was gone! There was no explanation. No call. No, 'I couldn't handle this'. No, 'I had a girlfriend who was away for four moths so I thought I'd just mess with your head until she came back'. No, 'I'm really a madman parading as a sane, suited, working individual'. No 'I meant to explain but I really can't do any long-term commitment'. None of the above. Just silence and voices in my head asking me if I didn't see the signs? No, for it looked exactly like a relationship to me.

But occasionally, when sleep hasn't quite caught up with me from the day, I still search the net for freebies, tenants for my spare room and a man. Old habits die hard!

Alias: **farfalla** | *Age:* **50** | *F* | ♀♂ | **match.com**

The first date? A fabulous evening. We met at Waterloo, under the clock in the time-honoured tradition, looked into each other's eyes and smiled. After several weeks of emailing and phone calls, it felt comfortable and exciting in equal measure. We wandered along the South Bank, found a restaurant and had a wonderful few hours of talking and making each other laugh, establishing contact. We walked back to Waterloo, arm in arm, under the pretty, twinkling tree lights ... we both felt happy and optimistic and lucky.

The next six months were blissful. There was daily contact – texts, emails and phone calls – we met regularly, we met each other's friends, we spent weekends together in each other's homes and arms, and we planned future holidays. We grew closer and became friends as well as lovers, and we were, I thought, happy. Then one day, quite unexpectedly, he announced that, much as he cared for me, he was going to seek a reconciliation with his estranged wife after five years apart. Ouch.

Alias: **Miss_Conduct** | *Age:* **30** | *F* | **Bisexual** | **Guardian Soulmates**

Here is the email I sent to Harry a couple of days after our date:

Hey Harry,

I had a lovely time on Wednesday (and Thursday). I really like your company, and I think you're handsome and beautiful. And I love that you lay yourself open and say what you're thinking and don't play games. I'm just not sure if I can do the whole sexual relationship thing. This isn't because the sex was not good – you gave me an orgasm on our first date for God's sake – but my sexual attraction towards men is a strange phenomenon. I don't consider myself gay, because I am incredibly sexually attracted to some men, but they are few and far between, and tend to either be gay or look disarmingly like girls, or both* (I had a very guilty crush on Boy George at the age of six).

I wish this wasn't the case but it is. I think you are a unique person and I love the way you are so open and honest and direct. So don't go worrying that you have seemed too keen or showed your feelings too much, because I think it's wonderful that you do, and wish more people were like that. I feel bad and sad that I have been careless with your heart; I guess I wasn't quite sure if or how much I felt sexually attracted to you on Wednesday night and just reasoned, 'I'll get into bed and see what happens'. But this was unfair and thoughtless of me.

I don't want you to think this means I consider you either unattractive or crap in bed – neither could be further from the truth – but it just didn't feel 100 per cent right for me. I think that's why I was not being very proactive, and rather selfishly did all the receiving and very little of the giving when we were in bed together.

I would dearly love to stay friends with you, as there are so many things I like about you; not just the ones detailed above, but also your inappropriate sense of humour and the fact that you can spell. And even write poetry. But I will understand if you feel mucked about and never want to see me again.

I hope this goes a little way towards explaining how I feel. If not, or even if it does, you are always welcome to phone me if talking by email seems a bit stilted. Or alternatively, you may prefer to cut off all contact and stick pins into a voodoo doll made in my image.

Louise xxx

* This does not mean I thought you looked gay or like a girl in your profile photo.

––––––––––––––

Alias: **farfalla** | *Age:* **50** | *F* | ♀♂ | **Guardian Soulmates**

Not everyone observes the etiquette of internet dating – messages are not answered and loose ends are left. Online dating is not for the faint-hearted. You have to know how to be kind and honest with strangers – possibly sensitive or vulnerable strangers such as the newly separated or divorced. With so many people on the site, it is likely that someone you could be happy with is out there; but if you don't meet them early on, how do you find strategies to keep going?

––––––––––––––

Alias: **AudreyB** | *Age:* **38** | *F* | ♀♂ | **Guardian Soulmates**

I would recommend keeping an open mind. Knowing what you are hoping to find is, of course, important, but getting stuck on seeking perfection in another is unrealistic, as it is in ourselves. Be honest in your profile and your communications. Be clear with yourself about what you are looking for. This may change over time.

I found that most people appreciated a response after trying to make contact, even if it's just a polite 'No thank you'. Treat other people as you would like to be treated. As someone said to me, it's like tumbleweed in the wind otherwise.

Alias: **spirograph** | *Age:* **31** | *M* | ♀♂ | **Guardian Soulmates**

At first you'll probably get a flurry of activity because you're new ('fresh meat'), but mostly from people you'd cross the street to avoid. This will make you feel good for a while, but then the sheer, grinding tedium of writing the same thing over and over again will lead you to save one message and then copy and paste it with minor changes to save time when you contact different people. Many women will ignore you. This is either out of arrogance, disorganisation or their 'popularity' (though having 200 fans who all look like murderers isn't that much of an achievement), depending on the person. You will toy with the idea on numerous occasions of just jacking the whole bloody thing in because it's such a waste of sodding time.

I'd like to tell you that it will all turn out for the best, except I'm not sure that it will. It might, but it might equally just cause you to become a borderline alcoholic out of sheer frustration, and to spend drunken evenings ranting about how there probably is a God, but he damn well hates you.

Alias: **Miss_Conduct** | *Age:* **30** | *F* | **Bisexual Guardian Soulmates**

I assumed that everything would be direct, clear, straightforward and ego-enhancing in the world of online dating. In fact, within a week of signing up for it, I realised that there was just as much opportunity for miscommunication, insecurity and rock-bottom self-esteem as there is in 'real life'.

Alias: **Lorimer** | *Age:* **47** | *M* | ♀♂ | **Guardian Soulmates**

To date, even to date online, is to open the door to a huge spectrum of possibilities. Once you open that door – even if it's barely ajar, you're only peeping and no one can see you – you need to be prepared. Prepared for the huge range of potential outcomes: the endless, noncommittal coffees, the sharp sting of messages unanswered and approaches rejected, the problem of gently letting down someone in whom you've no interest, the cold-sweat thunderclap of clicking so uncannily with someone you can't believe it was mere software that brought you together. None of which is easy. If you're rebuilding a life after separation or bereavement, or you've been outside a relationship for ages, these winds can be too buffeting for papery confidence to withstand. And I'm not saying there are rules or that even if there were they would help, but there's more than one way to look at how people behave.

My impression is that there are two basic models of dating, one from the US, the other the UK. The former's like one of those highly codified square-dancing events you might end up at if you're at the wedding reception of someone you don't know very well. Partners are taken, whirled around, danced with, then everyone budges up one. Identical things happen with different partners and so on. This way of dating seems more about the dance than the partner. Maybe I've watched too much TV, but I just have this sense of an implicit consensus that dating means seeing plenty of people, simultaneously, which becomes exclusive (i.e., serious) only by explicit agreement.

In the UK model you dance a variety of dances with the same partner. They're who you arrive and leave with and – though you might have never met them before, and might not see them again – while you're there, you're there together.

Under these (also unspoken) rules you try any number of dates, from one to who-knows-how-many, and when (or if) you reach the end of the line you start again at date number one with someone else.

It's something you feel, it's visceral. For example, I struck up a correspondence with Harriet, who lived over 250 miles away. We clearly had a lot in common. We wrote to each other often, sometimes about daily life's prosaic small change, sometimes about our pasts and things that mattered. We decided to meet, even though we kept puncturing the bubble of our expectation with talk of the potential for mutual repulsion and having to sit out the date in a cinema. The first available day was six weeks away; when her subscription ran out she didn't renew, and we communicated by email.

Then Sarah, who lived 60 miles away and was new to the site, got in touch. We instantly began to write: at length, in detail, candidly and often. Within days of our first exchange she had to go away briefly and volunteered her mobile number. She promised she'd turn it off, saying she just wanted to hear me on her voicemail to make sure I didn't sound like Mr Bean. We soon spoke, moved to emails and also arranged to meet, about three weeks before I was due to see Harriet. What to do? Tell them about each other and let them know, effectively, they were in some kind of eliminator to claim the (dubious) prize of dating me? Tell neither, see both, decide at leisure? I had conflicting advice, which aligned with the approaches outlined above: stick with one and one only, or play the field, it's just dating.

And here's what I meant about its being visceral: the date with Sarah was such a clear case of mutual connection there was only one thing to do. I emailed Harriet to explain why I wouldn't be coming to see her. I didn't want to over-egg it, because for all I knew – what with her living in a big city and being clever and funny and attractive – she might have been dating throughout our whole cyberacquaintance, and my slipping off her radar might have meant nothing more than minor inconvenience. As it was, she understood, and we agreed that, long-term (if there *had* been a long-term) those 250 plus miles would have been a huge, train-shaped obstacle to the development of anything significant.

So yes, there *is* an etiquette at work, but it's not something you need to learn so much as trust yourself to feel. It's like eating out: etiquette's also involved there, but you don't need a handbook to know that blowing your nose on the tablecloth isn't quite right. Some things you just know.

––––––––––––––––––

Alias: **Idina** | *Age:* **54** | *F* | ♀♂ | **Guardian Soulmates**

I was once a passenger in an old sports car that caught fire. My then boyfriend's car had a passenger door that was permanently stuck shut (you got out via the driver's door). We were in a slow-moving queue of traffic when I noticed smoke curling around my boyfriend's feet as he drove. Although I didn't normally comment on technical car matters, I pointed out that this was probably not a good sign. As he steered to the kerb, before he had even brought the car to a halt, I was out of the impossible-to-open door and standing on the pavement, with my back hugging the window of Hair by Jayne and my handbag clutched to my chest like a shield.

Many years later this uncanny ability to conjure up a rapid exit from an extreme situation surfaced once more. Th e email was friendly enough, the photo was pleasant enough, if a bit indistinct, and after a false summer on first signing up, my Soulmates message box had been empty for more than a month. And winter was coming. I suggested an exhibition I wanted to see at the Design Museum, and we agreed a day, time and meeting place.

I arrived at the said time. And waited. Outside, as arranged. In the cold, for around 20 minutes. His phone didn't pick up. Couples drifted into the museum, looking as if they belonged. I walked around in little circles to keep warm. Then, just as I was losing sensation in my toes, I got message number one: 'Apologies for delay; just arrived at nearby tube station.'

Ten minutes later I am still walking round in circles. Feeling mildly irritated. I text: 'Am moving inside 2 shop.' I examine every object in the shop as if the main purpose of my visit was to purchase a curated design icon rather than meet a tardy engineer. Many, many minutes and several ill-advised purchases later I gather that he got lost, probably because the tube station he exited from was not so nearby. But he's almost there now. I text: 'Am moving to café.' I purchase warming tea and find a spare table in a corner by the entrance, where I sit by myself and try not to look like someone whose arrangements are really poorly designed. And I wait.

More minutes pass. It's now an hour since we were supposed to meet, and entry to the exhibition is about to close. I am quite angry, suddenly. Enough. I start gathering up my possessions. As I do this, a portly, veteran version of the photograph strides in, without looking in my direction. Casting around the tables in front of him, he walks over to a woman on the other side of the café, who has the misfortune to have the same hair colour as me. A woman who shakes her head vigorously at him and his cravat. Next thing I know, I have travelled about half a mile in a blink, and I am back on the north side of the river.

Good job I was wearing trainers.

Alias: **SoSueMe** | *Age:* **56** | *F* | ♀♂ | **datingdirect.co.uk**

Sometimes it pays to be economical with the truth. On one site I withheld details of my disability. Let's face it, admitting you're 56, overweight and disabled isn't exactly going to have them queuing around the block now, is it? Mike was a great guy to break-your-dating-duck with – a retired firefighter, completely comfortable with himself and not fazed by my disability: 'I'll push you round Cheshire Oaks in a wheelchair if you like,' he offered gamely. After a pleasant couple of hours having coffee I realised that Mike wasn't looking for a partner: his daughters had bought his membership as a Christmas present, and he was just enjoying the experience.

Then there were the guys who professed to be 'cool about callipers' but who disappeared after the second or third date. Some guys run for the hills at the first mention of the D-word, while others stick around for a couple of dates but then dematerialise.

Not that I've been short of offers. I've had guys in their 20s and 30s chatting me up, despite my insistence that I'm old enough to be their mother. One chap, though, was so daunted by the prospect of dating a disabled woman that he sent this text: 'Sorry to learn about your disability. Probably won't choose to have a relationship with you. But I feel sorry for you. May I offer sex only for you?' Eh?

I did meet someone I thought had potential. He told me I was a nice person, he liked me, and we got on very well. He wasn't put off by my disability, despite being a fitness advisor who runs for fun several times a week. Dates were rather sporadic, but we always had a good time when we got together. No problem with the D-word then. His problem was the C-word. Not only could he not commit to any kind of regular relationship, he couldn't even commit to the occasional Friday night. After letting me down several times at the last minute, it was curtains for Running Man.

I'm now more savvy when I scan profiles and read between the lines. For 'No picture, I'm camera shy' read 'I'm married and my wife will kill me if she finds out I'm on here.' Some research on one potential admirer (let's call him Alfie) revealed that he wasn't '63 and divorced' but '74 and married'. We didn't arrange to meet. Months later, out of the blue, I had an extremely vitriolic email from Alfie saying, 'Well, that wasn't very nice, going off like that without even saying hello! OK, I'm a bit older than my profile says but you're nothing special.' Chortling to myself, I realised that it was sent to me in error.

I replied 'Blimey! I bet you feel better for getting that off your chest!' A sheepish response came from Alfie, complaining there were too many Sues on the site.

Some men look gorgeous and sound interesting – on their profiles. Chatting online and on the phone enables you to weed out the dross. Why waste time meeting someone who's dull as ditchwater? Example: I was watching a TV documentary, reading a book, painting my nails *and* chatting on the phone to a guy and was still bored witless. In the end I said 'Am I keeping you up?'.

The latest interest came from Mickey in LA, who said he was a widowed geologist with no family who travelled the world performing important geological explorations. Within days he was talking about us spending the rest of our lives together, how he would come over to the UK so we could go travelling (all at his expense, of course), oh, and how he couldn't stop thinking about me blah, blah, blah. The only thing was that he didn't seem able to string a sentence together. Call me old fashioned, but I do like a properly constructed sentence, even in a chat room. I would write long, carefully crafted paragraphs to him, and he would simply reply 'OK cool'. I challenged him (politely), and he took umbrage. I said that if it was going to work, our conversations would have to be a bit more 50:50. He said he was working in Brisbane for a couple of weeks, but then I had a chat message from him one lunchtime. I replied: 'If you're in Brisbane it's the middle of the night. Shouldn't you be asleep?' 'brb' he wrote (for chat virgins brb = be right back). That was two weeks ago.

It's liberating to discover that some blokes actually prefer a well-upholstered woman, even if she isn't an Olympic athlete. 'I may not be a four-minute miler,' I say, 'but I like to think I make up for it in other ways ...'

Happily, I now feel a lot more secure about my sexuality and attractiveness than I did at the beginning. Overall, online dating has been a life-affirming experience.

Alias: **Ms_E** | *Age:* **34** | *F* | ♀♂ | **match.com**

After embarrassing myself horribly with a previous date and making every bloody mistake in the book, I was determined not to be put off but to learn from it. So, I wouldn't make it obvious if I liked someone, I wouldn't start crowing to friends about how I had 'finally found him' and I certainly wouldn't be staying overnight for at least … six dates? Six weeks even. My friend recommended reading *The Rules*, which, of course, is largely a load of rubbish, but there were definitely a few things I could take from it. Not being so utterly available was one of them.

Sam had been 'winking' at me for a while, but I had ignored him. I now decided it was time to meet him. He met me enthusiastically in the bar. He looked like a demented Rick Astley – his quiff was at least twice the size of the original version and he had huge goggly eyes. He was not 'the full ticket', as my dad would say, and I knew this within five seconds. I suppose there is no box to tick on your profile for being a bit mad. But he was sweet, and he was keen for us to go to dinner at a famous sushi restaurant in Ealing, one I hadn't been to before. I will be forever grateful to him introducing it to me – I have taken at least five more dates there since, and it is truly fantastic.

Sam had suffered horribly at the hands of bullies during his school years. He told me about all this at length and also how he had remained a virgin until just last year. After just half a lager Sam's face went bright red, and he lost enough of his inhibitions to go on to tell me about the night he finally lost his cherry. He was cheerful and brimming with enthusiasm for life and now girls. I found myself mentally writing the email the following morning explaining why it was best not to see each other again, but he never contacted me after that. We exchanged a quick peck on the cheek, and he bounded over the road to the tube station with his rucksack bouncing on his back.

I hope he found someone lovely – and equally bonkers.

I have retired from internet dating. For the time being anyway. Not because I've met my one true love (or perchance I have – more of that later), but because they wanted money. The dating site, not the men. Although sometimes I might have been tempted to pay the men. Services rendered and all that. If only any of them had. But I wouldn't have been able to anyway. I have a lot of wonderful things – cats, daughters (sorry, the other way round), a rural idyll, dandelions and a small widget to make coffee akin to amphetamines. Money, being the root of all evil, not buying you love, and being hard to come across, I don't have.

I could have just left my profile up, but I worried that some poor fellow would see it, fall deeply and irrevocably in love with me and then find that, due to lack of funds, I could never speak to him, and that he would become deeply embittered, kill himself by throwing himself off a motorway bridge, cause a massive pile-up that included various world leaders on their way to a peace summit and so miss their chance to save the world from war, destruction, pestilence and coffee akin to amphetamines, and so we would all die of war, destruction, pestilence and coffee akin to amphetamines. Th us rendering internet dating obsolete.

Internet dating turned out to be a lot like shopping. I go into town, and in the very first shop I find some shoes that are really nice. But then it's the first shop. Maybe there are better, redder, sexier, more shoey shoes in the other shops. I spend a tiring day/week/year/lifetime trawling, inspecting, smelling and trying on other shoes, only to decide that the very first pair of shoes was actually very nice. And so I seem to be dating the first pair of shoes. The shoes may or may not think this is the case, as shoes are unfathomable creatures. This pair particularly so. It may be that the shoes have, in fact, wandered off. For how can any of us tell if shoes fancy us? I certainly can't. I feel for the sake of utter corniness that I should make some joke here about shoes and soles and souls and soulmates. But I'll save you from that. PS Shoes – if you read this, the whole shoe metaphor thing was purely accidental. I do not now, and never have, thought of you as a pair of shoes.

Although if you'd like me to ...

Alias: **AliceInWonderland** | *Age:* **40** | **F** | ♀♂ | **Guardian Soulmates**

I kissed a boy and I liked it. Filey, May 2008. The beach, the waves, the ache. I've been fantasising about sex with a man since January 2007. I've looked on the internet and there's loads of them: handsome, my age, all within 15 miles of my postcode. It's time to take the plunge.

I meet Jason; I don't want to kiss him. I meet Adam; he doesn't want to kiss me. John doesn't even show up. Katie Perry is on the radio in the café while I wait for John: she kissed a girl and she liked it – and then she went back to her boyfriend. How did she get so wise? I kissed a girl, I liked it, I kissed some more, I married one. I always have to take everything to extremes.

Next I meet Glyn; his photo is so great I don't bother with more than the email it takes to arrange a coffee. While he talks, I watch his lips and imagine kissing them. I know they would be nice to kiss, but 10 minutes listening to the words coming through them are more than enough. This is hard work. Men are interesting. I am fussier than I expected.

What about this next one? Robert. Our emails are long, interesting, deep. This must bode well for kissing. I spot him coming down the escalator. He spots me. Bingo! Coffee extends to a meal. I can listen and talk to him at the same time as I watch that little scar on his neck and think of what it will taste like. Can he tell I'm thinking about what he might taste like? He's going on holiday the next day. We hover in the car park, and I want to kiss him, but no, that's enough excitement for one night. I haven't kissed a boy for 20 years; I don't want to rush. A tiny bit of me is still scared I might not like it.

We email through his holiday. My friends follow every nuance. He's back, we go out to dinner. Twenty Leeds speech therapists text to see if we've kissed. I collapse in the restaurant toilets and explain to the woman washing her hands that I am on an internet date. She is lovely. I want to stay there and tell her everything: he is gorgeous, he is interesting, I am terrified. I want to ask her: 'Does this mean I am not a lesbian any more?'. I thought I was, I liked it, it was OK. But why do I fancy this man? How can I tell him? What if it makes him not fancy me? That means I think he fancies me. Ohhhh! I can't go back out there! I go back out there. I go back to his house for coffee. It's too nice to spoil with premature confessions of complicated pasts. We hug as I leave, but I can't, I can't. I can't kiss him. I can't tell him. I can't make the leap. The hug is the kind of hug that knows we will hug again.

The meal was Friday evening. On Sunday morning, 20 Leeds speech therapists think I'm having a quiet day at home. I'm not. He takes me walking. He's brought Jaffa cakes, a flask of tea and an extra fleece. The conversation is fun, deep and open – except it keeps bumping into my past. The adventure is going too well to let the dodging and skirting continue. I take a deep breath and say, OK, it's only our third meeting but you know I have been skirting and dodging, well, it's like this ...

We are hopping over limestone pavements now. The conversation is freed up again, meandering happily like it might reach a great big ocean one day. We keep talking, and we notice birds in the sky, climbers on the cliffs. We stand very, very close to one another. It starts raining heavy, and we let it soak through everything it soaks through. He drops me home and yes, OK, he will come in for a cup of tea, what with his flask being empty now. I make tea, we drink tea, then the tea's all done and it's time for him to go. He doesn't wait until we're at the door. He goes for it in the middle of the kitchen. Mouth to mouth straight away. Brazen. The sexiness of it shocks me. My hungriness shocks me. We stand back, smile and move right back in for another.

Filey, November 2008, the beach, the waves, a different ache. I spent the summer having all of that sex I'd been fantasising about and more. Robert was the 'one' but he wasn't 'the one'. My internet profile is lying dormant for a while. I didn't find love, but I kissed a boy, and I liked it.

Chapter 5:
Dates from heaven

The ones to remember

There's no such thing as a great date. No ready-to-assemble, just-add-partner flat-pack. Despite the eleventy-squillion bytes of *where to go on a date* advice available on the internet (restaurant? salsa class? tenpin bowling?), there's no formula, no $\sqrt{(\chi + \gamma)} = fireworks$ that can be applied randomly to every person you date. The gourmet meal, walk by the sea and night under the stars that combine in a symphony of loveliness with one person will be muzak in the key of plinkety-plonk with another. If you've picked the wrong person for your Midsummer picnic on Chesil Beach, your oysters, figs and asparagus with hollandaise will suddenly become a massive, ridiculous joke. A great date is always a great date *with*. It becomes wonderful because of the dynamic between two people.

This is widely known in the dating world as 'chemistry'. Chemistry is touted as the missing ingredient that awaits you at the end of your journey from online to offline, that perilous transition from internet to 'real life'. Something that is just there, ready-formed and waiting for you to collect, like your dry-cleaning. 'Will the chemistry be there when you and your partner meet?'

If it's not, 'science' is on hand like some reassuring white-coated uncle, offering lab-tested certainties for the anxious. There are pheromone-based scents to make men more attractive.[41] There's a dating website called chemistry.com that riffs on the scientific lustre of the word: 'We'll tell you who and what ignites chemistry in you' and 'Get ready for some chemistry-inspired matches'. And, most magnificently, there's a DNA-match dating service that really takes this whole chemistry thing to heart, romantically offering you the 'buccal swab test' route to finding a DNA-compatible mate: 'We send you a DNA collection kit, the main component of which is a sterilized packet of cotton swabs. You rub the swabs on the insides of your cheeks. It's quick, easy, and painless. Drop the swabs into the pre-addressed envelope, and send them off to our laboratory.'[42] Tick tock!

It's not that there aren't major physiological and chemical attractors at work – steroids, sterols, hormones, face shapes, vocal textures, smells and atavistic procreational lusts – that invisibly yet powerfully affect our feelings for each other, or that the arousal associated with sexual attraction and pleasure isn't as real, measurable and involuntary as our flushed cheeks.[43] It's that chemistry is often assumed to be outside your influence: to exist independently, either there or not. A woman in a dating chatroom says, 'I'm waiting for it. I know it's coming ... ' There's a fatalism about this expectation of immediate fizz: if it's 'not there', some people swiftly lose heart and 'move on'.

But according to the anthropologist David Givens, we can 'create chemistry' even if it's not there at the start: 'Ordinary courtship goes over a period of weeks and months, and it builds up and adds up and eventually you get this kind of chemical bonding.[44] Eye contact and discussing personal subjects can accelerate this chemical bond.' As a relationship starts to mean something, our levels of pleasure-giving dopamine rise. In a match.com survey, over two-thirds of the respondents (68.3 per cent) agreed that they needed 'to know someone for a period of time before falling in love'. Mutual attraction may not be instant. When 41-year-old ex-Londoner **DaPopester** met his drama teacher girlfriend, **SnowieMunro**, 36, he found her 'slightly scatterbrained': 'She did most of the talking – she had all this nervous energy – I thought she was a bit crazy to be honest! She's very ebullient and talkative anyway but it turns out that that's how she behaves when she's nervous.' Four weeks later, they were engaged.

The signs are that more and more people are giving chemistry a chance. Despite employment gloom, housing woes and a general case of the mopes, dating is on the up. The recession has been kind to the cyberdating industry: match.com reports a membership rise of 35 per cent in the six months to June 2009. But, as the blissed-out folk in this chapter show, the great news for daters in cash-strapped times is that the raw materials of heavenly dates are creativity, time, conversation and trust. Which cost precisely nothing.

Honesty is where it all begins, and you can't get freer than that. Start as you mean to go on. 'As both of us were completely honest right from the beginning', says **DaPopester**, 'that honesty has carried forward into the relationship' (see p. 155). Honesty is about openness, and not simply the absence of lies. Your soul must wear its high-vis vest: to allow others to know you, you must let yourself be seen. As **DaPopester** continues, 'I saw something in her on our first date. She gave me the impression that she had a lot of love to give and was capable of receiving it' (see p. 153).

The next ingredient for a recession-proof date is the capacity to dream. 'Imagination is everything. It is the preview of life's coming attractions,' said Albert Einstein – and he should know. The desire to enchant someone makes you creative, and few pleasures can beat that of delighting someone you love. **SnowieMunro** sings 'Summertime' on a beach, a cappella, to woo her man, **DaPopester**. Despite his initial embarrassment, he is seduced.

Then there's one of life's greatest gifts: time. Uncounted, freely-given, irreplaceable time. People miss plays and trains and skip dinner under the influence of love: 'At eight o'clock that evening, the third bottle of champagne had been opened, the meal hadn't so much as made it out of the marinade and the play had started half an hour ago' (**ArtyTheatreBoy**, see p. 139). So don't even think about clock-watching. Great dates will not be rushed.

Again and again, in their stories of life-changing dates, people describe extraordinary conversations: talk that is free-flowing, honest, egoless and funny. And the greatest conversations – those foreshadowings of great relationships – are utterly egalitarian. As the historian Theodore Zeldin writes, in a study of intimacy through the ages, 'Conversation … demands equality between participants. Indeed, it is one of the most important ways of establishing equality.'[45] **DaPopester** describes this rapport during his magical first date with **SnowieMunro**:

> She laughed at what I had to say. There wasn't a lot of interrupting, that 'Oh yeah, I've done that as well' thing that people do when they aren't really listening to you, just chipping in with their own stories. We were really talking about and connecting to the little stories that mattered.

It's the small things that are touching. The knowledge of someone's thoughtfulness on your behalf, for instance, that precise considerateness that can make tea bags the perfect birthday tipple: 'He came to mine with a dozen red roses and my friend Helen said you could tell they weren't from a garage. He bought me tea bags too; red bush, instead of pink champagne, because I don't drink. "Isn't that thoughtful", my Mum said.' (**AliceInWonderland**, see p. 142). Or the pleasing triumph of scandalising teenagers with your public displays of affection: 'On the Millennium Bridge, we're like foreign exchange students; we stop halfway for more kissing, leaning over the Thames. It's one thing we have really got in common, this kissing. We like it so much, and hey, we're in London, who's to stop us? A raggy teenager goes past and mocks "Get a room!" I break off in giggles and I nearly punch the air: Yo! 39 today and no one ever shouted "get a room" at me before! *Je suis arrivée!*'

The location is your stage: whether it's the wide openness of the coastline (see p. 131), or the complex glamour of the city (see p. 141), it will become part of the play. Forty-year-old **AliceInWonderland**'s insight at the artist-installed cracked floor at the Tate Modern reminds her briefly of sorrow, adding wistful depth to her day: 'I have something inside me just like it and I want to know how long it's going to be there and how they are going to fill it back in and not leave a scar for the next exhibition.' More modest backdrops become part of the story too, such as a bakery with its plentiful entertainments, described with deadpan delight by **RedAdmiral**, 72 (see p. 144).

Your location can even *create* the chemistry, firing up adrenalin in the service of desire. The psychologists Arthur Aron and Don Dutton carried out their 'shaky bridge study' in the 1970s: men who walked along the 5ft wide Capilano Suspension Bridge in Vancouver – which rocks terrifyingly above rushing water – found the encounter with a woman they met in the middle far sexier and more romantic than did those who met her on a low and stable bridge just 10ft above the river. Th e differences were large enough for the researchers to conclude that the men on the shaky bridge had confused the excitement of fear with the excitement of desire. Not surprising, as the physiological response to fear, anxiety or challenge – flushed cheeks, racing pulse, pumping adrenalin – is remarkably similar to sexual arousal. So wobbly bridges, scary movies, fairgrounds and unfamiliar places can create an additional thrill: your mind will transfer the exciting rush of adrenalin to the person you are with.

Challenges may be more intimate, like the warm, flirty, boundary-testing dares that show one person's confidence and invite the other to show theirs. **DaPopester**'s challenge to his date, **SnowieMunro**, for instance, about the relative merits of champagne and sparkling wine. 'I said, "Bet you can't tell the difference between them," and she said "Yes I can!" so I suggested we do a champagne blind-tasting.'

For some, booze is brilliant, but for **Jane_G**, an honest cup of tea brewed in a field is enough to oil the cogs of conversation. Abstinence allows another kind of high: 'I consumed no alcohol during this period; I was in charge of all of my faculties so I was aware of what was happening and never had a doubt,' says **Charlie23** of his first date (see p. 6). A clear head also allows you to see clearly the attraction your paramour is revealing in gesture, as well as words. (On this front, you can be fairly sure they're pleased to see you if they enter your garden 'skipping'). (See **ArtyTheatreBoy**, see p. 139).

Where things do cost, you don't need to be lavish. Spartan pleasures can be luxurious: a grabbed station takeaway or an impromptu picnic. A great date is not a matter of throwing money at a situation. It needn't mean pricey restaurants or weekends away. And while you search for synchronicity and perfection, it's important to remember that some of the most enjoyable plans are those that go astray – as **ArtyTheatreBoy**, 34, discovered, when his romantic scheme for a picnic was gloriously derailed (see p. 140).

In the end, all that you really need for a great date is the 'someone': the gorgeous girl or boy who's able to match you in your crazy plans. That adventurous, big-hearted person who's ready, willing and able to come out and play.

Dates from heaven:
The stories

Alias: **ArtyTheatreBoy** | *Age:* **34** | M | ♀♂ | **Guardian Soulmates**

It was three o'clock. I was sitting at a rickety wooden table by the greenhouse at the end of my garden when Izzie arrived, skipping down the lawn with a selection of olives, a bottle of champagne and an iPod full of Barry Manilow.

The day had been well thought through, and as well as the previous hours scrubbing down the floors and surfaces of a single man's two-up two-down, I had spent the morning preparing an evening banquet of marinated duck (God bless Jamie Oliver). With theatre tickets for the evening and friends on stand-by for a drink after the performance, every possible eventuality had been thought of and any number of ways to keep my date entertained had been considered.

By eight o'clock that evening the third bottle of champagne had been opened, the meal hadn't so much as made it out of the marinade, and the play had started half an hour ago. Barry was on to his fourth rendition of 'Mandy', and Izzie and I were squeezing hands under the table like nine-year-olds playing thumb wars.

'This is just like being on holiday. I love it.'

'We should go – on holiday, that is.'

That 10-second conversation reached what we thought was the most natural of conclusions and we made plans for our romantic getaway.

Weeks later we landed in Pisa. Time-rich and cash-poor foodies, we had a simple plan: we would rest in the hotel for the night and then get up and set about making a cheap and delicious lunch and sitting on the banks of the Arno, watch Florentine life bustle over the bridges above us.

Our adventurous night before meant that our morning was accompanied by a hangover of Chianti, Grappa and chicken liver. It was 33° outside, and after an hour spent wandering the streets of Florence dodging hordes of Japanese tourists, it became apparent that rustic delicatessens were few and far between and that getting to the banks of the river would require picnicking in the grounds of expensive restaurants or abseiling down some imposing medieval walls.

Situations like these provide the ideal environment for really getting to know someone, especially someone you have known for only a few weeks. Hot, hungry, hungover, aching and now hulking round a bag that contained boiling white wine, warm supermarket salami, packets of sweaty rocket and cheese that had gone from solid to liquid in a matter of minutes, it was time to rethink our picnic plans.

Izzie realised quite quickly that I'm the type of man who doesn't function well without food or sleep. I was introduced to what she thinks of the world when she's been out in the heat too long and doesn't feel in control of a situation. Both of us were trying hard to hold on to our rose-tinted glasses. On a street not far from the Piazza Duomo my brain started to whir uncomfortably. Why was I here? What on earth was I thinking of, committing myself to a week in a foreign country with someone I had met online a few weeks previously? Had we really let ourselves get so carried away that afternoon? What if we kill each other? I felt like an idiot. At that point Izzie didn't so much walk as stomp off, out of sight and round a corner.

A moment later I heard a loud and excited 'Come here!' There it was, up a side street and in the middle of this Piazza, an area of raised decking that looked like a cross between a dining table and a John Rocca-designed boat. The decking was empty, as was the piazza, and reminiscent of the rickety table at the end of my garden: we had stumbled across the perfect picnic spot. We managed to get ice from the shop across the way, opened our wine and made our sandwiches while being watched by the owner and his friends. They waved and smiled at us, as did members of the public who walked past. We were content that our new-found happiness was visible to the world and, now settled in this beautiful and secret corner of central Florence, our potential argument was all but forgotten. It was one of those magical moments: everything was perfect; a cool breeze had started blowing through the Piazza, and, with our sandwiches and wine, we felt like backpacking teenagers. We toasted ourselves with our plastic glasses and kissed, losing ourselves in the moment.

In the background of our bliss we could hear noise and voices as we held each other, and initially tuned it out. It wasn't until we heard the applause that we looked up and found ourselves surrounded by about 20 Italian commuters and a chuckling driver. Our magical, secret, postmodern picnic table was a bus stop. We smiled back graciously, if a little sheepishly, and headed back to the hotel, laughing like teenagers in love.

Alias: **AliceInWonderland** | *Age:* **40** | *F* | ♀♂ | **Guardian Soulmates**

It was my birthday. OK, we'd only known each other a few dates, but we went to London together. He came to mine with a dozen red roses, and my friend Helen said you could tell they weren't from a garage. He bought me teabags too; red bush, instead of pink champagne, because I don't drink. 'Isn't that thoughtful,' my mum said.

We get the train from Leeds to London and share an earphone each of Nick Cave on his iPod. We hold hands on and off, rub around each other's legs every now and again. He reads Henry James and we disagree about whether there's such a thing as truth.

We walk from King's Cross to the British Library, where we browse anything to do with William Blake. We have lattes and tuna sandwiches in the café and say, imagine if we came here separately and were both writing on our laptops and then our eyes met over cutlery. We say yeah, we would have met one day anyway, the internet just made it faster.

We head into the underground and kiss on every escalator. I think of every visit I have ever made to London and every couple I have scowled at for their brazen escalator-kissing. My turn now – snog on!

We get off at St Paul's, and he knows stuff about people who hung out there at the time of the French Revolution. I can't remember that far back. I don't care, because already this is way, way better than last year when I just went to work and the school nurses took me to the pub at lunch time. On the Millennium Bridge we're like foreign exchange students; we stop halfway for more kissing, leaning over the Thames. It's one thing we have really got in common, this kissing. We like it so much, and hey, we're in London, who's to stop us? A raggy teenager goes past and mocks 'Get a room!' I break off in giggles and I nearly punch the air: Yo! 39 today and no one ever shouted 'get a room' at me before! *Je suis arrivée*!

It's the Cy Twombly exhibition at Tate Modern. He's a long-time fan of Cy. We look at the big crack in the floor – but not for long. There's no need to think about how fast we're going, no need to wonder about things like cracks. The Cy stuff is ace; we are excitable all the way. Do you like that bit? I like this bit. Oh look he's done that again on this one. Hey, there's another of those ones you like. No, this room's rubbish, he lost the plot here. Wow, look at this one. Oh, this is definitely my favourite. Can we go back and look at that one again? We're in there for hours, then we get hot chocolates and lemon cake from the café. We say, imagine if we came here separately and we saw each other in that big hall and our eyes met over those cracks. We say yeah, we would have met one day anyway, the internet just made it faster.

I buy a postcard as a memento of the day; I'll use it as a bookmark. He buys a big poster and says he's going to get it framed for his hallway. We're back in the main hall looking at the cracks. Like everyone looking down there, I have something inside me just like it and I want to know how long it's going to be there and how they are going to fill it back in and not leave a scar for the next exhibition.

It's my birthday. He thinks we should eat somewhere nice, except we're booked on a specific train like you have to be these days and if you miss it then it's going to be hundreds of pounds. So we skirt all round the station trying to find somewhere that looks like a birthday kind of restaurant but at the same time is still the kind of restaurant for people who need to book train tickets with discounted restrictions.

We find an Ethiopian restaurant. Hey, both of us have travelled, been around and that, but neither of us has had Ethiopian food before. We nearly don't get to try it tonight either as we've spent so long looking for it (food? love?) that there's not enough time to eat it. They put it in containers and we eat it on the train, almost warm. We sink into one another once it's eaten and doze all the way back to Leeds. Our fingers are too greasy to rub on one another's jeans. We get a cab from the station to my flat. Inside, we're ready to kiss again; we take our jeans off.

Alias: **RedAdmiral** | *Age:* **72** | *M* | ♀♂ | **Guardian Soulmates**

I've been out there this weekend trying to misbehave. On Saturday afternoon I met Magda at Theydon Bois. It was her choice of location, and we met in the station car park by the bottle bank. She was slimmer than her photo and, despite having lived here for 40 years, still had a strong Dutch accent. We gave each other a brief awkward hug and set off to find somewhere to become acquainted. Call it old fashioned, but I had already decided to pay for her tea – it's just the way I am.

We found a baker's shop that sold tea to drink on the premises and fortunately there was an empty table. For some reason, though, it was located just inside the door; as a result a queue of people formed from time to time, waiting to be served at the counter and standing alongside us. The service was good, however, and the tea arrived before Magda had explained the process whereby Gouda cheese is processed. She had grown up in Arnhem and recognised various shots of the town in the film *A Bridge Too Far*. In that scene where Anthony Hopkins is walking beside Sean Connery, well over their shoulders could be seen glimpses of the town she knew quite well.

The queue had almost diminished, and I was about to pop the question when the door banged open and in came four noisy young men wearing baseball caps and carrying skateboards. They wanted to know if there were any jammy doughnuts going spare. A lot of good-natured joshing began with the two young girls who were serving, who, I have to say, gave as good as they got. The thin girl with the ring in her nose did apologise for them and gave me a cloth to wipe up Magda's spilled tea when they had banged out again, but then very decently gave us two replacement mugs completely free of charge.

Apart from the confusion caused by her thick Dutch cadences, the battery in Magda's hearing aid must have been down because I had to repeat quite loudly my questions to her. Customers coming into the shop and standing in line beside us seemed to take an interest in our conversation; even twins in their double buggy gave us their wide-eyed approval. It did prevent me from asking her too loudly if she was still sexually active. Although Magda didn't catch my question, the twin's mother did and was waiting for her response. It did occur to me to repeat the question to those waiting and perhaps get a bit of a conversation going, but I thought better of it. For a long time I had been celibate, and the frustration that I felt might have clouded or coloured my motives, had made me impatient to connect physically with a warm and lovely living breathing creature again. If friends had been observing me they might have thought me a gentleman as I subtly attempted to woo Magda and appraise her for her erotic qualities. Depending on the success of such an exercise – should it take place – and the subsequent pillow talk, I was prepared to fall fervently in love with whoever could provide it. It was a done deal: make me feel alive again, and I'll love you until I'm not. Sorted.

The thin assistant was back trying to get the nozzle of the vacuum cleaner with its chrome extension underneath our table, so we took the hint and got ready to go. She rewarded us both with such a beam of good health and white teeth that I couldn't help wondering at my chances there. Outside on the pavement we had stepped into the path of the skateboarders, so there wasn't the opportunity for a quick kiss or even a cuddle; we parted, Magda hurrying off into a late misty afternoon, with assurances from each other we would keep in touch.

Driving back to Chingford I thought of her. She'd had lovely eyes beneath her bifocals, and although she possessed wrinkles her skin was smooth and she had a warm smile.

––––––––

Alias: **Jiri** | *Age:* **38** | *M* | ♀♂ | **Guardian Soulmates**

According to Soulmates, Jessica and I were a 96–90 match. And when we first met, about three weeks ago, I felt 'twinned'. There were so many shared passions and values – adventure, boating, camping, dancing, home-cooked food, to name a few. We even had the same laugh. We were more like old friends, and I hesitate to call it a date. We actually only ever touched to shake hands.

The evening ended with an early invitation to Jessica's narrow boat house-move-booze-cruise, from Coventry to Milton Keynes. Just the two of us for the first couple of nights. I had to fly out on business the morning after the second night anyway, so it worked. Two weeks later, we were phutting down the Coventry Canal. As before, it was like fire. It seemed as if we'd known each other for years, and I was reminded of Zhuangzhi's writings about 'friends who are friends without any special effort to be friends'.

On the first night a little too much vodka left us both sleeping on the floor of the boat. We vowed to stick to good beer and red wine, and another sizzling day followed, during which we managed to get into a fight (sober, of course) with another boat about which of us had reached a narrow bridge first. What camaraderie! The second night, mooring where I'd left my car, we feasted on Jessica's excellent rice and chilli, each glass of wine tasting better than the last, as they do. Jessica needed to get some work done, so we got into bed earlyish, she with her laptop, I with a copy of one of the Dune sagas. At that point, sharing a bed didn't seem odd at all. After what seemed like only a couple of pages of Dune, Jessica announced that we should sleep, as 'you have to wake early'.

Lights and candles were duly extinguished, and we made small talk about the stars shining brightly through the cabin window and the noise of the nearby motorway. Then Jessica announced that she 'always slept naked and did I mind!' All I could manage was a small squeaky sound, which was followed by vigorous movements from Jessica's side of the bed. I did begin to wonder about things at that point ... until Jessica began to snore. Which was actually a kind of release.

Moments later (seemingly), the sun was streaming on my face and the boat was rocking to and fro. It was the wake-up call of the early-morning boaters. A quick glance at my mobile confirmed that it was just a little past eight. Who needs an alarm? And it was the morning after. After nothing had happened. With a naked woman.

Getting up as softly as is possible in a narrow twin bunk, I was greeted with a cheery 'good morning'. We exchanged pleasantries, and I apologised for having to leave so early, at which Jessica replied 'At least you're not loving me and leaving me.' We both laughed nervously. I wanted out now, and after a quick brush and face wash I dressed and packed hurriedly, conscious of Jessica's eyes following me around the studio-plan boat.

Finally, I had my backpack on and was preparing mentally for the mad dash to Heathrow. Jessica held out her arms for a goodbye hug. I knelt down, burdened as I was, and managed an awkward hug. This was actually the first time we'd touched on the trip. Jessica insisted on pulling me closer, laughing that she wasn't going to eat me, 'yet'. The tension was electric. Trying to relieve it, I inquired casually whether she really slept naked. In answer, she pulled one of my hands under the covers on to her breast. It was really naked! That was like a lightning bolt, discharging the electricity. My heart felt like it was doing 200 beats a minute. The hug quickly turned into wild tongue probing and sucking and lip biting on both sides, as Jessica's attempts to grapple me into the bed with her were thwarted by my backpack jamming against the upper cabinets. Finally losing my balance, I fell back to the floor, and all we could do was laugh.

I decided that that was the best moment to make an exit, promising to return in two weeks, as I did my cool walk out the front door, and almost fell into the gap between boat and bank. It took what seemed like hours in the car for my heart to stop pounding like a jungle drum. A week later, Jessica is all I can think about, and it's difficult to get any work done. I want to call her, but I dare not. My tummy does a 1,200 rpm spin at the thought of meeting her again. I don't know whether to thank Soulmates or curse them, but I think I'm in love!

Alias: **NemoPut** | *Age:* **37** | *F* | ♀♂ | **Guardian Soulmates**

My best Soulmates date ever was with the man I consider myself very lucky to have been with every single day since, and I've felt this way from the start. Right from the outset, I knew he was different as he suggested a picnic in Battersea Park during the afternoon of a bank holiday Monday. The icing on the cake was that he would bring all of the food, the music, the blanket, the works. All I had to do was turn up. We both joked that as long as we didn't puke at the sight of seeing each other, it was bound to be a great date.

Between agreeing on the plan and our first date actually taking place there was a gap of a fair few days because I had to go away to a family function at the weekend. During this gap, we talked for hours and hours on the telephone, late into the night and really early in the morning. I just knew inside that this one was different and that this time it felt absolutely 'right'.

Even though we had not physically met, I felt a confidence I had not experienced before. I'd dated regularly online and had a number of perfectly nice times, but nothing like the old-fashioned courtship I was now experiencing. We seemed to get on so well through our emails and on the telephone that I thought it would be the world's sickest joke if we didn't get on in person. We'd been flirting like mad too, so I was full of anticipation.

Rain stopped play, however, or, more accurately, rain diverted play – to a picnic at my flat instead. Once I'd suggested relocating to my flat I couldn't quite believe I'd said it. All manner of things whirled round in my head, the main ones being whether he was going to think that I was more than just a little bit loose to make such a suggestion and whether he was an axe murderer, but I was so keen to meet him, and the rain was preventing me from getting my hands on all that lovely food he'd brought. To this day, he earns major brownie points with my girl friends as all the food was either homemade or from the farmers' market.

We sent texts all the way on his journey to where I live, and when he knocked on the door I thought I was going to have palpitations, I was so nervous. I opened the door and there was the smartest, sexiest, cutest man I could ever imagine. He came into my hall, and we hugged each other in a long and slow embrace. The rest is history – and the food wasn't bad either.

Alias: **Jane_G** | *Age:* **46** | *F* | ♀♂ | **Guardian Soulmates**

East meets West? I assumed it would be a case of East not meeting West. Nevertheless, I'd only been online a couple of days and couldn't resist lingering over his profile whenever I logged in. He was from Somerset, I'm from Essex. Surely, too far apart to meet, never mind start a relationship? I hadn't made him a favourite, but I suppose he knew I was interested in him. When I first noticed that there was an email in my inbox from him I was excited. It was a 'Hello, how are you, how's it going?' email. Quite polite. Not much to go on, but I just felt instinctively there was something about him I liked.

His name was Angus, and he was the first person I'd emailed on Soulmates. A day later he added a voice recording. I listened to it intently, several times. The message was all the more attractive for being uncontrived, unrehearsed, even hesitant in parts. I began to look forward to his emails. He seemed intelligent and articulate. I loved his messages, succinct (not a waffler like me), occasionally witty, sometimes flirtatious. Our emails grew more intimate as time passed. He wasn't the gushy, mushy type, but his messages left me in no doubt that he was both passionate and imaginative. I couldn't help but daydream about meeting.

After the first week we talked on the phone. The conversations were easy, we laughed about stuff and nonsense, and I think I teased him a little. I was growing quite fond of this man in Somerset. One afternoon in mid-June he sent an email saying he wanted to meet me, even if it was only for an hour. He said he was having trouble getting me out of his mind after our correspondence, phone calls and photo exchanges. He didn't want to burst the bubble, but to make it real. He would travel to me.

My first instinct was to panic a little. This would be my first date for many, many years. What if, after travelling all this distance, it was a disappointment? What if our feelings for each other proved to be totally overwhelming? I told myself to stop dwelling on what might or might not be. Meet him and go from there. He said he would arrive on Saturday morning. We'd meet for one hour; a walk along the seafront, maybe a cuppa at my favourite little café. We agreed that a short date would remove some pressure from me, this being my first internet date. Because it was summer he said he'd bring his tent and camp overnight before driving back the next day.

Saturday was glorious – hot and sunny. Angus sent me a text message to say he'd arrived at the campsite, and I drove to meet him there. I scanned the field nervously. There were only three tents, and towards the left of the field was a tall guy staking out his tent. I recognised him immediately, though he seemed taller and slimmer than I had imagined. I parked alongside his car, as he turned and smiled in greeting. He was gorgeous, at least to me. Shaved head, big smile, nice lips!

Taking a deep breath, I got out of the car and walked towards him, smiling. Our first hug was like meeting an old friend, a warm, affectionate embrace. I kissed his cheek, then his lips found mine. His kiss made my knees go weak. Having been in email and telephone contact for a month before our meeting, our correspondence possessing an intensity I'd never before experienced, it was as if we'd already cut swathes through the usual rounds of first-date small talk. Our kiss was gentle, passionate and lingering. I closed my eyes – it was the kiss I had imagined. I'd been in a relationship devoid of intimacy for so long, that I had been worried that I'd forgotten how to.

We paused, smiling at each other, then laughed – our first meeting … in a field! We sat and talked, he boiled a kettle and we drank tea. After a couple of hours we set off for a walk down to the seafront. Finding a secluded spot on the beach, we set our stuff out and Angus went for a quick swim. We shared a leisurely lunch. It was warm, and I was happy. Afterwards we lay back on the blanket, entwined, looking out to sea. His hand slid under my blouse, caressing my back as we talked and kissed. He stroked my hair. I lay against his chest. It was perfect.

We made our way back to the campsite later that afternoon. We sat on camping chairs facing each other. Talking easily. I'd noticed that he had lovely hands, and he used them to massage my feet as we chatted. Had we really only met for the first time that day? I didn't go home that night. We lit candles and stayed up talking into the night.

My first internet date and my first camping experience. It was the most passionate night I'd had in years.

I moved to a fairly rural area in Cambridgeshire – I bought half an old farmhouse in a remote part of the Fens – and I couldn't see how I'd actually meet someone any other way. So I joined a dating website, but for a month only. I put on my profile exactly the truth: there is nothing on there that is not true. I am a 41-year-old working-class bloke from north London. I do go to the gym. I do have a motorcycle. I have been out of a relationship for a year. I've not over-egged my financial situation or what I do for a living. As you get older, you're not trying so hard to impress: you want people to like you as you. I tried to be honest in my profile and not big myself up. I wasn't going to say 'I'm into windsurfing' or something just because I'd done it once. I just put down a little about moving out of London and that I was starting to keep chickens. I wrote: 'The worst it can be is a pleasant half hour conversation. If you like what you read then drop me a line.'

Fiona's reply to me was just one line: 'I liked what I read.' I had to go back and reread my profile to see what she meant! I looked at her profile and liked her photo, so I wrote back. I joked with her about my profile only being worth five words! She told me she had put lots of effort in writing replies to people and often not had a response, so she was trying a different approach with mine.

In some ways online dating took away the embarrassment of having to go up to someone in a bar. I didn't feel I'd done any approaching – I'd just put what I had to say out there, and Fiona had come up to me, and said 'I like that.'

We batted a few emails backwards and forwards for three or four days, and eventually she gave me her number, and I got up the courage to make a quick phone call. We decided to meet. Because I'm always going to have a long drive when I meet anyone, I thought of combining a date with something I wanted to do anyway, so I suggested meeting on the beach at Skegness because I hadn't been there and I was thinking I'd go and look at the petrified forest nearby. That way, at least I would have seen something interesting if the date didn't work out.

I asked what her favourite tipple was, and she said champagne or sparkling wine, which is my favourite too. I challenged her with a 'Bet you can't tell the difference between them …' and she said 'Yes I can', so I suggested we do a champagne blind-tasting. We agreed that I'd bring the champagne and she'd get us fish and chips. We said we'd each bring a tent. We ended up at Anderby Creek instead of Skegness as it's much quieter.

It's daunting to go and meet a stranger in this way. We all have our insecurities about our looks – I wasn't too insecure but I was a little bit nervous. But when I saw Fiona get out of the car I knew we'd be well-matched.

So we put up our tents in the campsite. I've got a great big scouting tent, and she has a tiny little tent, so we had a laugh about how they looked next to each other. Then we went for a walk along the beach with her dog, and she said that I throw sticks like a girl. Fiona did most of the talking. She had all this nervous energy. I found her a bit wordy, a bit scatterbrained at first, but now I realise it was just because she was nervous and that's how she reacts when she's under pressure. When we walked on the beach she had a lot going on. But I thought she was a nice, witty, intelligent person, and I could see myself being friends with her. I have just a few, really close friends that I've had for many years – two of them are exes – rather than loads of casual friends, and friendships are important to me.

I brought Veuve Clicquot, Lanson Black Label and a six quid cava from Tesco. She bought the fish and chips, and she also brought a blindfold. And so began the blind-tasting. She failed to spot the difference, preferring the cava, which was funny, and I got them right. We had fish and chips with the addition of mushy peas with mint sauce, which I'd never had before. There was a bit of chemistry between us. There was a spark. There we were, sitting under the stars, near the sea, full of fish and chips, with the best part of a bottle of champagne still left. Her leg touched mine, which I thought was accidental at first, then it happened again, and I realised it was intentional.

She sang 'Summertime' to me. She's a good singer – she's a drama teacher and she's used to being uninhibited. It's not what I'm used to. I can be as raucous as the next person and I go to Glastonbury, but a girl singing to me is not something I'm particularly used to. I come from a family where you blend into the background, so I was a bit embarrassed about what the other people at the campsite might think, but then I thought, 'Why should I worry if someone else gets the hump about it?'

The next day we drove off to Mablethorpe, and she sat right on the other side of the van. I wasn't sure what she meant by sitting so far away. But when we got out of the van I took her hand, and she later told me it blew her away.

When you've been camping, you do look your roughest, so it's a bit of a test of whether someone wants to be with you. And when you come out of a long relationship you're not so sure of yourself, so I was thinking: 'This person is here, she's chosen to be here, and she didn't leave. She is deciding to spend a bit of this day with me.' She'd made me laugh, and I'd made her laugh. We held hands and I said: 'I don't want this day to end.' When she replied, 'Neither do I', it meant a lot to me. She's got a young son, she's got responsibilities, and yet she was saying she wanted to be with me.

I saw something in her on our first date. She gave me the impression that she had a lot of love to give and was capable of receiving it. Fi told me what had happened in her life and what she was looking for. When she was talking about some of the things in past relationships that she didn't want to repeat, I was thinking, 'Well I'm not like that, I'm not like that guy,' which really gave me confidence because I knew I would be different.

We gave each other our full attention. The fact that she felt confident enough to sing to me was attractive. She laughed at what I had to say. There wasn't a lot of interrupting, that 'Oh yeah, I've done that as well' thing that people do when they aren't really listening to you, just chipping in with their own stories. Fiona and I were really talking about and connecting to the little stories that mattered. I wanted to hear about her job as a drama teacher – I thought that was interesting and wanted to know why she decided to do it and what it was like.

Four weeks after we met she was going to Australia with her family for five weeks. We got close before she left, and for the first time in my life I wanted to make a commitment. I'd had no preconceptions about meeting a wife when I signed up to the site, and I've never felt I wanted to propose to anyone before. But in the short time I'd known Fiona there was a strong connection. Rather than bending down on one knee, I wanted to talk to her to find out how she'd respond. We both wanted to go into it with open eyes. There were sacrifices for me – I'd built a new life for myself, and I loved my new house in the Fens – but these sacrifices were worth making. We went and chose a ring before she left, which would be ready soon after she came back from Australia.

Her five weeks away were the longest five weeks I've ever had – and I'd only known her for four! We both knew where we'd go when she got back: it had to be Anderby Creek. We went back to the same pub, we had fish and chips to eat and bubbly to drink, we went to the same beach, I proposed to her, and she accepted. We're getting married next year, and at the reception we're having fish and chips and that cheap cava – not champagne – because it was the one that Fiona preferred.

This whole experience has blown my socks off. I have not felt like this in any relationship I've been in before. I never expected this. We've both been very upfront about each other's pasts. It feels very honest, very true. As both of us were completely honest right from the beginning, that honesty has carried forward into the relationship.

My mates were very concerned about me getting engaged to somebody after I'd known them for only four weeks, but I felt totally certain. I've laid myself bare to Fiona: my insecurities and whatever baggage I'm carrying. I've said 'This is what I don't like, this is what I do, these are my weaknesses.' I'd never opened up like this to anyone else in my life before. There have been times when I've tried to open up to people and they give you that sympathetic face and then there's the silence, as if they don't know what to say. Fiona genuinely listens, and she'll put her arms round me and give me a big hug. She treats me better than any other person of the opposite sex has ever treated me. She seems to respect my opinion and she listens when I speak to her. She has seen me with all my faults and she accepts me as I am.

My best friend said to me 'You're different.' And then he realised why: 'You're happy.'

Chapter 6:
Dates from hell

The ones to forget

Outrageous crudeness, breathtaking rudeness, Freudian slips and nervous tics, tongues hyperactive, tongues tied, toe-curling embarrassment and sexual harassment: it's all happening out there. Millions of the most stilted, weird and cringeworthy dates are just a few clicks away. Be prepared. Bad dates are as much a hazard of the cyberexperience as beautiful dates are a bonus. According to a recent study, one in three first dates will 'end in disaster': of the estimated 12 million internet-arranged first dates that British people will go on this year, 4 million of them will be dire.[46] That's a lot of experience to be chalking up to.

While the majority of dates are neutral – perfectly fine but lacking in fizz – it is the bad dates that truly linger, like sour milk on a car seat or a recurrent cold. It was no surprise that we had the highest number of submissions in this category of the competition: bland dates do not a good story make. It's the toothsome beau who's a toothless bore or the Ms Right who's dead wrong who will really spice up your anecdotes. There are few seasoned daters who have not had at least one weird, embarrassing or awkward date. If you stay on a site for more than a few months you can be certain of turning into a wry scrutineer of the human condition, a Bill Bryson of the amorous realm who can trot out a nice line in observational stand-up at married friends' parties. Sometimes there's nothing to be done on these cyberdates but yield to an overriding sense of the absurd and take a mental note ... for later.

Duff dates are part of the package. Normally when you meet someone there's a shared context – you know their friends, you work for the same employer or you've seen how they function in a group: but with online dating you are making contact with strangers. This anonymity can be immensely liberating. But the flipside is that you have *no* guarantee that you'll be meeting the person you think (which makes it all the more important to follow the safety advice later on in this chapter). Your decision to hook up for a date is based on some pretty slippery foundations: a hunch, the precision of the website's matching software, each person's honesty and judgement, and a massive dollop of serendipity.

Most nights-to-forget can be put down to a few simple ingredients: bad behaviour, bad luck, incompatibility and inexperience. Leading the bad behaviour walk of shame – at least from the point of view of those looking for a relationship – are the players: the men, and occasionally women, who want to get down and dirty before you've even taken your coat off, sleazoids who subject you to a stream of sexual innuendo that makes you want to burn your clothes when you get home. As **Ms_E**, 34, says of one of her dates, 'He got the conversation onto a sexual note fairly early on and I wish (as I have done so many times in the past) that I had had the courage to leave after the first drink. Politeness gets me into all sorts of trouble. And so I sat there, listening to the sexual innuendo for three long hours.' Filtering out these concupiscent chancers is tedious. **LoveCrumb**, 28, who has dated online since 2007, says 'I've got a lot better at spotting them over the years. Often it's fairly obvious when they're lazy about the writing of their profile, or come across as overly charming and perfect, or pushy and false.' The player reckons himself to be a bit of a Don Juan – the fictional character who has given his name to a psychoanalytic syndrome because of his need to gain self-esteem through sexual conquest. As with the real man on whom Don Juan was modelled, who was homosexual, the player has no love for the seduced: 'He loved chasing women, but did not like them; it was the chase that excited him.'[47]

While an up-front chat about sexual practices may be advisable if you and your date are considering becoming notches on each other's bedposts, generally, on a first date, it's just too much information: yet that doesn't stop 12 per cent of men and 6 per cent of women talking about previous sexual experiences the first time they meet.[48] **Cinnamon_Toast**, 27, describes the creepy advances made to her by a chap who was apparently ready to propose marriage within their half-hour date and narrated a range of sexual anecdotes before asking her, point blank, the least likely question of their short acquaintance: 'Are you attracted to me?' (see p. 182)

Allied to the active player is the passive player, who is even sneakier in his or her efforts to spend the night with their date – like the woman who was so sure she'd stay with **Freudianslip** after chatting to her briefly on gaydargirls.com that she knowingly missed her last train from London back to Essex, forcing the Londoner, out of pity, to let her sleep on the floor of her flat for the night. Or the man who, despite having agreed not to drink so that he would be able to drive home, proceeded to quaff several beers so that he 'had to' stay the night at his date's house, on the grounds that it would be 'too dangerous to drive home over the limit'.

Next in dating's carnival of creeps comes a band of pompous bores and narcissists: the rude, the patronising and the self-obsessed. These domineering swains came high on our daters' list of *bêtes noires*, for forgetting that the main purpose of a date is the conversation bit. Some of them see dating as a kind of tutorial in which they can display their knowledge to the captive 'student' in perfectly formed soliloquies and anecdotes. Others see conversation as a battle to be fought and won, decisively vanquishing the opponent, er, date. One would-be suitor turned to his date, **Global_Gadabout** (a 36-year-old Oxford English literature graduate), having subjected her to a one-on-one history lecture over the course of their brief acquaintance, with the question, 'Have you ever heard of a man called Robert Louis Stevenson?' (see p. 168). Another of life's legends told his date – **Ms_E**, a 34-year-old schoolteacher – that 'he liked comedy, particularly improvisation', and followed up with a corker: did she understand what he meant by 'improvisation'? (see p. 204)

As if being patronised within an inch of their lives was not enough, some of our correspondents have faced downright rudeness on their dates, as did **DemosthenesLisp**, a vivacious and elegant 61-year-old French woman who met a 68-year-old man through an online ad. His first words to her, as she walked towards him, were 'I wasn't expecting you to be so old.' Rather than leaving, she stayed. 'I've been brought up that way,' she sighs simply.

The varieties of rude are infinite: there are people who don't stand up to shake their date's hand, those who take phonecalls throughout the tryst, and some who chat another person up during the date. A recent study showed that 4 per cent of women and 2 per cent of men say they've called or texted another potential date in the course of a first date, while a staggering one in three men and one in 33 women can't even remember their date's name.[49] **AllyT**, 41, describes a rendezvous with a man who 'proceeded to talk incessantly about his life … never asking me a question' and 'took two calls on his mobile phone' in the space of a 45-minute date. **EllenO**, 47, describes the discouraging effect of being first blanked and then talked at by a Porsche-driving big kahuna, who spent the first part of their meeting ranting over the phone to a subordinate at work and the next in a 'non-stop monologue' about the highs and lows of his life. It turned out that Porscheman regarded conversation not as a free-flowing exchange in which two people find out about each other, but as an essentially competitive act:

> I do believe we have been there for 25 minutes before I manage to break through the ego chat and tell him that a) he talks too much and b) shows no interest in his date! He laughs at my forwardness and agrees he is a talker but that it is up to me to butt in and say my piece.

The one-way conversations don't end there: a number of people regard dating as a kind of free therapy, as me-time in which to 'share' psychoses and heartache with their date, confessing much too much, much too soon, as though in a session with an unpaid shrink. **Tigerseye**, 54, mentions that she had several dates with women who cried incessantly about their exes during the date (see

p. 239), while **Daisy_Daisy**, 39, talks about the lonely guys she encountered who were 'looking for a new mate, or should that be a female-shaped sticking plaster to fix their broken hearts, which have been so cruelly shattered by their evil exes?' Ex-partners turn out to be a popular topic of conversation: of the 1,300 singles polled by parship.co.uk, over a quarter (27 per cent) admitted to talking about their ex during the date. And some of these exes are not even ex. **SaucyPedant**, 44, describes a date in which the man she had believed to be single spent much of the meal ranting about his *future ex-wife* and his incomprehension that she wished to divorce him – before asking **SaucyPedant** to go Dutch on the tab (see p. 188).

Next in the parade of the badly-behaved are the liars and cheats. Along with the people who say they're single when they're not (apparently men from the north are in pole position here, with one in 10 admitting to having lied about their marital status)[50] there are the people who omit to mention details that some might consider relevant – such as the fact that their profile photo is actually of someone else. And there are those who lie about their height, weight, occupation, interests or looks. The long, short and wide of it is that deception is rife – but it's not as bad as people think. For the inglorious truth see Chapter 7.

Alcohol has a lot to answer for. In the parship.co.uk study, 14 per cent of women admitted to drinking so much on a first date that they felt out of control. We received stories of people drinking to excess and women being plied with drinks. A number of dates ended with one or both people getting rip-roaringly drunk; one young woman spoke of not remembering how she got home.

As bad as some of these dates were, at least both parties turned up. In their poll of bad dating behaviour, parship.co.uk found that 48 per cent of women and 30 per cent of men across Britain admitted to having arrived late for a first date. A significant proportion of people (12 per cent of women and 6 per cent of men) said they had taken advantage of their date's absence at the bar or in the loo to leave without saying goodbye. And one in 20 men and women said they had arrived at the rendezvous, glimpsed the person they came to meet and turned on their heel.[51]

Some dates are simply beset by bad luck. **Ishouldcoco**, 49, describes meeting his date at a pub where her ex-husband happened to be carousing with friends. In 36-year-old **Rosemaria**'s excruciating tale (see p. 179), a thoughtfully-chosen movie at the cinema turned out to be unforgettable – for all the wrong reasons. And in **Annie611**'s *Planes, Trains and Automobiles* odyssey of a date, everything that could go wrong did: after a sequence of pulse-quickening mishaps that were each, in turn, majestically resolved by London's guardian angels and her own indomitable spirit, she accidentally allowed her Johnny-Depp-a-like to slip through her hands (see p. 173).

And there are times when it can't be helped, when it's no one's fault, yet nerves, inexperience and bumbling ineptitude come together for a group hug. You're feeling the heat – in a bad way – and gaffes roll off your tongue with alarming ease. Like, 'Oh, you didn't say you were having a baby' to a woman with a round stomach. Or to a bald man: 'What colour is your hair when you grow it out?' Or to your elegant date: 'You look so elephant.' If great conversation stokes the flame of desire, poor conversation snuffs it out. There's nothing to do in those dreadful long silences but examine the weft of your napkin and think about happier times.

But beyond the errors, incompetence and deception that can turn a date bad, there is another factor to bear in mind: incompatibility. Also known as instant mutual loathing, a kind of chemistry in reverse, it's palpable, it's biological and it's real. You sometimes simply have to face the fact that you and your date are not destined for each other, not in this lifetime or any. So find your moment, be gracious, say goodbye …

… and chalk it up to experience.

TOP TIPS FOR A SAFE DATE

No activity is risk-free

With online dating, some of the risks of which you need to be aware include:

Unwittingly giving your credit card or personal details to a scam website

Someone claiming to be single who turns out to be married

Someone stalking you

Your personal safety being endangered

ONLINE
Choose a reputable dating website

Some sites have active customer support teams; others do not. A good customer support team will hand-check profiles and photos to ensure that they comply with the website's terms of use, weed out fake profiles that are fronts for criminal rackets, protect you from being spammed, and help you if you are stalked or harassed on the site. If you are unsure of the site or have concerns, call the customer support number to make sure it works.

Research other users' experience of the site. Check the website's terms and conditions for the steps it takes to protect your identity and its policy if you are harassed by other users.

Paid websites have fewer problems than free ones: credit cards act as identity checks, making scammers reluctant to join.

Protect your privacy

Choose an anonymous profile name. Don't use your surname, phone number, email address or postal address on your profile or in correspondence with other members.

Don't reveal personal information such as where you work, the ages of your children or your date of birth – which can all be used to identify you. Experienced fraudsters can put together a picture of you with surprisingly little information. Be careful what you say while chatting – you could be giving away more than you think.

Set up a separate web-based email account for online dating which doesn't include your surname. Use the website's in-site email until you are ready to go it alone.

Report bad behaviour
Established websites have a code of practice, which aims to keep the place free of offensive or abusive content. Report anyone who behaves badly to you to the customer support team, forwarding abusive or inappropriate emails to the site's moderators. Block anyone who makes you feel uncomfortable, or behaves coercively to you.

Bad behaviour includes harassment, abuse, coercion and threats; criminal use of the site; uploading fake profiles; spam and solicitation; copyright infringement; and requests for money.

If someone writes something suspicious to you, save a copy of the screen by holding down the ALT key and press the 'Prt Sc/Sys Rq' key at the same time. A Windows PC will take a snapshot of the screen. Open up a new Word document and paste the image into it, making sure to add the time and date of the conversation before saving it.

Use the cyberdating tools
Most websites allow you to communicate anonymously with other members until you're ready to meet. You don't need to reveal your personal name or email address unless and until you're sure you feel comfortable doing so – which may never happen. You want to be reassured that their

behaviour is consistent over time. If you have any worries or doubts, follow your instinct. Someone's refusal to send a photo, or more than one photo, for instance, might suggest that the image is not theirs. If photos are blurred and grainy, they may well predate the era of the digital camera. Ask for recent ones. Nicely.

Don't be afraid to ask for more information to check that his or her story tallies, and be aware of anything that smacks of a copied and pasted letter.

You can Google them once you know their name.

Contact
If you decide to call them, withhold your number by dialling 141 first.

Be honest
Dishonesty is one of the main causes of anger and frustration on online dates. Don't be fooled into thinking that bending the truth will allow you to jump the queue for someone's affection. Your lie will only tarnish you in the other person's eyes.

MEETING UP
The first priority is your safety. Plan everything with that in mind and stay clear-headed in case you need to leave a situation quickly.

Meet in public
Don't agree to be alone with someone, don't go home with them, and don't invite them to yours until you are absolutely sure of them.

Inform others
Tell a friend where you're going. Arrange an exit procedure,

for example a blank text to a friend who is on standby to call you with a reason to leave.

Make your own way

Plan you exit strategy in advance. If you're not in the same town, meet during the day: don't risk missing the last train home and the last vacancy in a B&B. Be flexible but don't be beholden to your date.

Stay sober

Drinking too much can cloud your judgement and lead you to overestimate your compatibility with your date. Disturbingly, 11 per cent of men and 14 per cent of women say they've drunk so much alcohol on a first date that they've felt they weren't fully in control of themselves. And don't leave your drink unattended – it could be spiked.

Guard your privacy

Keep the details of where you live or where you're staying to yourself until you know the person – even if you feel comfortable on a first date.

Practise assertiveness

Become confident in your ability to say, politely, 'Thanks, but no thanks'.

Politeness

Don't be scornful if you are rejecting someone – you can do it kindly – but never, ever, put politeness above safety.

Be realistic

Keep your expectations in check. Don't go on a date expecting the earth. Bear in mind that people can – and do – tell little white lies and giant red ones all the time. They could have invented everything about themselves and you wouldn't know it until you met.

Use common sense

Get your antennae working. Take precautions and use your instinct just as you would if you had met someone on a bus.

Value yourself

Remember that most people are not predatory: enjoy your experiences but keep your wits about you. And above all, know your own worth.

Dates from hell:
The stories

I'd met Gordon in the Pentlands some months previously – we'd chatted when he and a friend stopped for a rest while I enjoyed a flask of tea – and when his profile appeared on Soulmates it seemed like fate. Th e meeting and his strong physical resemblance to a friend of mine made me feel I already knew him. That, and my subscription's imminent expiry, prompted me to curtail the lengthy email exchanges that had typified my internet dating experiences to date, and we agreed to meet at the National Portrait Gallery one Sunday morning.

Even their excellent home baking couldn't hide the fact that the conversation as we sat in the coffee shop was stilted, so I hoped the exhibition of *Vanity Fair* portraits from Hollywood's heyday in the 1930s and the magazine's reissue in the 1980s might ease the situation. Unfortunately, it soon became clear that he was only humouring me, and when he skipped stunning sepia photographs of Katharine Hepburn and Josephine Baker only to be mesmerised by a naked Gisele Bündchen on horseback (fair enough, but not tactful), I began to sense that our aesthetics, at the very least, were at odds. It seemed unduly harsh to make a love of old cinema an absolute requirement for a romantic partner, although, to be honest, it would probably help, so at his suggestion we progressed upstairs to an exhibition on Scottish industrialism, where things went rapidly downhill.

My admission that, having been educated in south-east England, my knowledge of Scottish history was fairly sketchy, was apparently interpreted as 'I know nothing about anything at all' and I was suddenly Eliza to his Professor Higgins. I was forbidden to read the labels beneath the paintings, and obliged to listen to his version of their subjects' achievements, which was initially amusing in a boy-substituting-telling-you-stuff-for-actual-conversation fashion but increasingly felt like mental blitzkrieg. In another room a portrait of Flora McDonald prompted a treatise on the Jacobite rebellion, to which I tried to contribute the information that I had, in fact, visited Culloden and found the desolate battlefield profoundly moving. This was swept aside.

In desperation I found myself dropping into the conversation that I had studied English at Oxford (a detail usually kept well hidden to avoid the assumption that daddy drives a Roller and I regularly bathe in champagne) in the hope that the cliché would at least convince him that I was not a fluffy-headed nincompoop. It had no impact whatsoever.

As we emerged into the rainy Edinburgh afternoon Gordon looked a little forlorn. He admitted that our date hadn't gone terribly well but wondered if perhaps we could go walking in the Pentlands together some time. I felt suddenly sorry for him, speculating that he had perhaps been emotionally crippled by the kind of upper-class education that makes it hard for a chap to see a woman as a real human being capable of independent thought and hesitantly agreed.

He offered me a lift home. I pointed out that, with the tram works disrupting the city's traffic, I'd be faster on foot. He pointed out that the rain was torrential. I weighed it up, figured that he was a fundamentally decent man if a bit short on social skills, broke all the rules that had kept me safe in years of solo international travel and got into the car. It was battered and musty and had dog hairs on the seat, for which he apologised, but was oddly endearing, in a tweedy kind of way. Then he set off in the wrong direction. I calmly pointed this out while trying to work out if I should be hurling myself from the moving vehicle. He said he knew, but 'wanted to show me some things first'.

Under the circumstances I should be grateful that what he wanted to show me were his father's former drinking club, his own old school and his rugby club, but it was another lecture tour. 'Have you ever been to Stockbridge before?' 'I've lived in Edinburgh for eight years. Of course I've been to Stockbridge.' And the classic: 'Have you ever heard of a man called Robert Louis Stevenson?' which finally broke me. 'I don't know what I've said or done to convince you that I'm a complete f—wit, but yes, I have heard of Robert Louis Stevenson.' It would have been unforgivably rude if he'd been paying any attention, but he ploughed merrily on with his tale of where the idea for *Treasure Island* had come from. Spotting a newsagents, I expressed a sudden desire to purchase an *Observer* and made him drop me off.

In retrospect, I was lucky that I'd only been patronised to death. The internet's illusion of familiarity can be deceptively dangerous, and if I have another go at web dating I'll be a lot stricter about adhering to the recommended 'rules of engagement': pick a public place, don't share too much personal information too soon, and never, ever admit to an ignorance of Scottish history.

Alias: **Ms_E** | *Age:* **34** | *F* | ♀♂ | **match.com**

Piano-tuner Pete's photo looked exactly like Colin Firth in *Fever Pitch*, and Colin Firth in *Fever Pitch* is the sexiest man ... ever. I remember being in the cinema (unfortunately accompanied by my dad and brother) and salivating at his curly hair and sexy Arsenal pants. I was excited.

In real life, Pete did not look like Colin Firth. At all. He also had a limp, which I suppose you wouldn't reveal on your profile, and, of course, with the right person, anything can be overcome. But Pete was wrong, right from the very start. We sat down with glasses of red wine and within half an hour Pete asked me when was the last time I had had sex. I replied that I didn't think this was an appropriate question. Why, when was the last time he had had sex? Pete revealed that he had had sex on Tuesday night. Already sensing Pete wasn't going to be a goer, I enquired who this was with. Pete told me about a park, by the Thames, where he went to meet men. So, he had sex with a man on Tuesday? Yes. Did bisexuality bother me, he queried. Um, no, but, well, you know.

Pete then went on to tell me that he was 'highly sexually charged' and, in fact, 'hired' himself out to husbands who wanted to see their wives shagged by another man. Interesting. Did he ever get involved with the husbands too, I enquired. Sometimes, but only manual stimulation, no kissing. Nice.

Keen not to anger him and to get out of the date unscathed, I remained polite and inquisitive throughout. I went on to discover that Pete was 44 and divorced with three children (not, as he had stated on his profile, 35 and 'never married'). Even more 'interestingly', Pete was also engaged to a 22-year-old Polish woman who lived in Warsaw. But he liked his own space and was in no rush for her to move over here, he informed me encouragingly.

Pete had never heard of Rufus Wainwright and suggested that I play him some back at my flat. I assured him that, as it was a school night, I wouldn't be taking him up on his kind offer. At this, Pete leaned over and told me he could guarantee me 'at least three orgasms'. I kissed him on the cheek and said I'd be in touch.

Alias: **SaucyPedant** | *Age:* 44 | *F* | ♀♂ | **Guardian Soulmates**

It was that tricky third date. Number one had been a long and lazy lunch on the patio of a country hotel. Number two was drinks in a real ale pub, followed by a rather promising snog in the car park. Now number three was on the horizon. Number three is the clincher. My previous foray into the internet dating world had involved a third date where the potential soulmate had taken me to the supermarket to buy ingredients for dinner (we went Dutch), which we ate on our laps watching TV. There wasn't a fourth.

'You could come to my house. I'll do a curry,' suggested Max. Max was a lovely bloke, tall and bear-like, with an offbeat sense of humour and lots of interesting anecdotes about travelling in Asia. He was kind and attentive, gave lovely hugs and was a pretty good kisser. I drove hopefully into the estate where he lived and was impressed that the houses were all huge detached villas with well-tended lawns.

I rang the bell. Max answered and swept me into a huge hug. 'Come in, it's so lovely to see you!' I followed him into a kitchen, which seemed to be something from a living history museum, complete with yellow Formica units and nicotine-stained walls. Sitting at the kitchen table was a man with very bad skin and fuzzy ginger hair. He stood up and held out his hand for me to shake. 'Lou. I've heard all about you!'

'This is my lodger, Sam,' Max explained. 'And this is Stig.'

An enormous dog, with the same ginger tones as Sam, bounded into the kitchen and attempted to mount my leg. Max made some tea, and Sam and Stig retreated upstairs. 'We could eat soon or we could go upstairs for a snuggle,' Max suggested. I wasn't too keen on going upstairs and 'snuggling' as the lodger and his dog were up there. 'Don't worry, Sam's been on the vodka all afternoon, he won't hear us.' I cringed at what sort of noise we might possibly be making.

'Why don't you show me the garden?' I said brightly. The garden was beautiful. A huge lawn, surrounded by mature shrubs, descended to a pretty stream, across which was woodland.

'Mind the dog poo,' warned Max. I looked down for the offending item and realised that there wasn't just one of Stig's little presents. The whole lawn was littered with dog faeces in varying degrees of decomposition, ranging from dried up, shrunken piles of excrement to huge, fresh, steaming turds. I also noticed Max's footwear – nylon socks under sandals. We went back inside.

'Haven't you started cooking yet? Do you need some help?' I offered.

'No, no, everything's in hand, I made it yesterday. Nothing like being prepared!' Max pointed to an aluminium pan on top of the grubby stove. 'Prawn curry! All the flavours have been marinating together on there since last night! Just needs warming.' He set about cooking some rice, and I looked around the kitchen. On the worktops were piles of newspapers, packaging and post, all covered with a coating of dog hairs. As I tried to focus through the net curtains and dirty windows to the garden beyond, Max came up behind me, put his arms round me and sniffed my hair.

'You smell gorgeous babe.' (Babe?) 'We've got 10 minutes while the rice cooks – fancy a cuddle?'

'Oh! Only 10 minutes? Shall I set the table?' I changed the subject.

'We'll have to eat in the kitchen, there's a motorbike in the dining room.'

'That's fine! Oh look, the rice is boiling over!'

The table was more Formica. On it there was an ancient juicing machine, a compost bucket filled with rotting vegetables, a pile of takeaway menus, four empty plastic milk cartons and a film of yellowish grease. Oh, and a hair brush, which either belonged to the lodger or his dog, as it was full of ginger hair.

'Do you want a fork or a spoon?' asked Max.

'Oh, whatever you're having.'

Max plonked the dish of rice and day-old prawn curry in front of me, a spoon stuck in it. Politeness made me eat, though I was thinking about how many types of food poisoning were multiplying in it. Thoughtfully, he also placed a roll of toilet paper on the table. 'Just in case you need to wipe your mouth!'

'Would you like a beer?' Max offered me a can of cheap lager, having secreted away the bottle of wine that I'd brought with me.

'No thanks, I'm driving! And I have to get back for the cat!' I thought about the huge pile of cat food I'd put out as I'd set out hopefully earlier that evening.

As we finished our meal, Sam lurched downstairs. 'I'm going to stay at my mate Johnny's – give you two lovebirds a little privacy!' He winked lasciviously at me. 'I'm sure I'll hear all the juicy details tomorrow! Eh Max?'

'Actually, I have to go!' I squeaked. 'Now!'

_____

Alias: **Annie611** | *Age:* **28** | *F* | ♀♂ | **match.com**

'Have fun but be careful. Some of them are only after one thing.' My brother was giving me a pep talk on online men with dishonourable intentions. 'Take Seth – he's seeing a different girl every night.'

Seth was on the same dating site as me, one of his many sources of ladies. My head translated my brother's advice: 'Oh Seth? He will Drive – You – Wild.' I'd heard of this guy. You probably have, too. In fact, you've probably slept with him. I knew that his aspirations for online dating wouldn't share my own saccharine hopes of brunches and bluebirds, but my brother's caution was like a dangled carrot. Intrigued, I looked up Seth's profile. And yes. He would. No witty commentary, no shared interests, no self-deprecating humour, but he looked like Johnny Depp. I thought I was more evolved, but sometimes that's really all it takes.

I winked. He wrote. We bantered. I told him my brother had warned me against him. This entertained him, and he asked me out. I'd just won tickets to a comedy gig, and we agreed this would be an excellent first date. We vowed never to tell my brother. I holed up in the toilets after work to try to redesign my air-conditioned skin and screen-reddened eyes into the fresh and pretty features of the fluke photo I'd used on my profile. Off came my work outfit and my curtain-sized knickers. On went a miniscule red thong and an ambitiously tight black dress. I dashed out of the office, to the relief of the security guard who had been itching to go home. I felt fantastic. That quickly dissipated when I realised I'd left the tickets on my desk. Running back in panic, I found the building already locked.

I called Seth and he took it well, suggesting we try our luck anyway and promising me a good night either way. With a skip of my heart I jumped on the tube to meet him. Even now, whenever I hear the beeping of tube doors, I remember the horror of getting off that tube and realising that my handbag was still on it. I stood on the platform watching my phone, purse, keys, everything, disappear into the tunnel. Crestfallen, I headed up to the station office.

The staff were kind and patient, giving me forms to fill out and a phone to use so I could try calling my own phone. Not knowing Seth's number, I wondered sadly how long he would wait. After 20 minutes I gave my phone one last call – and it was answered. A lovely lady called Rose had rescued my bag. She was meeting family for dinner in Victoria, but was happy for me to come to meet her and collect it. I headed first to Embankment to see if Seth had waited, arriving frazzled and with no means to comb my hair, gloss my lips or deodorise. But there he was, looking even better than his profile pic, partly because he was holding a Creme Egg for me. 'I heard about your adventures, so thought you'd need this to cheer you up,' he explained. 'I received a call that put me in the picture. Kind of funny actually. It started: "Hello Seth. I believe you know my sister."'

It turns out that Rose had been so keen to reunite me with my bag that she had taken the initiative of looking up and calling 'Mum' with my phone. Mum, frantic that I was bagless in London, called my brother. My brother called my housemate Millie. Millie spilled all. Mortified, we went to collect my bag from the heroic Rose, then decided we may as well get something out of the evening and try to get into the comedy to catch the headline act. Back at Embankment we explained the saga to the doorman, who let us in to shut us up. And the comedy worked wonders.

As we hit the dance floor afterwards, the night looked bright. Four twirls in, my dress split to just above the waistband of my thong. I crumpled. 'Will this help?' asked a friendly dancer, offering me a tube of superglue that she'd brought for her fake nails. It certainly would! We snuck through an unlocked door – the mop cupboard, we discovered – to glue me back into dignity.

The bind was tenuous, but it gave me another hour of dancing before the glue and my pride could hold out no longer.

'Want me to walk you to the bus stop?' asked Seth.

'That would be great! But don't leave if you're having fun,' I emptily offered.

'You sure? Cool. Thanks!' Seth popped his tongue into my horrified mouth for a goodnight snog and turned back to dance. I went to collect my coat.

As I left, I saw Seth already dancing with another girl, one who was not sweaty or wearing a superglued dress or smelling of mop. With a bashful text to my brother, I headed home chastised.

———————————————

Alias: **GrammarSchoolGirl** | *Age:* **45** | *F* | ♀♂ | **Guardian Soulmates**

I pushed open the pub door. How hard could it be to spot a big red-headed guy in a fedora? This time I'd been more realistic with my expectations, my corners chipped off by two previous, woeful dates. Gillian was going to be on duty: lurking, best-friend lifebelt at the ready, in a nearby pub and ready to rescue me at a moment's notice. On the other dates I'd made frantic efforts to be someone else: thinner, less of a smoker, just generally, more of a lady. Euan's profile and eloquent emails were emphatic about his need for fat cigars and had at least spared me hours of smoking like fury to get a nicotine quotient in.

We saw each other simultaneously, robbing me of my opportunity to leave. He sat, sprawled on a couch, less a man and more a giant orange spider. He stretched out one of his huge claws to shake my hand. He was repulsive. He smiled broadly, showing stained black and tan teeth crowding his thin-lipped mouth. His wiry polo-necked pullover did nothing to lift the impression of a giant insect, stretching across his emaciated frame, its sleeves going on forever. The only thing that his profile had been right about was his height. His red hair was so filthy and run with grey that its colour was irrelevant. The fedora sat sadly beside him like a damp pub dog.

'So you're Ruth then? Very nice,' he slurred and rocked unsteadily to his feet.

'And you must be Euan.' I attempted a smile and tried to ignore his chin, bristled with rough stubble, and his dry lips, stuck together in the corners with a grizzly foam. He had already lurched towards the bar.

'And what are you drinking?'

'Red wine,' I mumbled, putting myself in the relative safety of a corner seat and holding my cigarettes between us like a talisman. He sat down opposite, as I'd intended, and looked at me through one eye, the other one clearly having trouble focusing.

'Nice of you to come.' He said it in an accusatory tone, one step down from threatening, dripping with sarcasm.

'You're not quite how I expected,' I said aloud, when I really meant, 'What a tragic waste of time.' The thought of my friend Gillian propping up the bar in a brightly lit pub, full of normal people, caused physical pain. He countered my every gesture at politeness with the same combative tone and belligerent sneer. Leaving became a very important issue.

'Excuse me for a second, would you?' I said, with a careless disregard for cliché. In the loos, I stabbed Gillian's number into her phone.

It went straight to answerphone. 'For God's sake,' I whispered, although there wasn't another soul in the decrepit washroom. 'You're supposed to leave your phone on. This is a nightmare with the biggest arsehole I've ever met. A pissed arsehole. I'm a bit scared of leaving on my own but I'm going to have to soon. Hurry up.' I flushed the loo for effect and went back in.

The creature had lined up another round of drinks. I downed mine almost in one. Wordlessly he went back to the bar, swallowing his pint as if he'd dislocated his jaw to do it. I found that I was talking for the sake of it now, unloading things I needed to complain about daily but wouldn't burden anyone I actually liked with. I was talking about the horrors of my job when Euan interrupted.

'You really have a problem, don't you? Listen to yourself with your whinge, whine, whinge – you love it, don't you?' His face contorted in a cruel snarl. As I opened my mouth to form the words that would end our hideous rendezvous, Gillian bounced into the bar. Euan's disparate personality switched straight back into the erudite gentleman mode of his emails, and he went straight to the bar to get more drinks.

'Get me away from the Ginger Nightmare,' I pleaded.

'What is he?' asked Gillian, wide-eyed with horror.

As Euan returned with the drinks, Gillian began an elaborate narrative about how she'd come to find me in the pub, completely by chance, and needed me to accompany her to a party. Halfway through, Euan interrupted. 'I have a PhD, I'm not a fucking idiot. You phoned her to get you. And why not?' he accused me, addressing the last half of the sentence to himself.

I picked up my coat and cigarettes. 'Absolutely fucking right,' I said and left.

———————————

Alias: **EllenO** | *Age:* **47** | *F* | ♀♂ | **match.com**

What's a girl to do? I'm getting ready for another hopeful coffee date, having negotiated the tricky virtual world of conmen, players and sex addicts to find a real guy. So here we are, Thursday afternoon, having exchanged flirty email messages and a phone call, and my hands are getting slightly clammy as I approach the coffee shop. My date, let's call him Jeremy, agreed to meet outside the café.

As I walk toward the entrance, scanning the city-centre crowd for the youngish-looking 50-year-old from the website picture, I spot The Guy. But hold on. He has his mobile clamped to his ear and is obviously giving vent to his annoyance with some work subordinate. Trying not to judge before I've even said hello, I nod to him and we both walk into the café. He continues to tear strips off this poor unfortunate who has not washed his company car properly, and I'm thinking 'This is a bit inappropriate.' I'm also feeling that I'm invisible, which does nothing for my confidence.

Eventually, he unclamps the phone and barely speaks to me while I find us a table. We order coffee, and he launches into a long-winded explanation of the grave injustice perpetrated on him. It turns out that apart from the company car, Jeremy also possesses not one, but two sports cars, one of which is a Porsche. I'm thinking 'Does he imagine this is impressing me?' I try to look interested, while this turns into an extended diatribe about the trials of his work, which, incidentally, he has had no trouble walking away from for this date, because he's such a company bigshot.

What follows is a nonstop monologue about the highs and lows of Jeremy's life. I do believe we have been there for 25 minutes before I manage to break through the ego chat and tell him that (a) he talks too much and (b) he shows no interest in his date! He laughs at my forwardness and agrees he is a talker but that it is up to me to butt in and say my piece.

This is not how it's supposed to go. I expected a little compliment, a lot of questions, some chat about mutual interests and maybe even a little flirting. But no, when the ego has landed, there is no room left for anyone else. This guy didn't need a date. He was totally in love with himself from head to toe, and on top of that expected a good deal of stroking and admiration. The friends who had encouraged me to embark on this crazy experiment in finding my soulmate had no idea of the calibre of specimens falling under the heading of available men over 45. But I was so intrigued by this guy's *modus operandi* that I thought 'Well I'm here now and if you can't beat them, join them.' So, making myself work harder than usual, I turned on the full force of my personality. Maybe he had a lot to get off his chest about the tribulations of his previous relationship, so it must surely be my turn now. I valiantly struggled on to make him laugh, connect with places we had both visited and find a softer side to that ego-driven personality.

By the end of a long hour, I was mentally exhausted and couldn't wait to make my escape. He surprised me as we were getting up to go, by telling me that I was very 'bubbly' and that he liked me. *Bubbly*! Not an adjective I would use on myself in a million years. How can human beings in their interactions get it so wrong? This guy actually thought there was chemistry between us and wanted to keep up contact. While he was quite attractive for his age, no way could I be around him again. I was relieved to disappear up the street, almost at a run, to get back to the safety of my car and return to regular life. And girls, if you see even more pictures of his cars than of himself on the profile you will know who will be the *real* love of his life.

Alias: **Rosemaria** | *Age:* **36** | *F* | ♀♂ | **Guardian Soulmates**

I met him online. He was just perfect: a Spanish engineer with deep brown eyes and gorgeous dark curly hair. Like me, he loved photography and ballroom dancing. He didn't mind that I had a young son. I longed to look into those eyes. After we'd exchanged lengthy emails three times a day for a week, we decided to have our first date. He suggested we meet at a local arts cinema, have a cup of coffee and see a film. The film, he said, was about immigrants – the topic I was researching for my work. How nice of him, I thought, to help me do some research and find something special for our first adventure out.

The coffee part went very well. Conversation flowed easily, and there seemed to be the promise of romance in the air. We bought our cinema tickets, took our seats and got ready for the experience. We laughed at the same ads and spent the first 10 minutes of the film looking at each other intently and unintentionally touching hands. Surely nothing could go wrong.

But then my jaw dropped and I covered my eyes in embarrassment. Glancing sideways through my fingers, I saw that my date had sunk so deep into his seat I could barely see him. His face was frozen in a mixture of mortification, horror and shame. Suddenly the film we thought was about migrant workers had turned into an explicit sex film, the screen filled with cruel and sadistic pornographic images.

Why we stayed I don't know. Dozens of people left the cinema, sickened by the scenes. The worst part was when a nurse broke an old man's jaw to punish him for eating food forbidden in the care home she was managing. Sophisticated movie-goers might be able to appreciate what the film director was trying to achieve, but we couldn't. I don't know how we lasted the 80 minutes till the end. Probably not looking at each other helped. Neither of us wanted to be the first to say anything or suggest leaving.

After the film we caught the bus home. The half-hour journey felt like an eternity. When the bus reached his stop, my date said hastily, 'I'll call you', and jumped off. I never heard from him again. I guess we both learned that sex on the first date can spoil everything, even if you are just watching it.

Alias: **Ishouldcoco** | *Age:* **49** | *M* | ♀♂ | **DatingforParents**

Our date seemed so sensible. We chose neutral ground – the village between both of ours – where the pub had a music night on Wednesdays, which looked an obvious time for our first date. It also served good food and a selection of real ales, which would be handy if things went badly wrong. So lots of options: if conversation flagged we could listen to the music; if things went well we could move on to a candlelit meal; alcohol could help us relax; and it wasn't too far home for us both if we wanted out or if things had gone better than expected. A perfect first date, we thought: if only we'd known!

Because it had a good music night and there was not a lot else happening on a Wednesday, it was a popular venue, and lots of other people chose it as a place to go. So before long a group of my friends rolled in and subjected us to endless ribbing when they spotted us on a couch together. Worse was to follow. Her ex walked in and started to give us the evil eye from across the bar. He pounced when she was making her way to the ladies, blocking her route to subject her to verbal abuse overlaid with physical menace. I promptly did the knight in shining armour bit and went to her rescue, which only resulted in a stand-off during which he was joined by a mate who wanted to contribute to the potential punch-up.

The music ground to a halt as they both hurled obscenities at us, and my pals took great delight in recording the mêlée on their mobiles so that they could taunt me with it later. Fortunately, the swearing and upset led the bar staff to ask my date's ex and his stooge to leave before anything kicked off.

We spent the rest of the evening with him moodily looking through the pub windows, mouthing what he thought of us and excitedly talking into his mobile. Fearing that he was lining up a welcome committee for us when we left the pub, we went out through a side door and I escorted my date home.

Alias: **Cinnamon_Toast** | *Age:* **27** | F | ♀♂ | **Guardian Soulmates**

My date's name was Mal Muttley. I knew from his photographs that he was not the physical type I normally go for – he was a lot larger in girth than ideal – but his messages were so amusing and genial that I thought I should give him a chance.

As soon as I saw him I realised that he was even more wrong for me than I'd anticipated. He was larger than his photographs had indicated, by a long way. Getting through the café door appeared to take some skilled manoeuvering and blocking out of the light. He was wearing a three-piece suit, which is unusual at 11:30 on a Saturday morning in Costa, and carrying a lavish bouquet, presumably for me. Wondering if he was about to redeem himself by announcing that he was on his way to a wedding or a funeral, I sat down to partake of coffee with him, after the obligatory kiss on both cheeks.

Ten minutes later I had been entertained by his stories of how, during his frequent work travels, women often propositioned him for one-night stands, only for him to discover after the event that they were already married. I could hardly help my eyebrow rising of its own volition at this, and apparently failed to keep a moralising expression from crossing my face. He then defensively asked whether I didn't get up to similar shenanigans. I said, in my best frosty voice, that I was not that sort of girl. His eyes lit up, and he said, 'Ooh, now you've become a challenge!'

Trying to brush this aside, I got him onto the subject of online dating and heard all about how he'd been knocked back after trying to kiss his last date. He interrupted himself mid-sentence to ask, staring intently into my eyes, 'Are you attracted to me?' I felt it was a little cruel to yell, 'No!' in response to this, and finally came out with the best I could manage as a compromise between tact and truth: 'I don't know.' Poor, I know.

He proceeded to put an immensely large hand over to my side of the table with the command, 'Hold my hand'.

After some seconds of horror-struck silence, I demanded shrilly, 'Why should I?', tucking both hands firmly under my arms.

'It'll help you decide if you're attracted to me,' he said. Undeterred by my refusal to hold hands, he continued to tell me how he was not looking for quick flings any more but for 'the future Mrs Muttley'. He then asked if I was assessing him as a future husband.

'Do you want me to be?' I quipped, and very much fearing that he did, decided it was time to leave. At just half an hour, this was my shortest date ever. On the way from the café to the tube he told me he wanted to kiss me. I was almost beyond even trying to be polite by this time and simply muttered that I didn't think that would be a good idea. From the look in his eyes when we came to say goodbye I could see that I was about to be enveloped in a very large hug. Doubting if I would emerge from this unscathed, I did my best dizzy act and, waving blithely, skipped through the barriers calling the ubiquitous dismissal: 'It was lovely to meet you!'

Back in my flat I made a strong cup of tea and sat at the internet, resolving never to give anyone 'a chance' again. Breathing a sigh of relief, I logged on to Soulmates only to find a message from Mal saying 'When are you next free? PS I want three children. You?' Aaarrrgggh!

Alias: **AnnieBGoode** | *Age:* **35** | *F* | **Bisexual** | **Guardian Soulmates**

She lived in the north-east but wanted to hear from women anywhere. There was no photo. I sent her a text from the West Midlands, a complete punt. We exchanged several more texts – her replies always faster and longer. She seemed nice, if a little 'yampy', like an enthusiastic boxer dog that needs to charge around the park.

One evening we spoke on the telephone. Alarm bells sounded when she said I was the only respondent worth pursuing, dismissing the others as too stupid or ugly. One of them had told her she was rather full of herself. Nevertheless, we decided to meet somewhere between our homes, and she suggested Bakewell in the Peak District. I'd never been to Bakewell and reasoned that, if the date was a disaster, I would have explored somewhere new. We arranged to meet on Saturday at noon.

Two days before our meeting she called to check that I was going to show up – she 'didn't think her little heart could take it' if I didn't. I assured her I'd be there. Her worries were sweet, but her high hopes for Saturday were just asking for trouble.

On Saturday morning I wasn't as fresh as I might have been. Nervous, I had drunk too much wine the previous evening and woken on the sofa at 4 am with a crick in my neck. But I made myself look presentable, and set off for Derbyshire. She texted me several times en route, and I suspected that she wasn't pulling over to send them. Catching sight of myself in the driving mirror I looked tired and pudgy-eyed. We hadn't exchanged photographs – we just had descriptions of each other. She'd asked me to send a photo to her phone. At the time I had an old mobile phone with no camera; I didn't want to send one anyway. She said not to worry – she liked the sound of me anyway. I rashly told her that I looked a bit like Demi Moore. This was true: several people had told me so – but not for about 15 years. Nowadays I looked like Demi Moore's slightly bloated cousin. Too late to worry about that now.

She was standing inside the entrance of the car park where we'd arranged to meet, looking hard at the occupants of every car that entered. I asked if she was Jo. She nodded and smiled, probably thinking, 'Demi Moore, my arse', but at least she didn't look horrified or too short-changed. The brakes on her car had failed mid-journey. She had navigated the Peak District with no brakes. Probably because she thought she was going to meet Demi Moore. She agreed that attempting the return journey would be stupid and arranged for a recovery truck to pick her up later that afternoon.

We headed into town. Bakewell is nice – marvellous if you want to buy Bakewell tarts and outdoor clothing. We started with a coffee in a quiet café full of middle-aged couples who'd run out of things to say and preferred to listen to other people's conversation, which I found a bit inhibiting. She was keen to shop. Ordinarily this would be fine, but it's difficult getting to know someone when they're rifling through a rack of waterproof jackets. Later, laden with carrier bags, she suggested lunch. We ducked into a pub and sat at a table with a drink – by the time we got there they'd stopped serving food. Enlivened by the noisy pub atmosphere, we had quite a good chat, but it was obvious that neither fancied the other or that we would meet again.

By late afternoon we really needed food, so we sat on a bench outside the public toilets holding polystyrene trays of chips as it began to spot with rain. She asked if I read *Diva* magazine. I said I didn't. She said it was full of ugly women. She wasn't the stunner her ad implied, but I kept quiet.

On our way back to the car park she stopped to buy a Bakewell tart. The bakery was small and crowded; I waited outside. Normally good with dogs, I went to say hello to a cute little border terrier tied outside. He nipped my hand hard and drew blood. In the car park we said goodbye. She waited for her recovery truck while I drove through a long and torrential downpour on the motorway with my hand wrapped in toilet roll.

The next day I texted her to say thanks and that I hoped she had got home safely. I also politely suggested that she might be less judgemental about any future suitors her ad might bring. She said yes, she would, and she'd also make sure she knew what they looked like before agreeing to meet. I hoped she choked on her Bakewell tart.

Alias: **Cornflower** | *Age:* **55** | *F* | ♀♂ | **Guardian Soulmates**

A Date with a Potter

You have such beautiful hands
small and neat with rounded fingernails
You know how to work the clay
making it your own
spending days and weeks on one piece.

So I have high expectations
that your hands will mould my body
seeking out its curves and crevices
bringing me to a peak of perfection
but your hands feel rough on my skin.

Your nails scratch down the edges of my back
and instead of centring me you lose me
so that I am not gathered in your hands
I skid off at different angles.
You scrape me up, throw me back in the bin
light a cigarette.

Alias: **SaucyPedant** | *Age:* **44** | *F* | ♀♂ | **Guardian Soulmates**

'Off on Big Date! Remember Escape Procedure!' I pressed 'send'. As I put the finishing touches to my make-up my phone beeped. It was my friend Jen: 'Just txt and I'll phone with emergency! Have fantastic time!'

'Now,' I said to myself. 'Remember, don't get too excited. Just because he's a 6ft tall, dark-haired solicitor who's prepared to drive 30 miles to meet you for lunch is no need to get carried away.' His photo showed big brown eyes, the kind that you could fall into, dark, slightly curly hair and a kind smile. We had said that we would meet in the hall of the hotel where he had booked a table for lunch, and I edged past a middle-aged man in an anorak to enter the grand hallway and stood nervously looking at the restaurant menu on the wall.

'Lou?' I looked round for Robin, but Anorak Man was standing in the way. 'Lou? It is Lou, isn't it? I'm Robin.' Anorak Man was extending his hand towards me. I gulped past my initial disappointment and held out my hand to shake his. It was like holding a limp, wet fish. 'You look lovely.' Anorak Man Robin was smirking at me. 'Shall we eat?'

'Oh, yes. The restaurant is this way,' I began, but Robin had shuffled ahead of me down the corridor towards the bar.

'I thought the bar was a better choice than the restaurant,' he explained. 'I can't be doing with fancy food, and the bar menu looks very reasonable.' In the bar I tried to listen to what he was saying but found it difficult to concentrate as I stared at the little flakes of dandruff that snowed gently on to his shoulders every time he moved his head. As he talked, tiny balls of saliva gathered at the corners of his mouth.

'I'll just pop to the little boys' room before the food arrives,' he said. After about 10 minutes he still hadn't returned. It did cross my mind that he could have found me so hideous that he'd escaped out of the back door, but he had left his anorak and his man bag. The food arrived. At last he entered the bar. He walked the length of it and went out of the door on the other side. Then he entered again, walked the full length of the room in the opposite direction and went back through the first door. I chewed on my sandwich as I watched this spectacle.

'Excuse me, but were you with a gentleman?' a waitress asked.

'Well,' I quipped, 'I was with a man, but I don't know if he's a gentleman!'

'He's outside in the corridor. He seems a bit distressed. Would you come outside?' I followed the waitress out to find Robin sitting on the floor with his head in his hands.

'Robin? Are you OK?'

He looked up, smiled, jumped to his feet and said, 'How are the sandwiches?' We went back into the bar and he tucked into his baguette. 'You must be wondering what all that was about,' he began. 'I have this ... condition. Have you ever heard of prosopagnosia?' I shook my head. 'Well it's also known as "face blindness". Sufferers can't recognise other people by their faces. Sometimes I don't even recognise my own wife. I couldn't find you, so I thought I'd wait for you to find me!'

'Your wife? I thought you were divorced!'

'We're separated. She doesn't understand me. She told me I was a psychopath. I'm not! I went to the doctor and asked him if there was a test for it, but he said he didn't think I was one. But that wasn't good enough for her. Just because I sat outside her office for a whole day in my car waiting to see if she came out with *him*. How does that make me a psychopath?' Surreptitiously I got my phone out of my bag under the table and sent a blank text to Jen. The Escape Procedure. 'I mean, Lou, do you think it's unreasonable for a man to send his wife flowers? Do you?'

My phone rang. 'Jen! What's up? The dog? But how? A cliff? Of course ... On my way.' I turned to Robin, 'I'm so sorry, but my friend's dog ...'

'I love that woman! I've given her the best years of my life! She'll never meet a man with as much love to give as me.'

I stood up and put my coat on. 'I have to go.'

Robin took my hand and looked into my eyes. '£9.36.'

'Pardon?'

'Your share of the bill. I think it's only fair that we split it down the middle, don't you?'

Neil 'winked' at me and I liked the look of Neil. He was conventionally quite good looking (ie not my usual type) and had all the right qualities: unmarried, own flat, good job. I warned Neil that I 'was not a skinny bird', but he insisted that size wasn't everything (retrospectively, I understand why he was so insistent on this) and said he was looking forward to meeting up. After a week of emails I felt that I knew enough about him for it not to be a total disaster, so I got ready for the date.

As I walked up to him at the bar, I saw Neil clock me. I saw Neil's face drop like a lead balloon. I clearly wasn't what he was expecting. Now I know I'm not Kate Winslet, but I also know that I'm not Tracey Emin. Somewhere in between and, at that time, about a size 16. There aren't many things that are more soul-destroying than seeing someone's negative reaction to you. It was awful.

I persevered. We chatted and drank, and he warmed up after a couple of drinks. A couple of drinks after that and he was positively all over me. He had never, he gushed, met a woman 'of my calibre'. I must confess that I was on sparkling form, and I began to like Neil. He was the right height, funny and intelligent. Surely this one was going to go somewhere! At last.

And? I was besotted with Neil. He phoned the next day and arranged a second date. The third date was the night after the second. Neil said he had never felt like this about anyone. Girls bored him, he told me. I didn't. I told everyone that internet dating had actually worked for me after all. I told my friends that Neil was potentially 'the one'.

On the fourth date Neil was an arse. He had one drink and said he was going home, which, when you have rushed home from a parents' evening, spent an hour getting ready and paid for a taxi, was not great.

On the fifth date Neil was even worse. He was argumentative, told me he couldn't understand why anyone would be a teacher and had a go at me for driving a car. Although quite a tubster himself, Neil let it slip that he 'couldn't wait' for my latest diet to start working.

Wounded, but not defeated, I pursued him. I phoned him to arrange a sixth date. He told me 'there was something missing' and put the phone down on me. It was then that I realised what an absolute idiot I had been. I have learned this the hard way, but I now know not to pursue someone who clearly doesn't fancy you, go to bed with them on the third date or flog a dead horse.

Chapter 7:
Porkie pies and whopping lies

Wishful thinking in cyberland

Dishonesty is the biggie. It tops the bill of people's negative assumptions about online dating – and acts as a powerful deterrent for those wavering singletons who might otherwise sign up. Even online daters themselves – 86 per cent of them – believe that others misrepresent their physical appearance in their profiles.[52] But is this perception of online duplicity true? Is cyberdating really a festering swamp of liars, fibbers, scammers and cheats?

The good news is that there's no truth to these allegations. Actually, that's a lie. One recent study of 80 online daters carried out by researchers at Cornell University concluded that more than 81 per cent of people did indeed tell porkies in their profiles.[53] The vast majority of them only fibbed a tiny bit. A small minority of them fibbed a lot: 13-pounds-of-fat, three-inches-of-height, someone-else's-face-on-the-photo whoppers.[54]

A number of contributors to this book have certainly waxed cynical about the online fictions they've encountered during their dating adventures, from the barest-faced baloney to the sneakiest sham. On page 203, **Ms_E** tells us about her date with an improbable diving instructor, and on page 200, **PolkaDotSoup**, 27, about hers with a self-styled model. From the many scathing stories contributed by women about men lying – dripping with wit and fury in equal measure – it would seem that there's a small but significant minority of men out there who have latched on to online dating as a way of punching above their weight. Economical with the truth during the initial, online stages, they can skirt round the mental checklist many women would apply face-to-face (attractive? fit? clean? polite? fun to be with? considerate? own teeth? listens?). A number of women have turned up for their dates, freshly buffed and beautified, only to find that the man on the bar-stool is a smelly, leery impostor who bears no resemblance to the groomed, dapper photo in the profile. 'It's infuriating,' says **Belladonna**, 39. 'These guys seem to think they can use the internet to have a date with women they wouldn't have a snowball's chance in hell with in the real world.'

'People sometimes lie, and you can't beat yourself up too much for not spotting a lie,' says 28-year-old Londoner **LoveCrumb**, who has dated about 30 guys over the past few years:

One of the strangest lies I was on the receiving end of was from a man with a black and white photo who had stated his eye colour as brown – but on meeting him, his eyes turned out to be blue. Height is another thing men frequently exaggerate. Being quite a tall girl I always tend to knock a couple of inches off in my head from what they've stated on their profile. I've also come across guys who avoid ticking the 'finance' occupation box when they're actually investment bankers, and even a couple of stated teetotallers who turned out to be alcoholics!

In the meantime, many women are not entirely honest either – as **MilesAway**, a 29-year-old lawyer, found out when he encountered a woman playing a bizarre game, the rules of which were known only to herself:

You often find yourself corresponding with several people at once. I'm quite time-poor so I tend to take things at face value, and I was in touch with, among others, these two girls who both seemed quite interesting – bright and up for a laugh. One of them lectured in communications theory and the other

worked in marketing for charities or something. I remember
the marketing one looked pretty funky and had an asymmetric
haircut. She emailed me and sounded quite keen to meet up for
a coffee, which I was open to. I emailed her back to say yes and
to ask whether she could meet me at the Barbican café. I didn't
hear back for a day or two, so just assumed that she'd changed
her mind. She hadn't, but when I finally got my acceptance
email, entitled 'Barbican', it was from the other woman – the
lecturer! It turned out that these 'two women' were in fact one
and the same person. What's quite scary is that I wouldn't have
suspected if she hadn't slipped up. When I looked back at the
two profiles I could see that the heights and age were identical
and there was a remarkable similarity in writing style, but her
whole image and dress-sense in the photos looked so different
from one profile to the other.

MilesAway never found out whether this was an elaborate
verification ritual or some kind of psychological game, trusting the
hairs rising on the back of his neck instead, and ending all contact
there and then. **Reliable_runner**, 28, tells of another fabulist who,
despite an active, if secret, heterosexual life, successfully passed
herself off as a lesbian for several hedonistic months in the salons
of gay London, in order to have her last walk on the wild side before
settling down to marriage with her boyfriend (see p. 202).

Our contributors have been frank about their own discreet bending
of the truth too, explaining the reasons for their 'strategic self-
presentation' – those little white lies by which they present their
optimal selves on the site. Sometimes they're motivated by the
spirit of self-improvement. Twenty-one-year-old London woman
2leggedtree says: 'I've been really honest in all areas of my profile
apart from smoking. I think I've said I smoke less than I do so that
I could meet a non smoker. I'd like to quit. My friend and I made
profiles that were completely orientated around the men that we
wanted to meet. I wanted to meet an athlete so I lied a bit here
and there so that I would be able to find someone more athletic.
Obviously if I'd met an athlete in real life it wouldn't have worked
out. I think he would have been a bit disappointed!'

One of the most common deceptions is geared to beating the computer's matching system, which uses parameters rather than precise figures in order that people can search by, say, age-ranges and height-ranges. As **sugar_hiccup** says:

> I'm actually only 5ft 3in but I put 5ft 4in on my profile because loads of people wouldn't want someone shorter than that. I think psychologically people think of that as the cut-off. One of the drop-down boxes has 5ft 4in as the minimum, so if you put 5ft 3in that instantly puts you in a completely different category and you won't come up as a match in a huge range of people's searches. I value honesty but you have to work within the limitations of drop-down boxes.

Tweetybird, 45, encountered a man who described his age as 49 on the webform but admitted to being 58 in the prose description, saying that he had 'only written 49 in order to come up in the online searches'. Depending on your point of view, that's either a major con or a pretty astute piece of honesty: he was claiming to have the qualities to confound people's prejudices against his age, if only he could get the chance to show them. At least he didn't leave it to the date to come clean.

Constructing an idealised public self – accentuating the positive, eliminating the negative, latching on to the affirmative – is something we all do all the time in CVs, job interviews and social settings to get what we want. This may explain the delicious statistic that 'only one per cent of online daters listed their appearance as "less than average"'.[55] The whole thing is complicated by the need not only to look good but to compare well with others on the site. The dating pool is a competitive place that sometimes has all the charm of a candlelit bath with sharks: the temptation to manage other people's impressions of you in order to gain the edge can be irresistible.

Take the profile. A trawl of the hobbies listed on two large dating websites seemingly reveals that Britain is in the throes of a scuba-diving craze. There is apparently no activity quite as popular with singletons as exploring the sea-bed with an oxygen cylinder strapped to their backs. They're a modest bunch, so you won't find wetsuits on their porches, their underwater movies on YouTube or any noticeable change to their well-larded physiques: no, this new British obsession only surfaces on dating profiles. And while these singles have discreetly been laying waste to the great coral reefs of the world, they've also left no mountain unclimbed and no savannah unsafari'd, while simultaneously ensuring that our national passion for salsa is undimmed.

This low-level lying was borne out by a recent study by Catalina Toma and Jeffrey Hancock of Cornell University and Nicole Ellison of Michigan State University, which revealed that deception in online dating was 'frequent, subtle and intentional'. Researchers compared the height, weight and age declared by 80 online daters (40 men and 40 women, all heterosexual) on their profiles against actual measurements taken at the research centre and their age as specified on their driving licences. Around eight in 10 of the participants massaged the facts. Just over half of the men (52.6 per cent) lied about their height, as did 39 per cent of the women. Women and men both lied about their weight, with slightly more women underreporting the pounds (64.1 per cent) than men (60.5 per cent). When it came to age, almost a quarter of the men were untruthful, as opposed to 13.1 per cent of the women.[56]

A separate study at the University of Chicago found that men and women lie differently. Comparing measurements given in daters' online profiles with national census data, the research team found that men's major areas of deception are 'educational level, income, height, age and marital status', and they estimated that, in the US at least, 13 per cent of online male suitors are married. Women's lies, meanwhile, focus on weight, physical appearance and age. Women appear to understate their weight more and more as they get older – 'by five pounds when they are in their 20s, 17 pounds in their 30s and 19 pounds in their 40s'.[57] Attempts to understand these discrepancies have concluded that 'daters sometimes engage in deception to meet the expectations of the opposite sex'.[58] So, men lie about the qualities they believe women will find attractive (height and social status indicators such as education, occupation and career), while women enhance those attributes they believe will attract men (their figures and looks). This goal-oriented deception is hardly surprising when men claiming incomes exceeding $250,000 receive 151 per cent more emails from women than men claiming incomes less than $50,000.

The difference between the sexes was strongly marked when it came to tolerance of deception however, according to Toma, Hancock and Ellison. All the participants in their study believed that lying about 'relationship information' was 'less socially acceptable than lying about any other category', but 'men considered it more acceptable than women to lie about their social status ... their occupation ... education ... and marginally about their relationship status [i.e. whether they were single, divorced or separated]'. The researchers guessed that 'perhaps men wanted to give themselves more leeway in deceiving about characteristics that would make them more sought after by women'. The same was not true in reverse, however: women were no less forgiving of 'lying about age or physical attractiveness, characteristics that are considered important for women in attracting men'.[59] This difference between men and women in their tolerance for online lying may go some way to explaining why women on internet dates are, in the words of Michael Norton of Harvard Business School, the co-author of a study on disillusionment with cyberdating, 'much, much more disappointed than men'.[60]

This deception carries through to the visual realm. Many daters are suspicious if there is no photo with a profile, and it turns out that this caution is partly justified – some of these shrinking violets are no doubt the covert marrieds. People who posted photographs were 'significantly more accurate about their current relationship information than those who did not post a photograph'. Yet among the photos that *are* posted, a number of them are old or misleading. Some women who post photos of themselves in their younger days – sporting those size 8 clothes that are currently mothballed at the far end of the wardrobe – seem to be using the promised date as a kind of WeightWatchers meeting. They propose a date four weeks hence and calculate on losing a quarter of their excess weight every week, neatly dovetailing their romantic calculations with their weight-loss goals. 'I've lost 44 pounds since I've started [online dating], and I mean, that's one of the reasons I lost the weight so I can thank online dating for that,' said MaryMoon, a Los Angeles-based woman interviewed for a study of strategic self-presentation. She described how she used dating to help her kick-start her metabolism: '[After] the first guy ... hit on me, I checked my profile and I had lied a little bit about the pounds, so I thought I had better start losing some weight so that it would be more honest. That was in December, and I've lost every week since then.'[61]

Photoshop has unwittingly become the fibber's best friend. **Jellyfish**, 46, a council employee, explains his rationale for doctoring his photograph: 'I have used online dating for one year. I have had just one date. It is near on impossible to attract a mate this way if you look like me. But I remain optimistic and am hanging in there. Moral is – photoshop your pic and be patient.'

There is a tiny problem here that the Photoshop evangelists haven't grasped: if you arrive on your date not looking remotely like your photo, you are instantly at a disadvantage. Your enraged date will despise you for playing fast and loose with his/her time, money and, most cruelly, hope. You have a few seconds to get out of the dog house, during which you will have to come up with a better spin on your hoax than 'Once you get to know me, you won't mind that I am shorter and not as good looking', the lines that **Tweetybird** was offered by way of appeasement after being persuaded by some prize-winning flim-flam to devote her Valentine's evening to a fake (see p. 210).

Beyond the opportunistic fibs geared at netting the best partner, there is another form of deception that afflicts internet dating as it does the whole online community: predatory fraud. Like social networking, online dating is a potential target for fraudsters and robbers. One man in Detroit, Terrance McCoy, was sentenced in October 2009 to two years in jail after stealing the car of a woman he had met online for a date.[62] Claiming to have left his wallet in the woman's car after sharing a meal with her at a restaurant, he simply 'asked for the keys and drove off'. Dating websites with poor or non-existent customer services teams can find themselves inundated with fake profiles from spammers and scammers: ostensibly real people's profiles, they turn out to be marketing ruses, fronts for prostitution or ads for other websites. Unsuspecting daters can find themselves clicking to places they *really* don't want to go. One clear advantage that paying sites have over non-paying ones is that the information embedded in a credit card makes it only one step short of an ID card: the sheer fact of paying for a subscription brings an additional filter and identity-check.

In the US, where internet dating technology has been used – and abused – for several years longer than in the UK, online dating and social networking sites have 'figured prominently' in scams reported to the The National White Collar Crime Center. Its Internet Crime Report 2007 refers to fraudsters who use these sites to arrange meetings with people in order to commit 'romance fraud'. The architecture of the fraud reads like the step outline of a bad movie, so clunky is each new manipulation of the poor victim's credulity. Yet a lot of people have fallen prey to this kind of scam – more than the numbers reported as many are too embarrassed to come forward.

After meeting someone at one of these sites, the fraudster tries to gain a person's trust through false displays of affection. In most cases, the fraudster lives far away, usually in another country. The fraudster expresses an ardent desire to visit the person, but the fraudster cannot afford to make the trip. The scam is successful when the two agree to meet and the fraudster convinces the victim to send money to cover his travel expenses. Then, invariably, an unforeseen event (often an accident of some sort) prevents the fraudster from making the trip (or, at least, so goes the fraudster's lie). The fraudster lands in hospital, and now the victim's money has to be used to cover medical expenses. The fraudster's brother has been kidnapped, and now the money has to be used to set him free. The fraudster was mugged on her way to the airport, and now she has no money at all. In any event, the fraudster always needs more money; and, if the fraudster's success continues, he is able to obtain more money from the victim while making more promises to visit.

> The fraudster, however, always has an excuse for missing the plane, and the rounds of false promises and excuses continue until the victim loses patience and stops sending money.[63]

Like other forms of fraud that take advantage of our better nature, romance fraud relies on the possibility of truth. Even when that possibility is very slim, we might wish to hang on to it rather than lose the delightful mirage of erotic union with the fraudster or his/her surrogate, wallow in despair at human ignominy, or face the fact that we've been taken for a schmuck.

Women are not suspicious enough about profiles and subsequent emails, according to one study of 740 women by Dr Paige Padgett of the University of Texas, which found that 30 per cent had sex with the man on a first date; of these, three-quarters did not use condoms. The study argues that, while online communication can be a good way to verify details about someone in advance of a meeting by providing opportunities for cross-checking information, it can also very quickly create a false sense of security and familiarity: 'The high frequency and intensity of email communication prior to meeting in person cultivated acceleration of intimacy for the individuals involved and may have affected some women's decisions to engage in risky sexual behaviours.'[64] Whatever the sense of security generated through email correspondence, however, no one should give out their personal details (even personal email addresses can be traced) or agree to be alone with a stranger they have met online, until they have reassured themselves they are safe (see safety tips, see p. 162).

But it is important to remember that, as these studies show, most people are decent, if a little prone to exaggeration. And there are fraudsters who would fleece us in every walk of life – but they are few and far between. The fact that some of them operate online simply means that people need to remain circumspect and realistic.

And there's some bittersweet reassurance in knowing that the scale of the fibs in dating profiles – despite some very tall exceptions – is modest and strategic rather than sinister. Despite knowing they are not being wholly truthful, online daters express qualms about lying too much. There's a tension: on the one hand, they wish to emphasise their positive attributes and present themselves as appealing; on the other hand, they feel the need to put forward their true selves, complete with quirks and shortcomings, because ultimately they are looking for the understanding and acceptance of significant others.[65] Online daters are, after all, hoping to meet their correspondents in person, and most are seeking long-term love. Much as people might want to control and perfect the impression they give to others, there is another desire that is far greater: to be loved and accepted as they are.

Porkie pies and whopping lies:

The stories

Alias: **PolkaDotSoup** | *Age:* **27** | *F* | ♀♂ | **udate.com**

I had just got a new flat and was living on my own. I had tried the clubbing scene with no luck so had decided the way of the future was to try the internet. I enrolled on a dating agency called UDate, and I thought that, because you had to pay for it, it would be peopled by honest, decent men looking for an honest, decent woman – me. How wrong I was!

The first man I met from UDate looked drop-dead gorgeous in his photo. He sounded lovely, too, and we had a lot in common and had a talking relationship for several weeks, during which I kept asking if he had any other photos, but he said he didn't have a digital camera. We finally arranged a date – for February 14.

On my profile it said I was between 5ft 6in and 5ft 8in. His profile said he was between 6ft and 6ft 2in. We had agreed to meet at my local pub, two minutes walk from my flat. He was catching a train from London and stopping in a B&B down the road from me. I was really excited about meeting this 'hunk' but very nervous too. I walked into the pub, looked around but could see no sign of this guy, so I went to the bar and ordered myself a large dry white wine (just to calm my nerves, of course).

I was still casually looking for this guy, wondering whether I had been stood up, when I felt a tap on the back. I turned around and couldn't see anyone stood there, then I looked down … Oh no!

'Hello, Maddie,' he said.

'Hello. Who are you?' I said.

'Your date, Steve,' he replied. He was no more than 5ft tall. I wished the ground could have swallowed me up there and then. I asked why he didn't look like his photo and couldn't believe his response: 'Well', he said, 'If you'd known what I really looked like, you would not have agreed to see me, would you? So I put a picture from the Next catalogue online to attract your attention. But once you get to know me, you won't mind that I am shorter and not as good looking.'

'Help! Get me out of here!' I was thinking, but I smiled, trying not to show my disappointment – especially given the distance he had travelled. But after three minutes of listening to him, I realised that not only was he downright ugly, he was downright boring too. I am afraid I said I was going to the ladies and escaped out of a side entrance. I did feel bad about the distance he had come, but he had been dishonest. And hey, if you agree to go on date, you at least have a right to know who you are meeting!

Alias: **Cloudwatcher** | *Age:* **49** | *F* | ♀♂ | **Guardian Soulmates**

His profile was a tad over-egged. For 'a management executive who likes to paint' read 'temp admin clerk at a pen factory who likes a spot of DIY'.

Alias: **Reliable_runner** | *Age:* **28** | *F* | ♀♀ | **gaydargirls.com**

I met someone I thought was *perfect* for one of my best friends. I'd been enticed by an artistic profile picture, a shared dislike of mustard and the general display of poor grammar by other users 'currently available to chat' into an exchange with a very bright French girl. As we 'chatted' it seemed that we shared more than just a dislike of mustard (all varieties). We were both in that place between depression and desperation that you can find yourself in following the breakdown of a long-term relationship. I was genuinely relieved that this person didn't seem to want to have sex with me any more than I did with her. Instead, I found great solace in discussing, with someone totally anonymous, the sordid details of a miserable affair and subsequent relationship termination that had left me feeling pretty dreadful.

I should have left it there. There was no need to meet. I'd had my online counselling session and given my expert opinion to her. After all, I *really* wasn't looking for a new relationship. Nor did I particularly need any new friends. But we met. We were both 'online dating' virgins, and it started to feel peculiar not to know what this person, with whom I'd spoken relatively intimately, was really like.

We met in a bar in Soho and within moments of meeting this slightly haughty, olive-skinned slip of a French woman, I knew that my best friend, Ruby, would sacrifice a lung to go out with her. She was perfect. Beautiful (in an obvious way), bright, brassy and, the number one criterion, a little bit mean. I orchestrated a meeting – London Pride – so it was perfectly easy for them to go their separate ways if my hunch was wrong. Needless to say, the end of the evening saw them disappearing off home together and barely surfacing for a month of, by both accounts, pretty mind-blowing bedroom action (not that I needed to know that). But something just wasn't right.

I knew that Frenchie (as we called her) had been with a man as her previous long-term partner – we'd had long email exchanges about how she couldn't be with him any longer after a relationship with a woman at work had made her realise what she wanted (i.e., women).

In itself, this wasn't a problem at all. She was just cagey and would sometimes be incommunicado for days at a time.

I thought I'd probably made a mistake when I introduced them, and my suspicions were confirmed when Ruby received a phone call from Frenchie's boyfriend telling her that she'd probably better not see any more of his girlfriend. They'd just moved into a new house together and it would be better for everyone that Ruby did not interfere. It was quite reasonable really, but a surprise nonetheless. Ruby was devastated, and I felt terrible.

Frenchie disappeared overnight – from Gaydar, from Facebook and her phone was disconnected. I guess it had been her last big fling before she settled into home-owning bliss with her boyfriend. We'd all been duped, and it was pretty discombobulating. Ruby, wounds licked, confidence restored, found her perfect partner on the same website around 18 months later. I've not used a dating website since.

Alias: **Ms_E** | *Age:* **34** | *F* | ♀♂ | **match.com**

Stuart was Scottish, 6ft 4in and local. After a couple of brief emails I thought, why not? We arranged to meet in a pub in Ealing for a drink and a chat. As I walked into the pub I caught sight of his face and recognised him. He waved, and I gradually made my way towards him. As the rest of him came into view it was with slight horror that I realised his photos were years out of date.

He was enormous. Morbidly, morbidly obese. Like Channel 4 documentary-sized. I'm surprised he managed to get out of bed. Now, I'm no stranger to extra weight, but this was ridiculous. I felt a bit angry to be honest – he hadn't even ticked the 'few extra pounds' box but had described himself as 'about average'. Did he think I wouldn't notice? I glanced at the barman as we introduced ourselves and caught him grinning. I suspect he'd probably picked up my surprise at Stuart's size. But being polite and well brought up, I greeted him warmly. He wasn't going to be the love of my life, but he might be a nice bloke, I thought.

I thought wrong. Big Stuart was a twat. He bought the first round – a diet coke (!) for himself and a glass of wine for me. He then proceeded to drone on about how depressing internet dating was and how annoyed he got when women 'misrespresented themselves' online. Looking back, I wish I'd pointed out the irony of this complaint. One woman he met claimed to be 'bubbly', but apparently on their date she was quiet. I'm not bloody surprised.

He was one of those people who talk constantly and boringly about themselves, and even when he did ask me a question he brought the subject straight back to himself. He was arrogant and self-obsessed. His profile stated that he was a scuba-diving instructor. When was the last time he went scuba-diving, I enquired? About six years ago was the answer.

Stuart moaned about his ex and how she forced him to do DIY all the time. Stuart bragged about his sports car (how on earth did he tuck that massive belly behind a steering wheel, I wondered?). Stuart told me he liked comedy, particularly improvisation. Did I understand what he meant by 'improvisation', he checked? I wanted to thump him.

I didn't have the nerve simply to finish my drink and go, so I agreed to myself to buy the round back and then make a sharp exit. Would he like another drink, I asked? Why yes, Stuart replied, perusing the wine list. He ordered a large glass of Rioja costing £7.50. I was speechless. I went up to the barman and said, 'That idiot has just ordered a large Rioja. I'm never going to see him again. Shall I get it?' The barman agreed I shouldn't, and so I plonked a small glass of house red down in front of him and said nothing.

Stuart went on to reveal that sometimes he took his Sooty and Sweep puppets out to the pub to 'entertain' his mates – his sense of humour was 'out there', he assured me. It was around that point that

I gulped down my drink in about three mouthfuls, said goodnight and hurried off.

Alias: **SoSueMe** | *Age:* **56** | *F* | ♀♂ | **datingdirect.co.uk**

Laurent was just what I needed on a wet Sunday afternoon in February: he was tall, dark and handsome and wanted to chat with me online.

To be precise, Laurent is from Cameroon and totally gorgeous. He was currently living about 10 miles from me, but a quick squint at his profile revealed, well, not much really because it was written in Spanish. I don't speak Spanish. 'He's probably looking for a British passport and a meal ticket,' I thought. 'He's only 38 though. What's the harm in chatting online ... ?'

A couple of hours later I suggested that it might be better if he looked for someone nearer his own age. Laurent assured me that he had Spanish residency and didn't need a British passport. He just wanted to meet me. So, what's the harm in meeting for a coffee?

We got on well, laughed a lot and he was extremely attentive. Afterwards he sent me an email: 'hi Sue, i cant stop thinking of you, thinking of how lovely a met you. i can forget the smoothness of your skin, you are so tender!!! i could have been kinssing you during one more hour. Since last night i am missing you. it would have been a pleasure to be by your side. take care darling. laurent xx [*sic*].'

Laurent's written English definitely needed some work – but then we did share the universal language of 'lerve'.

On our second date, as we passed a bookshop, Laurent mentioned Barack Obama's autobiography: 'If you see it, perhaps you could get it for me,' he said casually.

'Well, you're passing Waterstone's on your way to the station, so you could pick it up there yourself,' I said. I felt he expected me to buy it for him – but why?

But I'm only human, and I liked Laurent. I wanted it to work out and chose to ignore any warning signs. Then one day I was driving him to the station and we passed a second-hand car showroom. Suddenly he announced 'I need a car – nothing too expensive, perhaps about £1,000.'

'Blimey!' I said, 'I didn't think you had that sort of money.' Probably not the required response.

Then, during a phone call, Laurent told me that one of his sisters in Cameroon had TB and he'd had to send money to Africa to pay for her medical treatment.

'Oh dear,' I said, sounding concerned. 'I didn't think you had any money.' Again, probably not the response he was hoping for.

Sadly Laurent had to return to Spain because his tourist visa had run out. He's still there. He phoned me out of the blue a few months ago, asking me to be his sponsor. He said: 'If you could just write a letter, Sue, saying that I am your boyfriend and that I will be living with you, I'll be able to get my visa.' I declined, wondering how many other women had received the same request. Safety in numbers, as they say.

Alias: **AllyT** | *Age:* **41** | *F* | ♀♂ | **Guardian Soulmates**

Mmm. Why wasn't there a photo? He was witty, intelligent, funny and charming, and we really did click online. My workmate warned me never to correspond with someone who didn't have a profile photo, but I was excited. It was my first foray into online dating after a sceptical start, and I was soon as addicted as my more savvy workmate. Waiting to see who had chosen me as their favourite, who had sent me a message, I felt so popular. It was like a whole new world opening up.

He sounded amazing, and we had so many things in common, shared tastes in music, literature and art. He had recently moved to Nottingham from London for work and didn't know many people locally. He loved great music, and we swapped stories about Nick Cave and the Bad Seeds gigs. He was an aspiring writer, and I looked forward to his emails. He made me smile, and he made me laugh. I felt a connection with him and began to dream about the possibilities of a relationship.

After a few weeks of daily correspondence he suggested that we should meet. I was excited but nervous too. Would our online connection exist in the real world? I suggested a rendezvous at my favourite art house cinema. He said he would be the one reading the latest Sebastian Faulks novel. It was a lunch-time meeting, which my workmate recommended in case a 'quick getaway' was required.

I walked towards the cinema, my heart beating fast and beads of sweat on my forehead. This was a milestone: it was my first encounter with someone I had met online. I walked up the steps tentatively, the promise of potential propelling me forwards. I scanned the downstairs café. It was busy as usual, with several lone males present. A book caught my eye: Faulks. In an instant, I looked from the book to the hand holding it, along the arm and upwards. My feet felt like doing an about turn, but I drew breath and moved towards the reader.

'Hi, I'm Elizabeth.' He stubbed out a cigarette (it was in the days before the ban).

'Hi, I'm Paul.' His hand felt moist in mine. He smiled broadly. And now I realised why there was no profile photo. Several teeth were missing, and those that remained suggested a long history of smoking. I have always been rather partial to a freshly shaven bald head, but his had an unfortunate egg shape. Anyone wanting to call me a totally superficial bitch might like to note that I was willing to overlook his physical shortcomings had he charmed me with the wit that had captivated me online, but he proceeded to talk incessantly about his life in London, never asking me a question and periodically calling me 'darlin'. He carried on smoking and took two calls on his mobile phone during our meeting. I felt like sliding under the table. After 45 minutes I was calling time. I told him that I had an urgent meeting to get back to at work.

The next day I got an email saying, 'I really like you. Let's meet again?' After that I followed my workmate's advice about profiles without photos.

Alias: **Ms_E** | *Age:* **34** | *F* | ♀♂ | **match.com**

Randal said he was 6ft. In fact, he could not have been more than 5ft 9in, which is an annoying and pointless lie to tell if you ask me. It's not as if I wasn't going to find out about that one. And before I am accused of being shallow, I think everyone is allowed to have their prerequisites, and height is one of mine. I feel like a drag queen when I'm with a shorter man. I also wear heels and 5ft 9in versus 6ft 2in is not a good look. Or, it's not a look for me, at least.

Alias: **Saes** | *Age:* **55** | *M* | ♀♂ | **Guardian Soulmates**

Although I live in North Wales, I'd been exchanging messages with a lady from Derbyshire because my mum still lived there, and I could stay over in order to be handy for meetings. We arranged to meet for afternoon tea in a hotel in Buxton – it was a touch refined for my taste but perhaps she was a 'nice' person, I recall thinking. I arrived there (early as ever) and eventually my date joined me.

It was a bit of a shock, to be honest. She was clearly at least 10 years older than she had advertised – maybe more – and kept her white gloves on for the whole proceedings, presumably to hide her hands. Now I've no problem with older ladies, but fibbers are a different matter. Nonetheless, I was polite to the extent of feeling thoroughly chivalrous: I poured her tea for her and engaged in chit-chat, while inside I really couldn't wait to make my escape.

After a long, long hour she excused herself for nose-powdering activities, and I took advantage of her absence to pay the bill and prepare for a polite farewell. I waited for her to return, but alas (or should that be hooray?) after a quarter of an hour there was no sign of my date. I had a minor panic as I felt that at her apparently advanced age she might have collapsed in the ladies, so I asked one of the waitresses to check the toilets – only to discover that she'd done a runner. Well, I didn't shed a tear; just paid for the tea!

As I had a bit of time on my hands I decided to have a mooch around the market. Now Buxton market isn't the biggest in the world, and a wander round takes only a few minutes. I was just about to leave when who should I notice but my date, hob-nobbing with a group of similar-looking ladies. To my amazement they all proceeded to get on a waiting coach that bore the sign 'Trip to Buxton'. The cunning minx had booked me as afternoon entertainment – together with a free pot of tea – as part of her pensioners' day out.

Alias: **Cloudwatcher** | *Age:* **49** | *F* | ♀♂ | **Dating for Parents**

There was no photo. He told me he had blond hair and blue eyes. Maybe he did once upon a time, but the little bit of hair he had left was grey and very definitely combed over his head. Don't do it boys – you'll get found out.

Alias: **Tweetybird** | *Age:* **45** | *F* | ♀♂ | **match.com**

I am busy updating my internet profile, which reads like something I'd have written to my French penpal in the 80s, when I see I have a message. It's from Stub2009, an unfortunate, somewhat pathetic-sounding username, but hey, mine is not much better! Tweetybird. Makes me sound like one of those hairdressers who won't shut up.

OK, Stub, let's have a look. His 'catchy' introduction line reads: 'Tall, handsome, witty male looking for a female who can return serve ... Up for the challenge?' Well, I was looking for a relationship, not a fight, but he describes himself as tall and handsome (though the photo does little to justify this claim). He could be my Colin Firth. The photo is grainy, his face looks like an anagram, and he's standing by a huge globe that is bigger than his head, no doubt a trophy of all the places he has been to. He has travelled extensively through Africa, canoed down/through/in or over the Victoria Falls, been trekking through Namibia and climbed Kilimanjaro as well as a host of other mountains I've never heard of. He is, however, 'equally happy with a cosy night in with a DVD and a nice bottle of red'. How many times have I read this before? So far he sounds about as deep as a puddle.

Aha! Now we get to the really interesting bit: he travels to work on the A24, but if there's a traffic jam, he takes the M23, though generally he doesn't like motorway driving. He prefers to look at the countryside on the A24, which goes past Box Hill, and no doubt he has climbed its sheer face, risking life and limb – in an epic *Touching the Void* type scenario – and lived to tell the tale.

He likes women who are feminine, slim and attractive, who like cooking and have similar interests to him, and we now find out that, as well as climbing things, he likes football and golf. On the telly. Most women would find more excitement in an Ikea flatpack, and if I had to watch golf, I might lose the will to live.

His politics? He used to vote Labour 'until they took us into an immoral and illegal war'. Blimey Stub, have you paused the golf to make a cutting-edge political statement, or is this just your way of letting us all know you are a Tory, because they've never taken us into any immoral or illegal wars, have they?

I've got as far as 'interests and activities', which read as follows: 'friends, going out, staying in, cooking, television, cars and drumming.' No mention of the intrepid mountaineer I thought I was about to date, and apart from the random 'drumming', the list of things is so obvious I am surprised he did not add breathing in and out or letting his hair grow.

He also adds that he doesn't want any 'time-wasters', presumably because there is still some part of the A24 that remains unexplored and there's so little time. Now he says he's not actually 49 – he's 58 – and that he just put 49 'for search purposes'. He cannot possibly be my Colin Firth, because Colin was born on September 10 1960 and is therefore really 49.

Alias: **PlusOne** | *Age:* **39** | *F* | ♀♂ | **Guardian Soulmates**

I saw a profile on a dating site that looked interesting: tall male, good-looking, single, 38, good job. It all looked very promising, so I sent a 'hello' and received a reply within a few minutes. We got chatting online and then on the phone. He sounded shy but quite nice, and we decided to meet in a local bar at 8pm a few days later.

On the night of the date I got to a nearby bar over an hour early with a friend just so I could prepare myself and calm my nerves. The friend was going to leave 15 minutes before my date was due to arrive, and I would go to the bar where I'd arranged to meet 'Ben'. While we were at the bar a guy kept winking at my mate and smirking at her. Needless to say, she avoided eye contact and ignored him. We had a drink, and the man came over to our table. He smelt of damp clothes, stale beer and ciggies. He was about 50, 5ft 3in tall and had a bald patch with a straggly mullet *à la* Bill Bailey. We tried to ignore him, but he just stood next to us, winking at Sara and gesturing for her to join him. She politely asked him to go away, and he looked quite hurt but simply retreated a few feet and kept on watching us.

Sara and I decided to leave and go to the bar where I was due to meet Ben, only to be followed a few minutes later by the odd man. This was too much for me, so I asked him why he had followed us to the bar. He looked quite shocked and said he fancied my mate. I told him that my friend was married and not interested. He quickly replied that that wasn't a problem: he'd take me out instead! I laughed and told him that I wasn't available either.

The man shrugged his shoulders and left the bar. At 7:55 Sara left, and I went to re-do my make-up. When I returned the creepy man was standing at the bar again. At 8:15 my date hadn't turned up so I sent him a text to check his arrival time. As soon as I sent it I heard the man's phone bleep. He read the message and looked at me and smiled. He swaggered over – yes, *swaggered* over – and introduced himself. It was Ben.

I nearly fainted. So much for the tall, good-looking, 38-year-old! I somehow managed to shake his hand when he jabbed it at me and told him he looked a little different from his profile. He simply shrugged and said, 'Yeah, well no one tells the truth on those sites. Look at you.'

With that, I picked up my bag and left.

Alias: **UtterlyAlly** | *Age:* **37** | *F* | ♀♂ | **Guardian Soulmates**

It was a dramatic choice for our first meeting: 'Outside York Minster near the camp Emperor,' he had written. Standing in the cold February afternoon, the statue of Emperor Constantine did indeed look camp, with his arm draped languidly across his throne. My date already had brownie points for location and humour.

Our initial correspondence via Soulmates was sparky and sharp. I worried that he was going to be too quick for me. The decision to meet up was largely due to my technical incompetence as I was unable to upload a photo. He seemed a little concerned. I suggested meeting up quite early on so that he could 'see the goods'. He agreed. At this stage, I had a false name and had lied about my age, shaving off two years so that I fitted into his ideal age range.

He was late. The Minster bells chimed four o'clock. I began to wonder if the middle-aged man holding a carrier bag was him. I thought about going home. The middle-aged man looked as though he was waiting for someone. A group of teenagers started to climb on to Emperor Constantine, taking photographs. Then he appeared, looking like a smarter version of his profile photo.

The date went well. He had lovely eyes. He didn't seem appalled at my appearance. We nattered. Emperor Constantine smiled.

I told him my real name about a week later. I told him my real age about two months later. We're now married and so, of course, no longer keep any secrets from each other.

Chapter 8:
My search is over

Finding love, bliss and happiness on the internet

We are fantastically compatible: formed for each other. Lucy is my ideal in so many ways, unquestionably my partner for life. I doubt we would have met any other way, and yet I have ended up with someone most of my friends could have picked for me. We're engaged, and plan to get married in the summer. I just feel 'Wow! That was lucky!' **sugar_hiccup**, 41, ♀

It is very rare in this jigsaw puzzle we call life that you come across the other piece that fits so perfectly next to you. I found this in **NemoPut** and feel truly blessed to call such a beautiful, intelligent and wonderful woman my soulmate. She is my urban safari companion and I love her very much. **Vapourtrail**, 37, ♂

Soulmate, other half, kindred spirit, fellow traveller, beloved: there are many names for the person who awaits us at the end of our quest, at least in the traditional story of love. Finding the promised land of a deep, loving union with another person seems unlikely in a world where there is so much loneliness and sorrow – like beating the bookie at impossible odds or snatching joy from the jaws of disappointment. The lifelong partnership that is one of our culture's enduring images of love is, in practice, rare. But is this ideal of a marriage of souls, of a union with 'the one' – notwithstanding loss of lust for them, other playmates on the horizon and our unfeasibly long lives – even what people want?

It seems that the answer, perhaps surprisingly, is yes, but with a pretty pronounced caveat: not at any cost. In the recent *LoveGeist Report 2009*, match.com found that 95 per cent of people wanted a long-term relationship.[66] Even allowing for a certain 'social desirability bias' (respondents skewing their answers to sound more appealing), these figures challenge the view that the net is full of 'players' and that men are 'four times more likely to be looking for no-strings sex than women'.[67] The *LoveGeist Report* only found 45 participants in their trawl of over 11,000 people who were explicitly *not* looking for long-term love.

Interestingly the survey suggested that it's not only the image of the HNG (Horny Net Guy) that we need to consign to the recycling-dump of history, but a raft of other outmoded stereotypes too. First up, the idea of women as fluffy romantic airheads who have overdosed on Mills and Boon and, in a state of romantic catatonia, await the coming of their one-and-only. The report found, in fact, that single men are far more classically 'romantic' and inclined to believe in 'the one' than women: 'They held a general belief that there would be one person with whom they would have a deeper connection over and above all possible others.' Women, both single and married, were more realistic and level-headed. Single women in the study's focus groups went so far as to say that they 'believed it was dangerous to think that there was just one person out there for them', and married women endorsed that view, saying that 'different people are right for different stages in their lives'.

The approach of 29-year-old north London teacher **sparklehorse** to online dating is about as far from gushing romanticism as you can get: 'I didn't think I was going to meet the love of my life on a dating website and I've never even had a romantic image of meeting "the one" anyway,' she says. 'I do have an idea that there's not just one person for everyone – I think in reality there are probably lots of people that any of us could be with. It's just about whose company you enjoy.' She took a supremely rational approach to the limitations of online dating from the start: rather than refining her 'preferences' infinitesimally to ask for the moon on a stick, she set them in a far more modest way. 'I think you'll never find anyone who ticks all your boxes, so in a way there's no point in having the boxes. But it is a good way of ruling out what you know you *don't* want,' she says. Her only absolute no-nos were smoking and religion, which she felt 'would be a barrier'. And she did insist that potential mates had to be based locally:

> I live in Kentish Town in north-west London. Central London was OK but south or south-west London was out. I always wanted to meet close to home so I wouldn't have far to travel. Because I wasn't taking it too seriously, I was quite laid back about it. I didn't want it to take an hour to get there or for it to be a big deal, because I might not care about them.

sparklehorse found that this even-keeled attitude led to appreciative and enjoyable encounters with 14 people she would not otherwise have met. 'It's actually really interesting to meet new people – it's a nice way of spending an hour or two,' she says.

The 15th person to contact her sounded promising. But there was a problem. 'Leon contacted me through the messaging system. When he told me he lived in Brixton, my initial reaction was, "He lives on the other side of London, and I can't be bothered!" But then he emailed that he worked in Archway, just two tube stops from Kentish Town, so I thought "all right"'. They exchanged just two emails before Leon suggested meeting for a drink. **sparklehorse** liked that: 'My theory is that you need to meet people. You can tell within an hour of meeting someone whether you're going to get on.' And they did. Really well.

> It was an easy, relaxed conversation, and quite funny and fast-paced. I liked the fact that he could change subjects and move on with ease. Afterwards he sent me a really long text message, three messages long, which I now know is not really like him. I thought, 'That's nice, he likes me too'.

Her response – in keeping with her anti-romantic courtship style – was rigorously low-key. She sent Leon a single text thanking him 'for a nice evening', which is what she did after every first date. No frills.

No hyperbole. 'I went with no expectations, so if I'd had a nice time, that was lovely.' Soon after that, they met again. After the second date, **sparklehorse** started to think that it might become more serious. Within a month they were in each other's company all the time.

Again and again, in this book and elsewhere, online daters show that they do, passionately seek romance: but they want to be *really* sure they've found it. Almost two thirds of the huge sample of women in the LoveGeist report (62 per cent) claimed to have become choosier about who they would date than they were last year, as did 43 per cent of men. It seems that these days we not only seek happiness, including the happiness of love, but that we regard it as an entitlement. Stacks of self-help books and therapeutic doctrines are geared to helping us find it. And online dating embodies the promise – in the words of Gaydar.com's homepage, 'What you want, when you want it' – that satisfaction is an achievable state.

We browse romantic possibilities, experimenting with different people and different types of relationship, in order better to know what we do and don't want. The dream of 'settling down one day' persists: but, like everything in our modern lives – childbirth, leaving home, marriage, retirement – it has been postponed to a later date, shunted further along the timescale of our lives. We postpone decisions about long-term relationships (the average age for women to marry now is 30, and for men, 32) for three reasons: because we can – our longevity sees to that; because we want to exercise our individual choice in the best way we can, to find quality; and because of our fear of 'failure'. There is a widespread lived experience in this country of the emotional fallout of the high rates of divorce during the 1970s and early 80s. According to the historian Stephanie Coontz in *Marriage: A History*, people who experienced divorce in the US at that time – either as children of divorcing parents or as spouses – do not want to relive the heartbreak and so avoid marriage altogether.[68] Britain now enjoys its lowest divorce rate since 1981; we also have the lowest rate of marriage since records began (despite over 50 per cent of people allegedly hoping to tie the knot[69]). The generational caution works both ways – people want to get it right as desperately as they don't want to get it wrong.

It is clear why, in this context, the internet has become *the* romance technology for our times – it seems to enable the browsing/research process that will find us the 'best', our 'perfect match', while reducing our chances of 'getting it wrong'. It does so by blending the two great traditions of partner-selection that the world has produced – the arranged marriage and the love-match – to come up with a third option.

For much of human history, even in the romantically-obsessed west, the blinding sexual hunger of people who have just fallen in love has been deemed the enemy of marriage. According to Coontz, 'For most of history it was inconceivable that people would choose their mates on the basis of something as fragile and irrational as love and then focus all their sexual, intimate, and altruistic desires on the resulting marriage'.[70] Many societies have frowned upon love in marriage. The 12th-century lover's manual, *The Art of Courtly Love*, argued that 'True love can have no place between husband and wife', and most nuptials in the West were arranged – by families and matchmakers – until the mid-18th century. And then a new form of marriage was born, which broke with thousands of years of tradition: the love-match. It was egalitarian and utopian, invented by English radicals at the time of the French Revolution. Over the next two centuries, this modern style of self-chosen partnership has been freighted with new cargoes – romance, politics and sex. *Et voila*: modern marriage.

Online dating puts the arranging back into the love partnership to form a unique third option, which could be called 'arranged romance'. The arranged romance dovetails the pragmatic values of traditional matchmaking with intangibles that were never part of matchmaking, but very much part of romantic love – compatibility and desire. People are choosing their partners not only on the basis of romantic love and sexual attraction, but in terms of a much broader compatibility. This is where online dating's 'preferences' come into their own.

There was no peculiarity for **sparklehorse** about meeting this way. 'It's natural that our generation dates online: we do everything else online. If you think of your grandparents, they used to go to dances:

that's how they did it in their day. It's better to be in control of finding someone yourself. You're your own matchmaker.'

It is the romantics' prejudice against matchmaking that underpins the last traces of squeamishness about online dating. It seems less spontaneous, more calculated, than accidental meetings in the flesh. There is nothing new in the disparagement of these digital classified ads. As HG Cocks has shown in *Classified*, his illuminating history of the personal ad, 'Ever since the 17th century, advertising for love has been accused of being cold and unromantic, calculating and even just plain sad, in spite of the fact that large numbers of people actually did it.'[71] There's an almost puritanical implication that it is somehow wrong to want to direct your life by putting yourself in the way of the greatest number of potential mates. As though you're disobeying the Fates, or some fundamental rule of nature; or being too presumptuous about the happiness you might be allowed.

In a witty article denouncing online dating, the Australian writer Bridgid Delaney claimed that while traditional dating is based on 'trusting the randomness of life', online dating is oppressively 'clinical' and mercantile.

> I'd rather ... love in the real world, taking chances, risks, trusting the randomness of life and the mysterious alchemy of serendipity than favour the clinical approach favoured by '1.3 million REAL singles!' casting a cool eye over photos and blurbs, shopping for a mate.[72]

It is alleged that the mechanical nature of online introductions is at odds with romance. But saying a love affair is unromantic just because it began on a website is like saying Lake Ullswater is less beautiful because you arrived there by car.

The people who have recounted their stories for this book, with such sincerity, grace and wit, have shown that the sometimes clunky process of mate-searching on the internet does not freeze human warmth, obstruct romance or crush spontaneous love. Their stories of meeting their life-partners online resonate with simple gratitude at the sweet music of chance. **MissJones**, 51, meeting the love of her life in her hometown of Wigan says:

> It's amazing to think that he was only a few miles away but I may never have met him. When we were young our paths may have crossed several times – at college, in any number of pubs in town, outside the Casino as he left the Saturday rock night and I waited for the Northern soul all-nighter to begin … We can't believe our luck.

There's a much messier element of serendipity to online dating than its critics might suggest (Will your one-and-only's subscription have ended the week you joined? Are you even on the right website?). What internet dating gives you is heightened serendipity – a few more hooks on which to snag chance. A number of contributors describe how they narrowly missed their future loves for years – uncannily failing to meet them, despite living in the next street or working in the same building – until they combed through their environment with an online search. As **PreachersSon** says:

> I was one of the first subscribers to Soulmates in 2004. Fortunately for me, so was a beautiful but overlooked (by all sensible men) woman under the moniker of **FestivalGirl**. Despite the fact that she was far cooler than me and that I failed her profile test, 'Applicant Must Be Able to Cook', she agreed to a date. And then another. And, heaven help her, she risked buying a house with me. We were married this summer. The twist in the tale is that **FestivalGirl** and I had worked at the same university since 1999 but never crossed paths. So Soulmates succeeded where our employer failed.

The romance between **ArtyTheatreBoy**, 34, and **Kizzy**, 36, was similarly hatched by chance. Without realising it, they were already connected at three degrees of separation before they met: **ArtyTheatreBoy**'s best friend was a mate of **Kizzy**'s friend. Yet it was unlikely that they would have met because they lived in different cities. Online dating placed them within reach of each other, allowing several coincidences to cascade. 'Slightly jaded' after a series of unsatisfying dates, **Kizzy** clicked on one of the random 'featured profiles' on Guardian Soulmates one evening, which belonged to the intriguing **ArtyTheatreBoy**, someone who would never have fulfilled her search criteria. It was the equivalent of the Lottery's Lucky Dip – a random digital encounter with someone she would not have looked for. Drawn to his 'witty, interesting, yet self-effacing' profile, she fired off a message. 'We very quickly found ourselves exchanging brilliant, well written and funny emails,' he says, 'or at least hers were – almost every day.' They lived two hours apart, but, thanks to a chain of gloriously unlikely coincidences that brought them to within five doors of each other, they met (see p. 139). The internet had reduced those three degrees of separation to one: 'I have quite by accident met my best friend and lover and lately now only really stop smiling to whisper silliness or steal magical kisses,' says **ArtyTheatreBoy**.

There is a sense that cyberdating can get to the parts that other forms of romantic introduction can't reach; and, in so doing, make relationships a possibility for many people who might otherwise have had to bow out of love. It has enabled many people in their 50s, 60s, 70s and 80s to find new partners – previously impossible because of the dearth of opportunities in a culture that caters to the young.

Scribulous had romance in her sights, but on her own terms:

> I had been looking, though not wholeheartedly, for a soulmate for a long time. I'm 68 and was not at all sure it could happen. On the other hand, I did have a romantic belief that there would be someone who could love me, adore me and value me, about whom I could feel the same. But was this an unrealisable fantasy and would I have to settle for much less? As well as fairly standard requirements (intelligent, funny and taller than me!) I knew my soulmate would need to be courageous and adventurous and up for challenges. Guys who are cautious, indecisive, risk-averse, conventional, inflexible and parsimonious are not for me. I also knew I wanted someone who was fully available for a relationship.

While she was uploading her profile to Guardian Soulmates, a 62-year-old man named **Volcano444**, who nursed a similar wish for a life-partner, had re-dedicated himself to the task. Having lost weight, got a new wardrobe and tried everything from dance clubs to speed-dating, he joined a few dating sites: 'I soon discovered that British women are between five and 10 years more youthful than their male counterparts, both in looks and physical activity. So I decided on younger man, older woman.' Setting his preferences accordingly, he found **Scribulous**, who lived just a mile from his home. In a short while they had fallen in love in a way neither had expected nor experienced before. 'I have been with my soulmate, who is six years older than me, for over two months and we just love one another to bits,' says an enraptured **Volcano444**. **Scribulous** is equally delighted: 'we would not have met without internet dating,' she says. The internet has created a new way of 'putting people in the way of each other', increasing the possibility of a serendipitous meeting. **sparklehorse** is similarly categorical: 'Leon was someone I would never have met otherwise – even though we've found that we have people in common. I would never have met him as he lived in Brixton and I never went there.'

So what exactly *are* the chances of finding love this way? In a which. co.uk survey in February 2009, 62 per cent of the 1,504 online daters questioned said that they found it easier to meet people through online dating than any other way. Nearly a fifth of them had either married someone they met online or knew someone who had. Those are not bad odds. But they do imply that four in five went home empty-handed. Not everyone will find 'the one'. Fortunately, the 'fusion of two souls for life' is not the only relationship model we have. We are now just as likely to believe in the two or the many, and our society no longer judges alternatives as harshly as it once did.

If online dating is a way of saying 'I'm doing it on my own terms', the stories in this chapter reveal a quiet rebellion against other people's attitudes and social norms, as well as the delighted joy of discovering love. This arranged romance is leading to all kinds of relationships: unions based on love, equality, friendship, mutual support and the willingness to accept difference. They are snapshots of our culture, little reminders of the diverse ways in which human love can be expressed.

There are gay people getting married for the first time, injecting romance into a ceremony that had become an irrelevant ritual for many heterosexuals; there are older people marrying again, for the second or third time, well into their 70s and 80s; there are younger people choosing every detail of their weddings for themselves; there are people in 'middle youth' planning the ethical basis of their commitment ceremonies, devising their own weddings and choosing which guests they will invite rather than following a pre-ordained list written by the hand of duty; there are people embracing relationships that are free of ceremony and ritual altogether. People are making choices under the own steam – shouldering the risks of individualism but the responsibilities too.

Thanks to the chance meeting enabled by online dating, and very much in the spirit of autonomous choice that governs it, the 15th person who arranged to meet **sparklehorse** for a date eventually became not just her friend and lover, but her husband:

> We got married in Middle Temple: we rented out the garden and the hall and had a humanist wedding. We wrote the ceremony, with our celebrants. It's nice to be under your own control, doing things the way you like, taking charge. That's how we met online – at our own pace and on our own terms – and that's how we got married.

My search is over:
The stories

Alias: **Starling** | *Age:* **67** | *F* | ♀♂ | **Guardian Soulmates**

Last year I tried Guardian Soulmates, met some interesting, though not compatible, men and gave up. This January, impelled by chill, post-Christmas loneliness, and not least by the three-day free offer,

I tried again. I wrote a new profile, recorded a message, searched others' profiles and contacted half a dozen. One I had ignored last year because, having had two sad encounters with men his age, I considered him too old; and also, because his life sounded so full, I couldn't imagine how I should fit in.

This time I carefully read his profile and something about his style attracted me: a certain directness, a full facing of the facts, an unabashed display of his interests, a brave optimism. In the meantime, he had suffered a serious accident, though he didn't say how he was now affected. Several replies came, but only Edward wrote emails with a lightness of humour that encouraged me. He asked for a picture, which, with the help of the plumber, I managed to take on my mobile. What fun to master new technologies – I had just bought the phone.

We agreed to meet after a few days of sight-unseen flirting (another first for both) but had to wait a week because I was snowed in. His straightforward disappointment was touching and I determined to catch a train, even if it meant a journey compounded by bus interludes. He was sitting near the entrance to the gallery, and at once I felt, he is possible – though how could I tell merely from his posture, since at that distance it was barely possible to see the details of his face? I went up to him and moved to kiss him, realised my mistake by his movement, and amended mine to a handshake.

We went to the gallery's restaurant and he objected to the table suggested by the waitress. Fussy? But her table wasn't well positioned, so a man who chooses soundly. What we talked about, I have no idea at all. Walking to the gallery rooms, I wanted to hold him and gave him my arm – purely because he walked with a limp and a stick, of course. I was alarmed by the strength of my need to hold him. I liked enormously what he said about the pictures. He had previously suggested I go home for supper, assuring me the lodger would act as duenna, and now I did not hesitate.

I liked his house straight away: plainly beautiful, practical and modern. We had a wonderful supper prepared by 'the duenna', a lovely Spanish woman, but not before, goodness knows how, we were kissing – at which point she returned unobserved to the kitchen. I could not stay until the next night, by which time we had met both our daughters. I carried my case straight up to the bedroom. He had expected me to use the spare – but said he was delighted by such confidence. He asked me to move in, and I stayed, leaving the old house I had not dreamt of ever leaving.

Now, after seven months, I am ready to sell it, and at last I don't feel as though I am not living in a real world any more: my new life seems normal and I feel at home here. A country woman, I have become a townswoman, my dog and I have found walks, and we play in the parks. I live with someone who knows what I am talking about, who has read the same books, who has interests close to mine. Each of us has a range of experiences beyond these, which it is both exciting and peaceful to share; and we have hobbies and talents in common, to practise together. I find this love miraculous, immediately recognised and maintained as if somehow mysteriously resumed.

Edward invited his friends to a party and I was impressed by how delightful they were, and amazed by not being terrified of all the entertaining. Wanting our families to be in favour of our union, we visited each of our children and others important to us very carefully. One daughter, who had cared for her parents throughout her mother's last illness and then him through that terrible accident, found it difficult to accept someone new, but his family meet and talk often, and by the time we married, she was Best Woman and gave such a loving speech we are still moved to tears each time we read it – now in a wedding book given by one of my sons.

Reader, I married him – five months after we met, in a ceremony beautifully conducted by the registrar, a perfect blend of dignity and friendliness. When I entered the room with my son, we were as if bathed in a warm rush of the family's well-wishing enthusiasm. During these months, my dear husband has learnt to walk without his stick, and has restarted his voluntary work. Together we total 150 years and our love is passionate and a delight.

Alias: **SlightlyDishevelled** | *Age:* **35** | *F* | ♀♂ | **Guardian Soulmates**

Avoiding all the joyless dullards who cited sarcasm as being unattractive, I stumbled across Spike418, who had possibly the worst profile I've ever seen: three sentences at best and no photo.

Inexplicably, we embarked on an email correspondence, which morphed, swiftly, from my offering to be his dating guru (as I was dallying with another Soulmate at the time and had only logged back in to cancel my subs) into a literary courtship that would have put Elizabeth Barrett and Robert Browning to shame.

Four consecutive evenings of two-hour phone calls ensued, and our first date, on Friday, August 18 2006, lasted for three days.

We were, somewhat recklessly, living together within a couple of months, and we threw caution to the wind a year down the line and demonstrated our intention of a lifetime's commitment by merging our extensive vinyl (albums, not fetish clobber) collection.

Three (enthusiastically hedonistic) years later and it's bordering on nauseating the extent to which my family and friends revere the Big Man. Possibly relief, now that the underlying fear they'd have to deal with me as a caustic, aging spinster, spewing bile from my Shackletons high-seater and smelling faintly of wee, in my dotage, has finally been assuaged.

And so I thank you. My Plus One is taken.

Alias: **Kizzy** | *Age:* **36** | *F* | ♀♂ | **Guardian Soulmates**

Having been on Guardian Soulmates for nearly three months, I was starting to become slightly jaded with so-so dates, promising (but false) starts, and 'matches' not even matching up to their own profile, never mind anything else. Was I being too picky, too impatient or just looking in the wrong place? My subscription was due to expire shortly but I resolved to have one last blast, so arming myself with a glass of Pinot Noir, I fired up the laptop to peruse Guardian Soulmates' latest offerings.

As I logged on, one of the random 'featured profiles' on my homepage caught my eye and I duly clicked on his face. Alex would never have featured on my searches due to being an inch shorter than me, living outside my 'catchment area' and wanting kids (an option that I'd never really been able to envisage). Nevertheless, Artytheatreboy promised to be 'entirely creative, a little bit quirky and above all genuine'. This, along with a witty, interesting, yet self-effacing profile led me to bite the bullet and send what I hoped was a suitably pithy email into the ether.

What followed was an intense week of email tennis. And if the result wasn't yet love, it was certainly a promising match. Coincidentally I was attending a party in his hometown the following weekend, but in a cruel twist of fate he had plans to be in London, so I resolved to put him to the back of my mind and enjoy the weekend. At said party, my resolve weakened and I succeeded in boring my host rigid; waxing lyrical about this remarkable creature and how I fervently hoped the reality was as wonderful as the emails promised. It turned out that not only was she friends with him (and mercifully able to provide a glowing accolade), but he lived round the corner AND she had his mobile number.

Emboldened by Bobby Booze, I gave Alex a ring to impart the news of this amazing coincidence. He shared my childish jubilation, and to cap it all, his London plans had fallen through and he was back at home. After what must have been nano-seconds of deliberation, I invited him round to share some of the takeaway we'd ordered and five minutes later, he had somehow managed to intercept the delivery man and was standing on the doorstep with a bottle of fine wine and a pile of pizzas!

'The Domino's Effect' was instant, and within hours we were drinking champagne in his garden, celebrating the existence of ballet flats, naming our babies, and dismissing the two-hour difference between our homes as a mere glitch. We are totally besotted in a way that neither of us had hitherto thought possible, and spend every conceivable moment together.

Alias: **MarmiteLover** | *Age:* **61** | *F* | ♀♂ | **Meetic**

After 11 years alone, bringing up three children in France, I had an empty nest, and so I decided that it was time to take my single life in hand. In a determined gesture to broaden my horizons I signed on to Meetic. Of course I had the usual expectations – tall, handsome with tons of humour and buckets of money – but to these I needed to add a further condition: potentially successful candidates needed to know who or what were Monty Python, Shakespeare, Marmite and/or Rose's Lime Juice. This tactic was a feeble ruse on my part to limit French male candidates in general without running the risk of accusations of xenophobia. Why was I so keen to avoid a Frenchman? Because I'd already been married to two Frenchmen. This time I was determined to seek out an Anglophone – someone who spoke my language and understood my culture and, in particular, the English sense of humour.

For six months I applied myself diligently to the task of finding Mr Right. I answered sweetly and politely to the various 'impossibles', and I remained steadfast on the Anglophone decision, although it didn't seem to be bearing any fruit. Finally, a certain Charles Grant signed on. We chatted online and after prolonged phone calls decided to stop funding the mobile phone companies and meet. What a surprise! The English-sounding name was a pseudonym, and the very slight accent that I had detected on the telephone turned out to be French! Despite all my endeavours, I had found myself another Frenchman. By now I was hooked, however, so regardless of the treachery, I decided that this handicap could be overlooked since we happily discovered, miracle of miracles, that he liked both my bad French grammar and Marmite! It was a joy to be able to chat in my mother tongue with Charles and to eat Marmite on toast without being considered deviant. He is a huge fan of many of the great British comedy series, and I think he will soon be ready for a dose of the *Goon Show*.

However, elation at our compatibility was soon followed by despair, when he revealed that he was shortly to leave on a six-month expedition to the sub-Antarctic French island of Kerguelen. I had just met him, and now he was disappearing to the end of the world! But then, as if it was the most natural thing in the world, he asked me to go with him.

It was an act of folly. The journey there was an adventure. Kerguelen, which is 13,000 kilometres from mainland France and 3,000 kilometres from the overseas French *département* of La Réunion, is accessible only by sea. We had to navigate both the Roaring Forties and the Furious Fifties (the latitudes, not our ages – he was past 60 when we met, and I was almost there). The climate was inhospitable, and apart from the small team of scientists there to carry out scientific research, the rest of the population were penguins. The trip was filled with mishaps, some life-threatening, but we did get to know how each other functioned, and I did see how well Charles handled scary situations.

At home six months later, we decided that nothing much worse could happen to us and saw no reason not to get married. As a sexagenarian, have I learned anything about what makes a relationship work or how to find the perfect partner? I have no advice to offer, but I do think it's important that you have plenty of things in common, that you can converse easily with each other, that you look at the world in the same way and that you can laugh together. Going to the Antarctic is as optional as Marmite.

Alias: **Blushes** | *Age:* **41** | *F* | ♀♀ | **gaydargirls.co.uk**

Having explored, through my computer in London, the highways and byways of gay.com in Canada and the US, I went to a new chat room in 2005, gaydargirls.co.uk. The site attracts a lot of people who are not out, where a need for discretion is vitally important, as I wrote on my profile. Joining a gay British website potentially meant taking more risks in terms of my cover being blown, but I desperately wanted – and was ready for – a relationship.

gaydargirls.co.uk was then mostly London-based, and I met loads of interesting Londoners almost as soon as I went on the site. Among them were an eco-terrorist called TunnelVision, who was extremely funny online, and a civil servant who worked for the Department of Education and whose photo on her profile was of a female Che Guevara, which instantly won me over. I arranged to meet her for coffee, but when I saw her cycling towards me I thought, 'Oh Lord! This is not the revolutionary babe I was expecting!' We had a drink, however, and she turned out to be a nice, decent person. She invited me to a party at the home of a minister she was house-sitting for and asked me to invite a few of the people I'd been chatting to on gaydargirls.co.uk and felt I could trust. So I winked at a few regulars I knew, some of whom TunnelVision had also been chatting to, including someone who had uploaded a surfboard as her main profile photo. Absolutely nothing attracted me about this woman's profile, and the surfboard made me think 'What an idiot!'

Surf-girl was surprised I had winked at her. She later told me that she found my profile intimidating and would never have contacted me, but my wink encouraged her. We started talking online over the next few days, and I found her more and more intriguing. She was a Cypriot, finishing her law masters degree at the same university I had gone to, and she knew some of my old professors. I decided I wasn't going to invite her to the party after all: I had no intention of sharing her with anyone.

I was planning to play it cool and meet a couple of other women I had met online first, when Surf-girl emailed to say that she was going away to Lyons for a month and was leaving in two days' time. Now, a month in cyberdating is the equivalent of a year in the real world because of the intensity and speed of online communications. But I was working in Birmingham that day, and the day after that I had to go to Manchester. Our only hope was a brief encounter at Waterloo station on the morning she had to leave, just before her train left for France. She was waiting for me under the station clock at 8.30. We had only spoken on the phone, and I hadn't seen her photo, but she said it would be easy to identify her: her arm would be in a sling.

As soon as I saw her I decided I was definitely going to sleep with her. That thought was first and foremost in my mind. It had been such a long time, and she had a great figure, an enchanting smile, and she was tender and strong. Despite her broken arm, she was so full of life. She kept smiling and looking at me as if she was searching my soul. Within 10 minutes I was completely captivated. We talked about her trip, her studies and then, quite suddenly, she said she would take a later train, even though she needed to catch a connecting train in Paris. I persuaded her to go, promising to meet her the day after her return. In that short time I experienced a quality of attention and devotion that few people are ever able to give. She made me feel that I was the most important person in the world.

For our second date we met in a café at noon and parted at 11pm. A few days later I met her for the weekend at her house, and we made love for the first time. After that we just couldn't keep away from each other, and I knew she would be significant in my life. She asked me to break off contact with everyone I'd met through Gaydar and gay.com, and although that seemed a bit drastic I agreed, because by that stage I realised I had found the love of my life. Our meeting was entirely thanks to the internet, and it's unlikely we would have met any other way. Our only common ground was the university, but I rarely went back and anyway, I wouldn't have known she was gay.

She is the only person in my entire life with whom I have felt totally safe. And – who knows? – with her beside me, I may one day be able to express my sexuality with as much freedom and joy in the public world as I have done in the virtual one.

Alias: **BrownEyesBlue** | *Age:* **46** | *M* | ♀♂ | **Guardian Soulmates**

My friend Xiao Ming eventually badgered me into trying online dating. 'Everyone in Hong Kong does it – it's normal,' he said. I'd written a glowing testimonial for a friend on one website. He met someone shortly afterwards, and I didn't hear from him again. That's been a year now. In five years of being single I'd grown accustomed to my own company and enjoyed my way of life, but I felt there was something missing. As a man in my mid-40s, the only women I met these days were in off-licences, supermarkets and petrol stations.

'Oh all right then,' I said. The first night I put my profile up I watched amazed as a torrent of emails landed in my inbox, most from women 10 years older than me. I decided to play myself in, check the profiles of all the women I liked and not make any rash moves. I started a series of email conversations with a couple of women, and I resolved to meet one or two. I was so nervous on my first date that I nearly bolted. I went for a walk in the country with my second date but never heard anything afterwards. For the third date I sipped lemonade in a beer garden while a woman in her early 40s told me how teaching English abroad had left her sidelined and isolated when she came back. The fourth was a reiki masseur who was five days younger than me, not five years, as she'd stated in her details. I didn't care – these weren't the important details. My fifth date, an English teacher abroad, wrote me a series of beautiful and witty emails, but when we met she became extremely bossy and spent all the time complaining about the ex-pat community in Oman.

I had to go to Manhattan to work for a week, so I thought this would be a good time to take a break and take stock. They were all nice women, but none of them was right for me. I particularly didn't want to be bossed about. As I walked down Broadway, I decided that I'd have a rest from the whole idea. Standing in front of the Flatiron I told myself that I'd given it a go and it hadn't worked out. My life wasn't that bad, for God's sake!

Towards the end of the week in New York I noticed I'd been made a favourite by a woman who seemed a little different from the others.

She was pretty, worked at the university and had a foster son with whom she enjoyed singing songs and playing football.

'Hi. Your profile looks good and you seem very interesting,' I wrote. 'I'm in America at the moment. Could we meet up when we get back? It looks like you live near me.'

She answered: 'Thanks for getting in touch. Aren't we supposed to email each other for a while and then decide?'

If I had turned my head from where I was sitting, I could have seen the Chrysler Building. There was an air of unreality about this whole experience. 'Yes, but you never really know whether you like someone until you meet them,' I wrote. 'I don't want to email you for weeks and then be disappointed. Can't we just meet?'

The email went quiet. I went to Long Island for the day, where Carole King wrote 'Will You Still Love me Tomorrow?' When I got back there was an email from her. 'OK, I'll meet you,' she wrote.

When I got back to England we exchanged numbers and met outside a bar not far from her house. The conversation unfolded to a point where I found myself thinking: 'I like this girl. I want to see her again.' As we gathered our things to leave, I heard myself saying those words – and then hoping really hard she'd agree.

'All right. Why not?' she said.

I walked away, my heart leaping. I wanted to punch the air! And I may have done, once I was out of sight. What to do next? I had no idea. But sometimes you have to take a leap in the dark. And in three weeks' time we – me, her and her foster son – celebrate a year together. Last week Xiao Ming came for the weekend. As the three of us walked him back to the railway station, she took him to one side: 'Thanks for making him take the leap,' she said.

Alias: **RaspberryJam** | *Age:* **51** | *F* | ♀♂ | **datetheuk.com**

My 'new' husband and I met online, admittedly on a fairly raunchy site, but from there we quickly moved on to instant messaging and eventually phone calls.

I had been on my own with two sons for a few years and felt that I was recovered enough from a difficult split with their father to move on in my life and seek a new man. My date was from North America but had relocated to a remote part of the Scottish mainland, and although we lived 150 miles apart, in his opinion we were neighbours.

Both of us had had various dalliances with others we had met online, but when he finally came to visit me it was love at first sight. We got on so well within minutes and were hugely entertained by each other within the hour, and during that first evening both of us dared at last to hope that this time the chemistry was great and we might have a future.

The long-distance relationship was difficult to maintain, but reunions were particularly sweet. We got married at midsummer last year and there is no looking back.

Alias: **PlusOne** | *Age:* **39** | *F* | ♀♂ | **Guardian Soulmates**

Our first date was lovely: very polite, lots of getting-to-know-you chit-chat in at first a terrible bar and then a lovely pub. No kissing.

For our second date I had VIP tickets for the Kaiser Chiefs so I took him along. Chaste peck on cheek on the tube on our (separate) way home.

Our third date was, quite frankly, a bootie call. We started off with texts that got more cheeky as the evening went on. Then we had a polite phone call that got suggestive but was quite tame. Then at 2am I got a text from Rob telling me that he was still awake and I was doing 'bad' things to his head. Further increasingly filthy phone calls followed. At 3am I told him to get his backside over to my place, and although he lived nearly 20 miles away across London he arrived at 4am. It was hot! We were both grinning for the rest of the week.

That was two years ago. We're still together, are buying a home with each other and still love bootie calls.

Alias: **LadyDooLittle** | *Age:* **30** | *F* | ♀♂ | **Guardian Soulmates**

This story is about a very important man in my life: my wonderful dad. Shortly after breaking up with my mum, my dad – lost and lonely – decided to find a partner in cyberspace. I had visions of it all going terribly wrong and worried that he would perhaps forget to admit the 'bald' part of his profile or would end up with a money-grabber who would then discover that my wildlife-loving dad loves to pick mushrooms in the woods not just because they taste better, but because they are free (only joking, Dad – you're not quite that bad, but nearly!) After a few rocky dates – one even tried to sign me up for two years voluntary service overseas – he found the most amazing and wonderful lady ever.

Now, seven years down the line, they are married, and Joanna is helping me plan my own wedding next year. I couldn't have hoped for a happier happy ever after for my dad.

Alias: **Gumdrop** | *Age:* **30** | *M* | ♂♂ | **Gaydar**

My partner and I met on the internet seven years ago. I had decided that I was going to become a playboy and not look for anything serious, and I was quite sceptical when I heard about internet dating. However, I thought I would give it a go.

My first message was ignored, but on a second attempt (when I was a bit tipsy) I got a reply, and we agreed to meet. We exchanged photos. I think our profile names had a lot to do with the initial contact. I was Gumdrop (sad), and he was Trooper (I had visions of a rugged army type, but it was actually a reference to Abba). I was really scared and used my restaurant as a meeting point, getting one of the staff to pretend to be me so that I would have a way out if necessary. But I had no need to worry as we got on like wild fire. That evening we eventually moved home to listen to music and to have some coffee.

The next morning he returned to my house to help me fix the windows – I was renovating the house at the time – and we have never looked back. The funny thing is that we lived only about half a mile apart and we knew a lot of the same people, and moved in very similar circles, but we had never met.

Alias: **BarneyStubble** | *Age:* **30** | M | ♀♂ | **Loopy Love**

Eleven long years ago I calmly entered my debit card details on to a medium-sized dating site. The months pass quickly, and you can't look your bank clerk in the face any more because the repeated references to dating on your statement make you feel cheap and, in all honesty, a bit sad. Typical quiet evenings would be spent writing thoughtful prose to those few women I found interesting and who were interested in me. Internet dating became like another job, only one that didn't pay and, indeed, cost me money.

Meetings would be arranged. Sometimes no one would show up – perhaps they were hiding somewhere deciding that anyone who wore a shirt like that was not for them? I had dates with married women, soon-to-be-married women and, in one case, a man who 'kindly' turned up for drinks as his friend – my date and a woman – could not make it.

Year 8, month 99, day 3,010, several brief flirtations with online dating later and something changed. As the Disney song does not quite go, 'Some Day my Princess will Come'. And she did.

Alias: **VitaminD** | *Age:* **30** | *M* | ♂♂ | **Faceparty**

I understood what love really was when I met Fergus. We met online and we've been together ever since. The internet seemed like the perfect way for a non-gay gay to meet other non-gay gays. By non-gay gay I mean the kind of gay man who doesn't conform to the pink-wearing-poodle-flouncing-queen stereotype that props up many glittery, Abba-filled gay clubs across the country. Contrary to popular belief, I thinks it's fair to say that most gay men are non-gay gays. Or at least, they'd all like to think so. So it seemed the best way for me to find a non-gay gay without actually having to experience the camp exuberance of the gay scene was to use the internet. Surely I can't be the only gay man out there that doesn't like Kylie?

Thank god I was right! The internet was teeming with gay people from all sorts of walks of life and persuasions, and it wasn't long before I was looking at profiles and checking out pictures. Fergus caught my eye because his online profile made me laugh. One of his likes was something along the lines of 'I like to throw peanuts at old ladies.' He didn't look like a typical OAP hustler. In fact he was hot! Profile photos included a number of gorgeous buff topless shots, which were the cherry on the cake. I sent a message, and we exchanged emails that were always daft and made me chuckle.

I found out that he was the manager of a pub, and after a few weeks of messages and swapping photos we decided it would be good to meet. To defuse any awkwardness, I said I'd bring a couple of mates along and just have a drink while he was working.

A couple turned into five, and I'll never forgot the look on his face when we turned up.

Nevertheless, we started dating and hit it off instantly. After a year or so together we watched the film *Amélie*, and he nearly fell over when I said I'd never seen it. To this day I have no idea why I lied on my profile about it being my favourite film. I think I just filled it in quickly, and it was the first film I thought of. Thankfully, it was one of his favourites, and my white lie may just be one of the reasons our profiles seemed to match so perfectly. Within the first week of meeting I knew I loved him. Internet dating wasn't as bad as I'd thought.

Alias: **MissJones** | *Age:* **51** | *F* | ♀♂ | **Guardian Soulmates**

David had never tasted an olive until he met me. I'd never listened to a Patti Smith record until I met him. He was 'Because the night ...'; I was 'Miss Jones'. We met through Guardian Soulmates in May 2007 – on May 6, to be precise – and we've never looked back.

I'd had my profile on the site for a few months, had chatted to several men and even had a couple of dates. David had never used a dating site before and looked out of curiosity. I don't know what made him look at Soulmates, but he saw my photograph, read my profile and paid for three days' subscription. And that was it.

He told me later that only minutes after he'd posted his profile a Russian woman wearing a pink cowboy hat had looked at his profile, which scared him a little. We started chatting, first using Soulmates, then in private emails, and then on the phone. Then he suggested that we should meet. All that happened within a week. I told this complete stranger almost everything about me, and it didn't feel in the least bit strange.

I'm from Wigan – home of the Casino, Wigan Warriors, Stuart Maconie and the Verve. He's from Lowton, just a few miles down the road, home town of the female Ting Ting. We arranged to meet in front of the town hall. A friend dropped me off, and I knew within five minutes of meeting David that this one was different. We met again the next night and have been together ever since. I immediately felt comfortable with him: he was interested in me, and I felt no need to impress. I just knew. Instinct, I suppose. In less than a week he told me he loved me, and I had to say that I felt the same. I knew then that everything was going to be OK.

It's amazing to think that he lived only a few miles away from me, but I might never have met him. When we were young our paths may have crossed several times: at college, in any number of pubs in town, outside the Casino as he left the Saturday rock night while I waited for the northern soul all-nighter to begin. We are 50 and 51 and have both previously been in long marriages. We can't believe our luck. We are constantly learning new things about one another and so it follows, about ourselves. Cheers!

Alias: **Sufjan** | *Age:* **27** | *M* | ♂♂ | **Guardian Soulmates**

I recently met the man of my dreams – he is everything I could have wished for. I met Mr ILikeCycling in January after emailing for a month, and I am pleased to say that we are now boyfriend and boyfriend and very happy. He did like cycling, but now he likes me!

Alias: **tigerseye** | *Age:* **54** | *F* | ♀♀ | **Guardian Soulmates**

Twelve dates later and a few hundred pounds lighter, I was feeling somewhat jaded by the whole internet dating experience. A friend of mine once said: 'You have to kiss a lot of frogs before you find your princess', and I have certainly experienced a few close encounters in my search.

Take the antipodean academic, who turned up on a date drunk from too much champagne, don't you know; who tripped and fell head-first in the restaurant, cut her shin open and exposed her bloody leg to all and sundry for the rest of the evening, and who, on our third date – I know, I am forgiving – wanted to become my lodger. G'day!

Then there was the elusive blonde from Hackney, accessorised with Jackie Onassis sunglasses, whose photograph was taken down a darkened alley (I should have known better). She ended up pinning me to my own kitchen sink. Oh, and the policewoman who couldn't leave her husband and talked nonstop about the two younger women she was proudly seeing at the same time.

As time has passed, I have despaired at the let's-meet-up women who cancel, the yes-I-am-available women who nevertheless cry through the date because they miss their exes, the incessant-emailing women who never want to meet up and finally the let's-meet-up-but-have-I mentioned-I-am-slightly-mad? women. I have met a few lovely women along the way too, but the chemistry just wasn't there: and no matter how you try, chemistry cannot just be conjured up.

So there I was, thinking 'No more! I cannot go on, I'm going to delete my profile', when you emailed me. And I can honestly say, perseverance is the key word. I succumbed, renewed my subscription and met you in a local bar. You were my 13th date. My heart missed a beat, because there and then I knew you were the one: funny, attractive, articulate, intelligent and kind. I knew when I left that night that I had to see you again. And some months on – some very pleasurable months on – we are completely and utterly captivated by each other.

Alias: **MZEE** | *Age:* **83** | *M* | ♀♂ | **Guardian Soulmates**

A few days ago I read a year-old copy of *G2*. The cover story was by a grandmother describing her Soulmate experiences: the men she had met or had avoided. Although she failed to find a soulmate, her anecdotes were told with wit and style. My experience has ended so blissfully different from hers that I must write it down.

For a year I logged on regularly and met a number of pleasant, intelligent women, some of whom seemed promising and with one of whom I had a lively affair. I learnt two aspects of online dating. First, people who use Soulmates, unsurprisingly, read the *Guardian* and have similar attitudes to life – most profiles were by non-smokers who drink in moderation and prefer classical music to pop. Second, for the elderly seeking a soulmate there is the problem that most have houses, flats or cottages full of a lifetime's habits and material goods, which are difficult to move, discard or even sort into piles for Oxfam when one or the other decides to move in with their new mate.

This January, near the end of my year, I came across a profile of a grandmother who lived in the country, far from my London home, without a photograph but with a voice message, so I telephoned. She was snowed in, so meeting in person had to be delayed. There was a magic in her voice, and we swapped addresses and phone numbers. Over the following week we exchanged emails, phone calls and texts, becoming increasingly friendly as the days went by. When later we read and counted them, our exchanges were often two or three times a day. At the end of that week we met for lunch at Tate Britain and both found, at first sight, that there were no further questions to be asked or answered. The mutual recognition we felt at that moment was extraordinary and absolute.

As I had a lodger in the house (who also cooked the supper), I invited, like a male bowerbird, my putative soulmate home that evening, and later reluctantly took her back to her friend's flat. The lodger has insisted that when she came out of the kitchen she was surprised to find us in a warm embrace on the Barcelona chairs: to us there was no surprise because it seemed normal and necessary to be kissing a few hours after meeting. We met for lunch again the following day and came home that evening with her case. As she unpacked in the big bedroom, AS Byatt's *Possession* appeared on both sides of the bed, and identical mobile phones. Later we found that much of our domestic equipment was the same make (except where hers was better). Reading the same book and having similar tastes isn't essential, but it did reinforce the feeling that our meeting had a magical quality.

That first lunch was seven months ago, seven months in which we haven't been apart, and in which neither of us has wondered for a moment if we were being sensible. As we settle in as a couple, exploring our backgrounds, we discover similar interests, in spite of living on different continents for most of our lives and training in different disciplines: she studied psychology and philosophy, while I am an architect, passionate about painting and sculpture. It was some time before I discovered that my soulmate's second degree was in art, which explained her erudite comments, which I had assumed were simply because she is both sensitive and very intelligent. Whatever the reasons, we have great fun looking and talking about everything, including work in the Tate.

For a couple with 150 years between them, there are children and adult grandchildren to be told, hoping that they approve and understand the strength of our love for one another. My children are at the stage of life when they are bracing themselves for unexpected announcements from their young, so they were surprised and a bit shocked by their elderly parent's absolute resolve to share his life with someone whom he had only recently met. They also had memories of being brought up as part of a very happy marriage lasting over 50 years, but they soon recognised the qualities of my soulmate and came to understand and appreciate my love for her.

Five months after that first lunch we were married, surrounded by our children and grandchildren, and we continue to live a blissful life. Although they can see how happy we are, it doesn't seem appropriate to explain to our children how very un-platonic our life is – perhaps we are bodynsoulmates.

And Oxfam? My wife, finding ample green space – common, park and towpath for walking her (our) Labrador in this part of London – has decided to sell her house in the country: Oxfam is gaining a good deal of stuff, this house is fuller than it was and we still have some sorting to do. Among the papers she brought from the country was the year-old copy of *G2*, which she acknowledged as her story from another time and another life.

Winners and runners-up

WINNERS

SaucyPedant, page 57

Rebecca_01, page 82

Freudianslip, page 84

Upgrade, page 111

Marie_Mint, page 114

AliceInWonderland, page 131

ArtyTheatreBoy, page 139

Jiri, page 145

Global_Gadabout, page 167

Ms_E, page 169

Starling, page 223

RUNNERS-UP

AudreyB, page 31

Lorimer, page 59

Miss_Conduct, page 89

sugar_hiccup, page 96

SoSueMe, page 126

AliceInWonderland, page 141

RedAdmiral, page 144

Annie611, page 173

GrammarSchoolGirl, page 175

MZEE, page 240

Dating in numbers

31 rules were listed in *The Art of Courtly Love*, a 12th-century book detailing the principles of upper-class love. 'True love can have no place between husband and wife,' it proclaimed, showing that weddings were generally business arrangements between families, while romance occurred outside of marriage through discreet, covert meetings – the true predecessors of today's dates.

24 was the average age for a person to get married in 1851. It stayed more or less stable, even falling slightly during the 1950s, before gradually rising to the current average of 29.

15 million people in the UK are currently estimated to be single.

Half of these people are looking for a long-term relationship.

75 per cent of them have not had a relationship for more than 18 months.

Four is the average number of dates each of them will have in one year.

One in four people don't brush their teeth before a date.

43 per cent of people Google their first date before they meet them.

Lambeth in south London has the UK's highest percentage of single people.

Glasgow has the greatest deficit of males compared with females, while Reading has the greatest deficit of females.

4.7 million people in the UK have visited a dating website in the past year.

One-third of online dating users admit to lying in their profile.

One in five married individuals aged between 19 and 25 met their spouse online.

Half of all British men claim to be held back in their love lives by a lack of confidence (making them the least confident men in Europe).

88 per cent of women aren't bothered by baldness in a man.

3 per cent of those looking for a serious relationship will send a follow-up text immediately after a first date.

One in five people marry a co-worker.

Half of all workplace romances are over within three months.

30 per cent of relationships are ended face to face.

Notes

INTRODUCTION

1   '7.8 million UK singles logged on to find love in 2007', study by parship.
    co.uk, January 18 2008.
2   'Be lucky in love online', *Which?* survey of 1,504 people who had used an
    online dating site in the 12 months preceding January 2009.
3   Oxford Internet Institute study cited in 'We Just Clicked', the *Independent*,
    October 3 2009.
4   Theodore Zeldin *An Intimate History of Humanity* (Vintage: London, 1995).
5   'Credit crunches Cupid's arrow – UK singles spend £11.5 billion looking for
    love', study by parship.co.uk, July 21 2008.
6   Rufus Griscom, 'Why are online personals so hot?' in *Wired*, Issue 10,
    November 11 2002.
7   'According to Nielsen/Net ratings, match.com ranks second after Yahoo!
    Personals with 15 million members globally ... Th eir most diverse
    demographic is the senior group which accounts for 20 per cent of its users.'
    Raphaela Fischer, 'Game Just Got Hotter', onlinepersonalswatch.com,
    November 11 2008.
8   Carolyn Duffy Marsan, 'The Hottest Trends in Online Dating', *Network
    World*, February 7 2008.
9   Carrie Kirby, 'Out Th ere With Online Media: Gays and lesbians gain
    individual and collective strength from the internet', *San Francisco Chronicle*,
    June 23 2000.
10 Anupam G Mittal, interview by Mark Brooks, onlinepersonalswatch.com,
    August 11 2009.
11 'Online retailers "becoming more popular" than High Street shops', the
    Telegraph, March 30 2009.
12 HG Cocks, *Classified: Th e Secret History of the Personal Column* (Random
    House: London, 2009).
13 'The Marriage Market', the *Guardian*, 1964.
14 'Jupiter Research predicts that the number of paying members using online
    dating sites will increase from 2.6 million in 2006 to 6 million by 2011,
    creating annual revenues of more than £350m', 'Business Truth: Online
    dating', the *Telegraph*, December 5 2008.

CHAPTER ONE

15 '7.8 million UK singles logged onto find love in 2007', study by parship.
    co.uk, January 18 2008.

16 The response of NATFHE, the union of lecturers working in further, adult and higher education, to consultation 'Equality & Diversity: Age Matters' in 2003. 'Adult Education, for so long one of the glories of this country's education system, is being decimated. Th e hundreds of adult education lecturers who are being made redundant up and down the country this Autumn can bear bitter testimony to this fact.'

17 'Raw Dater' in *The Guardian Guide to Dating*, the *Guardian*, January 24 2009.

18 38 per cent of Britons work Saturdays against the EU average of 25 per cent (27 per cent of British people work Sundays against 15 per cent EU average and 13 per cent work nights versus 9 per cent EU average). 'Extended and Unusual Working Hours in European Companies, 2004-2005' *Eurofound*, May 14 2007.

19 Harry Wallop 'A quarter of British families will have no disposable income in 2009', the *Telegraph*, January 5 2009.

20 'Fate of the First Date ... The ex, lies and even pets on a first date', study by parship.co.uk, May 29 2009.

21 'The hottest trends in online dating', interview with Mark Brooks, editor of onlinepersonalswatch.com by Carolyn Duffy Marsan, *Network World*, February 7 2008.

22 'The LoveGeist Report 2009' by Dr Monica Whitty and Dr Tom Buchanan for match.com. Copyright Match International 2009.

23 'The hottest trends in online dating', interview with Mark Brooks, editor of onlinepersonalswatch.com by Carolyn Duffy Marsan, *Network World*, February 7 2008.

24 'The hottest trends in online dating', interview with Mark Brooks, editor of onlinepersonalswatch.com by Carolyn Duffy Marsan, *Network World*, February 7 2008.

CHAPTER TWO

25 Barclay Barrios speaking in 'Queerness, sexuality, technology and writing: How do queers write ourselves when we write in cyberspace?' Online conversation between a group of academics, www.acadianamoo.arthmoor. com/cuppa, January 21 2004.

26 Robert Epstein 'The Truth about Online Dating' in *Scientific American Mind*, February 2007.

CHAPTER THREE

27 The optimum length, the researchers found, for a first message sent by a man to a woman is around 700 words, according to OKCupid.com's research which sampled anonymous messages sent through its site. For women emailing men, the shortest messages fared best: the reply rate actually decreases when the messages were longer. Th e study concluded that messages longer than about 360 words (1,800) characters) actually

started scaring some people off. 'Online Dating Advice: Optimum Message Length and Exactly What to Say in a First Message', OkTrends, Official Blog of OKCupid.com, September 3 2009.

28 Rufus Griscom, 'Why are online personals so hot?' in *Wired*, issue 10, November 11 2002.

CHAPTER FOUR

29 'Britain's singles now prefer slow dating to speed dating', study by parship. co.uk, January 19 2009.

30 Kira Cochrane 'Should I follow any rules?', the *Guardian*, January 24 2009.

31 Study by parship.co.uk.

32 Theodore Zeldin p. 119.

33 Cited in Theodore Zeldin p. 119.

34 Study by parship.co.uk.

35 Study by parship.co.uk.

36 Dr Monica Whitty, Dr Tom Buchanan and Angus Watson, 'The LoveGeist Report 2009', match.com.

37 Barry Schwartz, *The Paradox of Choice: Why More if Less* (Harper Perennial: New York, 2005), pp. 77–9, 225–6.

38 Amy Eisinger, 'Too much of a good thing? Study finds online daters choose wrong people due to "cognitive overload"', *NY Daily News*, July 17 2009.

39 Mary Madden and Amanda Lenhart 'Online Dating', *The Pew Internet and American Life Project*, March 5 2006.

40 Sites with names such as plentyoffish.com, fishdating.co.uk, plentymorefish. com exploit this idea.

CHAPTER FIVE

41 Rumours of pheromones' sexiness have, however, been greatly over-estimated according to *The Smell Report* by Kate Fox: 'Androstenol is the scent produced by fresh male sweat, and is attractive to females (and other men). Androstenone is produced by male sweat after exposure to oxygen – i.e. when less fresh – and is perceived as highly unpleasant by females (except during ovulation, when their responses change from "negative" to "neutral")', www.sirc.org.

42 scientificmatch.com.

43 Physical arousal has been identified many times in controlled experiments: 'The sympathetic nervous system gets aroused. Blood pressure goes up a little, the skin may flush, the face and ears will turn red and there might be a feeling of weakness in the knees.' David Givens, interviewed by Kimberly Dawn Neumann for match.com.

44 David Givens.

45 Theodore Zeldin, p. 41.

CHAPTER SIX

46 'Fate of the First Date ... The ex, lies and even pets on a first date', study by parship.co.uk, May 29 2009.

47 Theodore Zeldin, p. 121.

48 Study by parship.co.uk.

49 Study by parship.co.uk.

50 Study by parship.co.uk.

51 Study by parship.co.uk.

CHAPTER SEVEN

52 Gibbs, Ellison & Heino, 2006 cited in 'Separating Fact From Fiction: An Examination of Deceptive Self-Presentation in Online Dating Profiles', by Catalina L Toma, Jeffrey Hancock, Nicole Ellison in *Personality and Social Psychology Bulletin*, Vol. 34, No 1023–1036.

53 Catalina L Toma, Jeffrey Hancock, Nicole Ellison.

54 Participants were asked to rate how accurately they had responded to the height, weight and age questions on their online profiles, as well as the accuracy of their profile photograph. Next, they were asked to rate the 'social acceptability' of lying about each of these areas. Then their actual height or weight was recorded and compared with what they'd written on their profiles.

55 Robert Epstein.

56 The researchers defined a 'lie' as a discrepancy of more than half an inch in height or five pounds in weight; they also asked participants how honest they had been in their profiles and found that the degree of dishonesty admitted to the researchers tallied closely with the degree of actual dishonesty on the profile – suggesting that the deception was intentional rather than accidental. Catalina L Toma, Jeffrey Hancock, Nicole Ellison.

57 Guenter Hitsch and Ali Hortaçsu 'What Makes You Click? An Empirical Analysis of Online Dating Meeting Papers' 207, *Society for Economic Dynamics*, 2005.

58 Buss & Schmidt, 1993, cited in Catalina L Toma, Jeffrey Hancock, Nicole Ellison.

59 'Separating Fact From Fiction: An Examination of Deceptive Self-Presentation in Online Dating Profiles', Catalina L Toma and Jeffrey Hancock of Cornell University, Nicole Ellison of Michigan State University, January 2008.

60 'In online dating, ignorance is virtual bliss', Jeanna Bryner, livescience.com, February 13 2007.

61 'Managing Impressions Online: Self-Presentation Processes in the Online Dating Environment', Nicole Ellison, Rebecca Heino and Jennifer Gibbs.

62 Man jailed for car theft on date, BBC News Online, October 2 2009.

63 Internet Crime Report 2007, National White Collar Crime Center, www.nw3c.org.

64 The study used a survey placed on various online dating services and targeting women. The survey was completed by 740 women of whom 568 said they had met someone in person. 30 per cent of women had sex on the first date, 77 per cent of whom didn't use any protection during the sexual encounters. Paige M Padgett 'Personal Safety and Sexual Safety for Women Using Online Personal Ads' in *Sexuality Research & Social Policy*, June 2007.

65 Nicole Ellison, Rebecca Heino and Jennifer Gibbs 'Managing Impressions Online: Self-Presentation Processes in the Online Dating Environment' in *Journal of Computer Mediated Communication* Vol. 11, 2006.

CHAPTER EIGHT

66 The study questioned over 11,000 single people, almost equally split between men and women, mostly aged between 25 and 34, 'The LoveGeist Report 2009'.

67 NetRatings survey 2005, cited in Natalie Hanman 'Logging on to find love', the *Guardian*, August 18 2005.

68 'Some of the increase in unwed motherhood in the 1980s and 1990s may have been a reaction against the rise in divorce in the 1960s and 1970s', according to a long-term study of daughters of divorced parents who 'said their mothers' experiences had convinced them that being a single mother was preferable to entering a bad or unstable marriage'. Study cited in Stephanie Coontz *Marriage, a History: How Love Conquered Marriage* (Penguin: Harmondsworth, 2006).

69 'The LoveGeist Report 2009'.

70 Stephanie Coontz, p.15.

71 HG Cocks.

72 Brigid Delaney, 'Online dating lacks romance', *Sydney Herald* April 6 2009.

ALSO PUBLISHED BY GUARDIAN BOOKS

A WORLD WITHOUT BEES

Alison Benjamin and Brian McCallum

The western honeybee plays a vital role within the planet's eco-system, pollinating 70 per cent of the food that we eat. Yet the future of the honeybee is under threat, and the rate at which their numbers continue to diminish, has led to fears that we are dangerously out of sync with nature.

A World Without Bees charts the fascinating history of the western honeybee and investigates the reasons for their rapid decline in numbers. Th is inspiring account will cause its readers to face the potential consequences of the honeybees' fragile existence, and cause them to look into the personal actions that can be taken to ensure their future survival.

'A timely and important exploration of the crucial role bees play in all our lives and the deadly threats they are facing.' Vince Cable, beekeeper and politician

'Benjamin and McCallum have trawled through a vast well of knowledge on bees, founded on millennia of observation and experimentation, and the result is a thoroughly readable book.' Jonathan Jones, BBC Wildlife Magazine

'A highly enjoyable, polished, well-researched homage to the honeybee.' Observer

'The success of A World Without Bees lies in its explanation of the challenges faced by the honeybee population and the intensiveness of commercial beekeeping.' Daily Telegraph

ISBN: 978-0852651315

RRP: £7.99

WILD SWIM
River, Lake, Lido and Sea:
The Best Places to Swim Outdoors in Britain

Kate Rew with photographs by Dominick Tyler

In this stunning, full-colour guide, Kate Rew, founder of the Outdoor Swimming Society, takes the reader on a wild journey through Britain, covering 200 rivers, lakes, tidal pools, lidos, estuaries and sea swims.

Whether you are a seasoned outdoor swimmer looking to discover a hidden fairy pool, or a young family seeking a fun day out, Wild Swim has all the information and inspiration you'll need to get you stripping and dipping.

'... like a glossy recipe book, only with pictures of delicious lakes and rivers where you would normally find soufflés and stews, and mouth-watering descriptions in lochs and oceans instead of recipes...' Craig Brown, Mail on Sunday Book of the Week

'A practical guide to pools and beauty spots combined with imagery that perfectly captures the freshness and freedom of elemental swimming.' Charlotte Ross, Evening Standard

'Will have you hunched on the sofa as though with a stash of love letters.' Antonia Quirke, New Statesman

'Packed with elegiac photography of boys on rope swings, laughter, swimmers in reeds and algae-green ponds that will sustain you all the way into the water, past the toe-dipping point of no return.' Matt Rudd, Sunday Times

'Covering swims from the Hebrides to Cornwall, this is also a guide to great places to pitch up for the day – usually at an easy distance from a good, steamy-windowed café.' Good Housekeeping

ISBN: 978-0852651223

RRP: £12.99

THE PROTESTOR'S HANDBOOK

Bibi van der Zee

Are you angry with bankers and politicians for screwing up the economy? Are you concerned about global warming? Are you desperate to make your voice heard, but don't know where to start? Then this is the book for you.

In The Protestor's Handbook, journalist and activist Bibi van der Zee reveals just how easy it is to plan, launch and fund a campaign. She gives step-by-step advice on putting pressure on politicians and businesses, and guides to all the tools in a protestor's kit, from letter-writing and boycotts to protest marches and direct action.

If you've ever wanted to stand up and be counted, this book will show you just how much you can achieve.

ISBN: 978-0852652114

RRP: £8.99

Guardian Soulmates
All you need for a good date
guardian.co.uk/soulmates
A COLD NIGHT
A LONG QUEUE
A SHARED COAT
A COUPLE OF
COCKTAILS
DANCING
MORE DANCING
SUNRISE.
theguardian